Moral and Immoral Whiteness
in Immigration Politics

Moral and Immoral Whiteness in Immigration Politics

YALIDY MATOS

OXFORD
UNIVERSITY PRESS

OXFORD
UNIVERSITY PRESS

Oxford University Press is a department of the University of Oxford. It furthers
the University's objective of excellence in research, scholarship, and education
by publishing worldwide. Oxford is a registered trade mark of Oxford University
Press in the UK and certain other countries.

Published in the United States of America by Oxford University Press
198 Madison Avenue, New York, NY 10016, United States of America.

Library of Congress Cataloging-in-Publication Data
Names: Matos, Yalidy, author.
Title: Moral and immoral whiteness in immigration politics / Yalidy Matos.
Description: New York : Oxford University Press, [2023] |
Includes bibliographical references and index.
Identifiers: LCCN 2022060583 (print) | LCCN 2022060584 (ebook) |
ISBN 9780197656259 (hardback) | ISBN 9780197656266 (paperback) |
ISBN 9780197656280 (epub) | ISBN 9780197656297
Subjects: LCSH: Emigration and immigration—Moral and ethical aspects. |
Whites—United States—Attitudes. | Whites—Race identity—United
States. | United States—Emigration and immigration—Public opinion. |
Emigration and immigration—Political aspects.
Classification: LCC JV6038 .M386 2023 (print) | LCC JV6038 (ebook) |
DDC 325.73—dc23/eng/20221220
LC record available at https://lccn.loc.gov/2022060583
LC ebook record available at https://lccn.loc.gov/2022060584

DOI: 10.1093/oso/9780197656259.001.0001

Paperback printed by Marquis Book Printing, Canada
Hardback printed by Bridgeport National Bindery, Inc., United States of America

For my beloved Poppy

&

Para mi mamá y papá, Lidia A. Peña y Julio C. Matos Divison, por ser lo suficiente valiente de soñar más grande para sus hijos

Contents

Acknowledgments

If you want to go fast, go alone. If you want to go far, go together.
—African Proverb

When I was seven years old, I migrated to New York City from Dominican Republic. I was a shy, non-English-speaking young girl, who over the years grew out of her shell with the help of so many. I have made it this far because I have been blessed a thousand times over by the Universe's intervention in placing me at the right place and the right time with the right teachers, professors, mentors, and friends.

In middle school and high school, still trying to grasp the English language, I was lucky to be taught and mentored by Kim Edwards and Bill Klann. They shaped my life in ways that I did not understand until much later. Growing up in Washington Heights, the mentorship and affirmation of Ms. E. and Bill grounded and inspired me. They praised and affirmed my efforts, which at that age was integral to my self-worth and my career aspirations. I could not have imagined dreaming as big as I did without having been supported, mentored, and cared for by Ms. E. and Bill. Thank you both for investing in me as a person and as a budding scholar.

When I arrived at Connecticut College, a small, predominately white liberal arts college in middle-of-nowhere Connecticut, I instantly felt like an outsider and an imposter. However, in my first year of college, I took Introduction to Gender and Women's Studies with Dr. Mab Segrest. At the time, I did not know the impact Mab would have on me and my life. I can tell you that without Mab, I would not be where I am today. Mab taught me a lot about feminist theory and women's studies, and a lot about myself. Years later, I still get to call Mab Segrest one of my most consistent and loudest cheerleaders. I also get to call her a friend and an ally. Thank you, Mab, for your kindness, your patience, your fierce leadership, and your generosity. My experience at Conn would not have been the same without having met Dr. Theresa Ammirati, Dr. Armando Bengochea, Dr. MaryAnne Borrelli, Dr. Sylvanna Falcón, and Angela Price, all of whom showed me understanding and kindness, and served as individuals who impacted me in positive ways.

As a result of my time at Connecticut College, I made the decision to go to graduate school. Beyond wanting to answer research questions, I wanted to emulate the wonderful teachers and professors I had had and provide the same kind of mentorship and affirmation to students like myself—students who need and deserve encouragement. Pursuing a doctorate in political science at Ohio State University (Go Bucks!) proved to be the best choice for me. At Ohio State, I had the pleasure of working with Dr. Kathleen McGraw, who believed in me and my work and was incredibly generous with her time. Beyond training me as a political psychologist, Dr. McGraw chaired my dissertation. During this time in graduate school I felt defeated. I didn't know if I was going to make it to the finish line. With Dr. McGraw's support and encouragement, I was able to successfully graduate. To be honest, "thank you" feels inadequate. Those two words do not do justice what your encouragement and affirmation meant to me during that time, but thank you is all I have. I am also thankful to my peers in the department of political science who made my first two years in the department and Columbus, Ohio, better. I seriously could not have made it through those two years without Dr. Nyron Crawford and Dr. Chryl Laird. Thank you, both, for welcoming me. Your generosity and kindness during that time did not go unseen or unnoticed. At Ohio State I met many wonderful people whose support was invaluable. Thank you to these individuals: Dr. Theresa Delgadillo, Yolanda Zepeda, Dr. Inés Valdez, and Dr. Maurice Stevens.

It was also at Ohio State that I met the most wonderful support system and sister-friends. I would not have made it through graduate school in one piece, mostly sane, without Dr. Delia Fernández-Jones, Dr. Tiffany Bourgeois, Dr. Danielle Olden, Dr. Eva Pietri, Mei-ling Rivera-Cerezo, Dr. Leila Ben-Nasr, and Dr. Cassie Patterson. I experienced a lot of laughter, dancing, eating, and tears with you all, and I am so eternally grateful for your presence in my life. Thank you for your friendship. In the last two years of graduate school, Delia, Tiffany, and I became sister-friends. Ladies, what an honor it has been to be your friend and to experience life with you in it. Outside of friends I made at Ohio State, I would be remiss if I didn't thank two of my very best friends, whom I have known for a very long time: Yoely Tavarez-Dunn and Dr. Taneisha Means. Yoely and I go back to middle school, and throughout the years she has been an invaluable part of my life, a strong supporter, and a great listener. Taneisha and I go back to 2008, when we roomed together at the Ralph Bunche Summer Institute at Duke University. Taneisha is my academic wife; she has seen it all and has gone through all of graduate school and beyond with me. I am so eternally grateful for your friendship over all these years. You are one of the kindest human beings I know (you kind of must be to understand my quirks and still love me), my friend; thank you for always being there for me. Finally, I am so thankful to Dr. Desireé Melonas and Dr. Nicole Burrowes. Desireé is a relatively new friend, but whose friendship was Godsent. Thank you, Desireé, for your kindness and your calming spirit. Nicole, thank you for being such a wonderful and steadfast friend and for all the walks in Philly that kept me going during the hardest time of the pandemic.

I could not have asked for a better set of amazing and supportive colleagues than the ones I have at Rutgers University, both in the departments of political science and Latino and Caribbean studies and across Rutgers. Thank you especially to Omaris Zamora, Hannah Walker, Kira Sanbonmatsu, Katherine McCabe, Lisa Miller, K. Sebastian León, Rick Lau, Stacey Greene, Nichole M. García, and Zaire Dinzey-Flores.

I want to acknowledge the participants in my book workshop, who took the time to read my work and provide invaluable and constructive feedback. My career would not be possible without the mentorship and investment of so many people along the way. I cannot thank you all enough for your friendship, mentorship, sponsorship, kind words, encouragement, and intellectual conversations: Marisa Abrajano, Lisa García Bedolla, Cristina Beltrán, Nadia Brown, Jessica Johnson Carew, Niambi Carter, Pearl Ford Dowe, Lorrie Frasure, John Garcia, Andra Gillespie, Cory Gooding, Kerry Haynie, Michael Jones-Correa, Tyson King-Meadows, Danielle Lemi, Paula D. McClain, Kim Mealy, Domingo Morel, Efrén O. Pérez, Tacuma Peters, the late Mark Sawyer, Valeria Sinclair-Chapman, Candis Watts Smith, Alvin B. Tillery, Sophia Jordán Wallace, Ismail White, Tiffany Willoughby-Herard, Janelle Wong, Jackie Yu-Johnson. Thank you to others I might have inadvertently left out and to those who have acted as sponsors without my knowledge.

Angela Chnapko and the editorial staff at Oxford University Press, thank you for believing in me and my vision for this book. It has been such a great experience working with Angela, and I could not have asked for a better editor. Thank you as well to Kate Epstein, who meticulously edited the manuscript and helped me clarify my ideas. Thank you to Jane Jones, of Up In Consulting, and Kali Handelman, both of whom helped me to the finish line. And the most heartfelt thanks to Nadine Mattis, whose stories, laughter, and food nurtured me along the way.

I want to thank my family. Thank you to my parents, my deepest grati-
tude for your love, your support, and your willingness to let me venture out
of Washington Heights, NYC, for college. Gracias a mi mamá, Lidia, por
ser el ser humano más valiente y compasiva que conozco, y por su apoyo
incondicional. Mi papá, Julio, por enseñarme a trabajar duro, dedicación,
puntualidad, y por su apoyo incondicional. To my sisters Julissa and Vianna
and brother Alexander for your love. To my nieces and nephews Biangelis,
Donathien, Donna Leah, Jael, and Madelyn, who have provided me with so
much joy, laughter, and purpose throughout the years.

Lastly, I want to thank my husband, Derick D. Dailey. Your support of me
and my intellectual life means the world. You kept me going when I doubted
myself during this process. Special thanks to Poppy; thank you for choosing
me and loving me.

Any mistakes are, of course, mine alone.

Introduction

Immigration attitudes are at bottom moral choices. The U.S. immigration regime is a racialized regime underwritten by whiteness, "a politicoeconomic system committed to white supremacy" (Mills, 1997, p. 106). As such, the moral and epistemological norms dictated by the system of whiteness also dictate immigration attitudes. Charles W. Mills (1997) calls this the racial contract: a political, moral, and epistemological system that explains how "society was created or crucially transformed, how the individuals in that society were reconstituted, how the state was established, and how a particular moral code and a certain moral psychology were brought into existence" (p. 10). The contract norms and races whites' moral choices. In the United States, the racial contract established a racial polity, state, and juridical system defined by a white-over-non-white racial order. All whites benefit from it, although, as Mills puts it, not all are "*signatories*" to it (p. 11; italics in original). Within this system, whites learn moral norms that regulate their behavior toward each other and other groups. Whites, then, operate on a "color-coded morality" (p. 16) that results in a distorted morality that motivates immigration attitudes. At bottom, the peculiarity of the racial contract sets their understanding of what counts as moral and thus clouds their understanding of immigration. This book extends our understanding of immigration attitudes by arguing that immigration attitudes are best understood by their relationship to whiteness, to the social status afforded to whites in relation to all racial others.

The moral choice that whiteness affords, that not all racial groups have, is the choice to continue to produce and reproduce a system structured on white supremacy—"a system of [white-over-Black] power relations that structure society" (Dawson, 1994, p. 199)—or to repudiate it. Immigration attitudes and whiteness are not the same, but they cannot be separated. Whites have the power, because of their white being, to define inclusiveness and exclusiveness; the ability to say, "You don't belong." Hence, in this project, I ask, under what conditions do whites choose to lean toward reproducing whiteness and/or repudiating it, and what role do predispositions play in the moral choices whites make about immigration.

Moral and Immoral Whiteness in Immigration Politics. Yalidy Matos, Oxford University Press.
© Oxford University Press 2023. DOI: 10.1093/oso/9780197656259.003.0001

Contemporary debate and discourse about immigration centers on a fundamental tension between framing the United States as a "nation of immigrants" or a "nation of laws" (Matos, 2018b; Negrón, 2019).[1] Such framing is a political strategy that can work to create new beliefs and make certain beliefs more accessible or more applicable to an individual's evaluation (Chong & Druckman, 2007). This discourse encompasses moral claims about belonging, who can be "American," and the "right" way to immigrate and to treat unauthorized immigrants, and whether immigrants contribute to U.S. society (Lakoff & Ferguson, 2006). Immigration policy has always been about defining who belongs. Those who are white, or perceived as such because of their whiteness, are automatically viewed as U.S. citizens. Due to their status as signatories and beneficiaries, whites work to perpetuate the definition of belonging and to define those who belong; the definition is narrow, exclusive, and racial. These claims are often politically polarized. Conservatives and Republicans often cite "law and order," describing immigrants as criminal because they "broke the laws" and view any leniency toward immigrants as "unfair" to people who immigrated the "right" way; meanwhile, liberals and Democrats call for more "humane" treatment of immigrants, referencing the United States' history as a "nation of immigrants"[2] (Abrajano & Hajnal, 2015; Chavez, 2001, 2013; Haynes, Merolla, & Ramakrishnan, 2016; Igartua & Cheng, 2009; Knoll, Redlawsk, & Sanborn, 2010; Lahav & Courtemanche, 2012; Lakoff & Ferguson, 2006; Sullivan, 2019; Wallace & Wallace, 2020). A 2019 survey by the Public Religion Research Institute (PRRI), which asked respondents whether immigrants make the country stronger because of their work and talent or are a burden to the United States because they take jobs and social benefits, indicates that immigration views align strongly with political leaning. While most respondents (62%) indicated that immigrants strengthen the country, 88% of those identifying as liberal or very liberal did so, compared to only 37% of those identifying as conservative and very conservative. With respect to party affiliation, the numbers were 82%, 32%, and 65% among Democrats, Republicans, and independents, respectively (Public Religion Research Institute, 2019b). Scholars have suggested a number of factors behind the increasingly anti-immigrant attitudes of whites generally and white Republicans specifically, including U.S. demographic shifts (Abrajano & Hajnal, 2015), whites' status loss (Jardina, 2019), whites' sense of being "strangers in their own land" (Hochschild, 2016), whites' supposed "minority" status (Gest, 2016), racial prejudice (Brader, Valentino, & Suhay, 2008; Burns & Gimpel, 2000; Pérez, 2010; Schildkraut, 2011), ethnocentrism (Kinder &

Kam, 2009), social dominance and authoritarian personality (Pettigrew, Wagner, & Christ, 2007), and nationalism (Citrin, Reingold, & Green, 1990).

Reflecting the influence of the racial contract, race and ethnicity also shape immigration attitudes. While 70% of Black, 77% of Asian, and 76% of Hispanic/Latino respondents on the same survey agreed that immigrants strengthen the country, only 57% of non-Hispanic white Americans did so (other racial categories had fewer than 100 respondents). Party affiliation largely explains this number: About 31% of white Republicans agree that immigrants strengthen the country while approximately 84% of white Democrats agree (Public Religion Research Institute, 2019b). Thus, the intersection of partisanship and race defines immigration attitudes among white Americans (Abrajano & Hajnal, 2015). Scholars have focused on this interaction in explaining attitudes as well as explaining party polarization and defection (Abrajano & Hajnal, 2015; Mason, 2018). However, I contend, this focus has ignored the moral psychology attached to immigration attitudes among white Americans.

Immigration attitudes carry with them an inherent value-based moral narrative that varies by partisanship precisely because parties set moral norms that encourage particular moral attitudes and behaviors. At bottom, I frame these moral attitudes of white Americans, and thus their choices, as choices that lean toward either sanctioning or repudiating white supremacy, given whiteness runs through the institution of immigration (Haney Lopez, 2006). Throughout this book, I examine whites' moral choices by partisanship and other key predispositions that are connected to whites' socialization and racialization in the United States. White Republicans and white Democrats use morally based justifications to support certain aspects of immigration (e.g., the DREAM Act, merit-based policies, and skill-based policies) that align with the moral values and principles that, in their minds, ground their party, while white Republicans, in particular, use another set of morally based justifications to support punitive immigration policies (e.g., Arizona's SB1070, hiring more Border Patrol agents, and anti-sanctuary policies).

Immigration has been at the heart of U.S. politics for centuries. This book examines the inherent moral, value-based nature of white Americans' immigration attitudes. I test my theory about the centrality of morality with a series of empirical models that take advantage of public opinion survey data as well as the roll call votes of elected officials.

In this work, morality does not reference organized religion, doctrine, or discourse—although of course the moral choice to accept and/or perpetuate whiteness as a hegemonic ideology may be rooted in religious beliefs (e.g., among white evangelicals)—in fact there is some research suggesting that moral and religious convictions are distinct constructs (Skitka, Hanson, Washburn, & Mueller, 2018). I also do not ground morality in the extant literature in philosophy, although of course one could. Conflating religion and/or Christianity with morality would only serve to occlude the ways in which religious formations are part of the structure of whiteness as a political project in the United States.[3] One only needs to know the history of chattel slavery to understand that often, both historically and contemporarily, what is religious isn't "good" or moral.

I define morality as value-based justifications rooted in a subjective understanding of what is "right" and what is "wrong" that motivate attitudes and behavior. These understandings, I argue, are raced. In a racially based society, like the United States, understandings of what is "right" and what is "wrong" depend on where in the racial order one stands. In other words, these understandings are intimately tied to one's social identity and the role that comes with being a member of that social group. In fact, two of the most prominent social identities in the United States are race and party identification.

Whiteness "generat[es] a sense of 'right' that is racialized: a white right," which affects the moral psychology of white Americans, their "conscious and unconscious framings of dilemmas and moral choices" (Mills, 1998, p. 157). My framework stems from Mills' concept of *Herrenvolk* ethics, which constitutes "a moral dividing line by which equality and subordination are reconciled" (p. 162). This kind of ethic allows white people to be "simultaneously committed to liberal egalitarianism *and* racial hierarchy" (p. 152; italics mine). As Mills argues, *Herrenvolk* ethics have influenced the dominant moral codes in the United States, as well as the West generally, in both practice and theory. Ideologies that ignore structures and systems of power dominate. Hence, white Americans' understandings of morality, what is right and wrong, is raced, given their racialized standing. Those who are systematically privileged see the world from that vantage point. Privilege impedes their understanding of the system of power that maintains their privilege and calls on them instead to justify inequality, if they see it at all, by attributing it to the moral failings of non-privileged groups. As Mills suggests, "The moral codes of the privileged will tend to adjust to that privilege and be shaped accordingly" (p. 142).

Party identification can reinforce moral codes, as it too operates with a set of moral norms. Partisanship, in particular for the Republican Party, reinforces the norms of white identity (Mason, 2018; Weller & Junn, 2018, p. 439). Thus, Republican Party identification becomes a vehicle of white supremacy and maintenance of the status quo, while Democratic Party identification helps to attenuate these norms and provides some whites the choice of a partisan identification that they deem more aligned with their views. My argument, however, is not a normative one that argues that Republicans are "wrong" and Democrats are "right," as that would be a simplistic attempt at explaining both parties. In fact, in both parties there is variation in the psychological underpinnings of party loyalty. Both white Republicans and white Democrats can deviate from party norms. My aim is to understand whites' immigration attitudes as moral narratives that vary by and within the two main parties in the United States. Moreover, I argue that morality and party are connected. The hegemony of whiteness is inherently embedded in U.S. political parties (García Bedolla & Haynie, 2013). Nearing the end of Jim Crow laws and the beginning of the civil rights turn in U.S. history, the Republican Party used identity politics to win over Southern white conservative voters who had traditionally aligned themselves with the Democratic Party. The Southern strategy appealed to whites' racial resentment and grievances (García Bedolla & Haynie, 2013) and was explicit in its racial appeals until the presidential bid of George H.W. Bush. Because of its continued success up to and including when Donald Trump made it explicit again, white identity and self-selection into the Republican Party overlap. This self-selection influences white political behavior. Indeed, white defection from the Democratic to the Republican Party in the United States from 1950 to 2008 has much to do with the intersection of race and identity—i.e., being white—and immigration attitudes (Abrajano & Hajnal, 2015).

The Centrality of Immigration in U.S. Politics

All whites in the United States trace their lineage to immigration and thus trace their privilege, willingly or not, to native dispossession, chattel slavery, exploitation, and racism. Immigration is thus a reminder of the precarity of their status as white citizens. It is a reminder of whites' moral struggle over the maintenance of white supremacy. The immigration of white ethnics in the 20th century thickened the boundaries of whiteness as they joined their white counterparts. White ethnics, with the help of the established white population and white institutions, did so by distancing themselves from Black

Americans and increasingly racialized Latinos by relying on an ideology of racism that blames these groups for the structural conditions they face.[4] At the same time, white ethnics claimed they had no role in this kind of white-over-Black racist ideology and the maintenance of it, because, in general, no one in their families had the means to trade or own slaves (see Novak, 1972). This kind of ideological thinking, namely a "just-off-the-boat innocence" in relation to white–Black relations undergirded by a moral logic that replaced a white-over-Black privilege for a "black-over-white victimization," is what Matthew Frye Jacobson (2006) calls a preface to neoconservative thinking. An individualized notion of racism at the expense of the structural features of race and attitudes that were anti-ameliorative toward programs such as welfare and affirmative action (p. 195).[5] This simultaneous claim to being innocent of racial oppression *and* taking advantage of all that white identity had to offer, alongside their white, "non-ethnic" counterparts, normalized and embedded whiteness in policymaking as neither a color, nor powerful (Frankenberg, 1993), precisely because of white ethnics' understanding of themselves as "off white" and just as victimized as African Americans. This new moral authority held by white ethnics gave way to "power evasiveness," to an ideology that asserts whiteness and power are not only elusive but also completely unrelated. Whiteness relies on white innocence, white homogenization, and white normalization to avoid accountability.

For whites invested in whiteness (and other citizens invested in whiteness), at stake in immigration policies and rhetoric is the unveiling of the fragility of whiteness. Immigration has become a legitimate avenue for the politics of whiteness, or the politics of citizenship. Through the immigration system, whites are complicit in a set of laws and policies that offers them full citizenship while extralegal practices, violence, terror, exclusion, and removal are enacted on non-whites as a means to defend the sanctity of a white democracy (Olson, 2004). It is a democratic system for whites, but tyrannical for non-whites. As Cristina Beltrán (2020) argues, "anti-immigrant practices offer nativists the increasingly rare opportunity to combine practices of overt racial domination with the invocation of law" (p. 23 fn 52). This invocation of law is but one moral narrative.

Whites continue to use the issue of immigration to evaluate where they are in the racial order, assess their racialized standing, and make decisions about immigration based on this evaluation. Anti-immigration attitudes secure whites' own (white) citizen status (Mutz, 2018). To be a citizen means to be fully American, and to have the privilege of white citizenship is to take advantage of all the rights that come with citizenship. The cultural defense of granting whites what Amy Brandzel and Jigna Desai (2008) call "normative citizenship" is a way of enacting whiteness. From its inception, U.S. immigration policy legally defined naturalization and citizenship as a white endeavor. Racialized bodies are treated as second-class citizens, obtaining what Vera Chouinard (2001) calls "shadow citizenship," which occurs when the law as written—which grants full citizenship to non-whites—is at odds with the law as lived, which denies it. As Brandzel (2016) puts it, "*citizen* is often used as if it were synonymous with being a 'good' or ethical participant in some form of social contract, therefore working to mark and reproduce proper—read, *normative*—behavior" (p. 13; italics in original). And more broadly, immigration attitudes are used to mask the larger political and moral project of the maintenance of whiteness, especially as it is manifested within U.S. party politics.

Because citizenship and American identity are strongly tied together, as Olson puts it, "Whiteness became the political color of citizenship. The significance of racialized citizenship is not that only white persons could become citizens; it is that becoming a citizen effectively made one white" (Olson, 2004, p. xx; also see King, 2002); whiteness and American identity should be examined. American identity and expressions of the importance of nationalism and patriotism are strongly associated with whiteness. In a survey, an overwhelming majority of white respondents selected an American identity over all other racial or ethnic identity labels, which members of other groups did not (Schildkraut, 2011). The form national attachment can take also varies by race (Sidanius, Feshbach, Levin, & Pratto, 1997; Theiss-Morse, 2009). It can also be the case that national identity supersedes other identities, like racial identity, and is viewed as its own social identity (Huddy & Khatib, 2007; Transue, 2007; Wong, 2010). However, for whites the strong historical link between Americanism and whiteness should nuance researchers' understanding of whites' conception of American identity as proxying conceptions of whiteness and thus exclusion. National identity can help whites orient their own racial identity, even if they do not admit to having one, toward ingroup loyalty and the desire to distinguish themselves from outgroups.

"On Being 'White' . . . and Other Lies"

In "On Being 'White' . . . and Other Lies," originally published in 1984 in the popular African American magazine *Essence*, James Baldwin (1998) proclaimed that "White" is "absolutely, a moral choice (for there are no white people)" (p. 180). He was, of course, referring to the fact that race is a social construction and not a genetic inheritance. Baldwin also argued that for white ethnics in particular, "becoming American"—which for centuries meant being legally white (Lopez, 1997)—meant learning to become white. Other scholars have echoed Baldwin's suggestion that white people are not white because of their skin color or ancestry but through a moral and political choice. For those wanting to become American, identifying as white, whether consciously or not, meant giving up their moral compass. This surrender involved and almost required them to discriminate against Black Americans and disassociate themselves from blackness (Harris, 1993; Roediger, 2005). The moral and political act of being white can also be defined as choosing whiteness. The moral choice is actively choosing to be white at the expense of non-white racialized groups, evident through daily practices of discrimination and racism as well as political behavior, including policy attitudes and preferences, that maintain the racial status quo.

An understanding of white identity and whiteness as a moral and political choice is missing within the field of political science, where it seems like we are moving toward understanding white racial identity (WRI) as an almost neutral category, a physical description. First, race, as Joel Olson (2004) argues, is not just identity: "The problem with limiting our understanding of race [is that] it leads to very little politics at all" (p. 6). Second, and relatedly, race is not a neutral category or an objectively political part of a person's identity. That is, racism and racial discrimination are not a product of deliberate and intentional actions by a select few. While such actions occur, they cannot explain structural racism and the systemic ways in which racial inequality persists. Thus, first, I contend that we ought to examine whiteness as both an identity that some white Americans may express and also a political category that goes beyond identity politics. This way we can fully capture how whiteness operates as an identity but more importantly as a moral and political choice that—unless those persons perceived to be white choose to do differently—maintains a racially based unequal system, a system of white supremacy.

A more thorough definition of white supremacy comes from Frances Lee Ansley (1989): "a political, economic, and cultural system in which whites overwhelmingly control power and material resources, conscious and unconscious ideas of white superiority and entitlement are widespread, and relations of white dominance and non-white subordination are daily reenacted across a broad array of institutions and social settings" (p. 1024). A white individual who is choosing to do differently, who does make moral choices to dismantle the current racialized U.S. system, may or may not express that being white is important to them because white supremacy was structured so that it continues to run with or without white racial identification. In fact, white supremacy has "become independent of feelings of racism" (Mills, 1998, p. 145), and "the crucial aspects of white supremacy may be perpetuated in the absence of racist sentiments" (pp. 145–146). Quoting Mills at length here helps undergird whites' group-interested moral decisions outside of the importance of white identification and whether it is correlated with racism:

> Once certain socioeconomic structures are established, questions of intent and the conscious aim to discriminate become less important to their internal dynamic. The system of accumulated, entrenched privilege can reproduce itself through motivation that is simply self- and group-interested, that does not want to lose access to differential opportunities, that does not want to probe too deeply into the past (or the present, for that matter). Whites do not have to be racist to want to keep their privileges. (p. 145)

I distinguish between WRI and whiteness to disassociate the two conceptually and empirically. WRI can be defined as an identity to which white persons decide to attach meaning. It can be measured and operationalized in different ways that get at identity importance, group identity, and group consciousness. WRI, however, is related to doing whiteness, but whiteness can take different forms. Because of this positioning, whites can still choose to *do* whiteness regardless of their racial identity. Whites can also choose to work toward dismantling the structures and systems that maintain white dominance. Hence, WRI and whiteness can exist in different configurations. A white individual who expresses that being white is important to their identity does not necessarily mean that they are prejudiced, or racist, nor does it mean that they are actively choosing to work to dismantle white supremacy. In other words, admitting to being white is a precursor to understanding whiteness and white privilege, but not everyone who admits to being white understands, is aware of, or wants to admit white privilege exists.

WRI is both an absence of an identity and an identity itself. In other words, being white does not only belong to those white persons who are aware of and attach meaning to their racial identity. Race is both an identity *and* a marker of privilege or subordination (Harris, 1993; Olson, 2004). This is what sets apart white identity from the racial identity of non-white racialized groups. Whereas being Black in the United States is both a cultural identity and a political category, being white has, at least historically, strictly been a political category (Olson, 2004, p. xix). And, I argue, it continues to be primarily a moral and political choice tied to political ends rather than cultural ones. As Olson (2004) puts it, "race does more than exclude, divide, degrade, and repress. It is also a productive form of power that accumulates humans into particular groups" (p. 16). Race is a system of "discrimination, hierarchy, and power" (p. xvii).

The current gap in white identity politics, which is the politics of whiteness, is that this understanding of the relationship between identity and whiteness is not fully examined and dealt with as part of how race works for those persons who are "called white by other whites" (Olson, 2004, p. 17).[6] Instead, the field is moving toward examining WRI apart from the moral and political project of whiteness, which has implications for how far we, as a country, can move toward abolishing the system of white supremacy. White identity (both the explicit expression of the importance of whiteness and whiteness as a privileged standing) is, by definition, relational. White elites' desire to prevent an alliance between the white working class and Black Americans gave rise to white identity. The invention of the white race (Allen, 2012) was in explicit contrast to the Black race (Roediger, 2005, 2007). The cross-class alliance, as Olson (2004) puts it, between the dominant class and the white working class conferred "privileges to its members, in exchange for which they guarantee the social stability necessary for the accumulation of capital. This alliance, W.E.B. Du Bois argues, produces two 'worlds' of race, the white and the dark worlds" (p. xxiv). Members of the alliance are defined as "white" while those outside the alliance are "not-white." White identity is relational, thus, being white is inherently also about outgroup attitudes.

White identity, thus, cannot be easily distinguished between ingroup attitudes and outgroup attitudes. For example, as Noel Ignatiev argues, the Irish sought to become American by allying themselves with the Democratic Party, "but the prerequisite of entrance into [the] institutions [comprising the party] was proof of whiteness, which implied a commitment to the degradation of African Americans" (Olson, 2004, p. 45). Although white identity in and of itself is not a manifestation of racism or prejudice, it is intricately related to them by way of hierarchy, discrimination, and power inherent in whiteness. An expression of white identity or white group consciousness also indicates whites' expressions of outgroup attitudes. Furthermore, an absence of racial animus does not mean ingroup favoritism solely motivates whites' racial identity (Jardina, 2019). Disentangling WRI from outgroup attitudes dismisses the history and definition of whiteness in the United States. Moreover, appeals to whites' sense of loss of status or their group position as justification for some whites' identity saliency *are* racially motivated and race-based appeals. In our political system, whites do not have to express outgroup hostility toward any specific group to maintain the system of whiteness. Whiteness is relational, and the invention of white identity is rooted in relational politics. WRI would not exist without the social construction of Black racial identity. Any examination of white identity politics must also consider how whiteness is maintained—above and beyond an identity—who is maintaining it, and who is choosing differently.

Whiteness is "something one does" (Olson, 2004, p. 19) rather than something one is. It is a marker of citizenship, and thus, a position of privilege (Beltrán, 2020; Olson, 2004). In a country committed to race neutrality, a civil rights legacy, immigration policymaking and attitudes toward immigration get used as vessels through which whiteness operates. Before the 1965 Immigration Act, immigration and white citizenship were closely aligned, legally and socially (Haney Lopez, 2006). Immigration has historically been a way toward assimilation and, in particular, assimilation into whiteness (Haney Lopez, 2006). After 1965, the explicit connections between whiteness and immigration became less apparent as the United States tried to appear colorblind and multicultural, especially amid the Cold War. However, those who wish to identify with whiteness use immigration policy preferences and attitudes to maintain the U.S. racial order that benefits whites under the guise of colorblindness. These attitudes, these choices, I argue, are inherently moral choices. And because race is a social construct, whites can choose a different role, as some have and continue to do.

The Role of Whiteness and Group Norms

Merging role identity theory (RIT; Burke & Reitzes, 1991; Hogg, Terry, & White, 1995; McCall & Simmons, 1966; Stryker, 1968) and social identity theory (SIT; Tajfel, 1978; Tajfel & Turner, 1979; Tajfel & Turner, 1986), provides a better understanding of the relationship between social structure and individual-level behavior. I argue that being white is both a social identity and a role, a role that has historical roots.

The colonial upper class hardened the racial caste of slavery to divide the "races" in the 17th century. An alliance between European indentured servants, enslaved Africans, and free Blacks as part of the armed Bacon's Rebellion in 1676 against Colonial Governor William Berkeley in Jamestown, Virginia, led to this hardening as a means of maintaining Berkeley's power. In the aftermath, "rich planters learned from Bacon's Rebellion that poor Whites had to be forever separated from enslaved Blacks. They divided and conquered by creating more White privileges" (Kendi, 2016, p. 53). These privileges included the right to commit any abuse of any Black person; if there was a response it was punishable by whipping (Kendi, 2016). By 1705, racist codes were enacted to secure chattel slavery, where Africans were rendered the personal property of slaveowners, throughout the Atlantic Coast. The Virginia Slave Codes of 1705 were the omnibus results, codifying chattel slavery and inventing whiteness (Allen, 2012). This invention gave poor whites a new role: As the armed defenders of planters' right to hold their enslaved persons, whites who did not own slaves were required to be part of slave patrols, to police enslaved people, and to prevent enslaved people's escape. In essence, Virginia lawmakers made slave patrols compulsory for non-slaveholding whites. Planters had to grant indentured white servants 50 acres of land upon freeing them, and Black people could no longer hold public office or land. Any property owned by "any slave" was seized and sold and the profits distributed to poor whites (Kendi, 2016, p. 68). Whites' role as defenders of whiteness would last through the centuries and become intimately interconnected with their identity as white people.

The emergence of a white identity as connected to the accompanying role that poor, working class, and landless whites played should prompt a deeper examination of WRI as more than just identity centrality. Examining WRI also means examining whites who continue to be committed to a role that maintains a system of white supremacy and whites who choose a counter-role. Although RIT does not see the meta category of race as a "role," I expand it to include race, not so much as a role in and of itself but the roles that come with being white, which is why whiteness is absolutely a moral choice. The choice is not to just say, I am white, but it is, more importantly, to behave in accordance with the norms, beliefs, and behavior that give meaning to being white.

According to the descriptive norm effect, individuals prefer to behave in certain ways when they know the behavior is in line with others' behavior (Sherif, 1965). Research shows that individuals can be encouraged to do the "right" thing (Bicchieri & Xiao, 2009), though they can also be encouraged against "moral" behavior (Abbink, Freidin, Gangadharan, & Moro, 2018). Self-categorization theory contends that individuals will also avoid conforming to the norms of a group to which they do not belong (Hogg, Turner, & Davidson, 1990; Turner, Hogg, Oakes, Reicher, & Wetherell, 1987). Such groups and the norms attached to them can be defined by race and, among other categories, political party further cements those group norms (Maxwell & Shields, 2019; Schickler, 2016). Norms, beliefs, and behavior are also set in place by political parties (Frank, 2004; Freeman, 1986; Grossman & Hopkins, 2016; Hogg et al., 1990; Mason, 2018). These norms have the potential to serve as the basis of an affective attachment to one's own party (Campbell, Converse, Miller, & Stokes, 1960) and social identity (Greene, 1999; Mason, 2018). The more whites identify with their political party, the more they will conform to that group's norms (Rimal, 2008; Smith & Terry, 2003).

These understandings shape my argument, and I contend that there is a gap in the scholarship of both white identity politics in political science and immigration politics about the intersection of WRI and whiteness. At the intersection of these two concepts and ways of moving around in the world for those individuals we call white in the United States are moral choices. Because race is not *just* identity and because race is about power, any examination of white identity politics must consider whiteness. Moreover, identity in and of itself involves norms (group expectations to which members must adhere) and moral codes that drive group norms, to which people in any given identity adhere and are psychologically pushed to satisfy (Tajfel & Turner, 1979; Turner, 1975). Thus, racial identity and norms are connected. Norms are also in relationship with one's understandings of the group's moral codes. These moral codes are racialized—they are shaped by race, and, for the dominant race, they are shaped by privilege. When a community "has been committed to group domination, the feedback and moral training it provides its members will necessarily be shaped, in ways both conscious and unconscious, by a model of the person and an identity normatively at home with the way things are" (Mills, 1998, p. 142).

Moreover, not only is one motivated to satisfy the norms of the group, group members also police such norms and thus members feel a social constraint to behave in line with group norms, which Ismail White and Chryl Laird (2020) call "racialized social constraint." Although White and Laird focus on Black political behavior, the concept, I argue, applies for whites as well. White Americans are also residentially segregated, and there are social norms of how to *do* whiteness. The institutions built around the maintenance of whiteness (e.g., the electoral college, the two-party system) are different from those built around blackness, but there are also norms built into these institutions. Much as whites police Black and non-white people, whites also police each other, and especially whites who fail to live up to white social norms (Davis & Ernst, 2019; Walton, 1975), individuals some call "race traitors" (Ignatiev & Garvey, 1996; Segrest, 2019).

During the civil rights era, "race traitors" were often brutally killed by other whites. William Lewis Moore was such a case. He planned to walk from Chattanooga, Tennessee, to Jackson, Mississippi, to deliver a letter to Governor Ross Barnett asking him to end segregation. On April 23, 1963, south of Collbran, Alabama, Moore answered the questions of Floyd Simpson, a white storeowner, about his beliefs and views on segregation and a few hours later he'd been shot to death, allegedly by Simpson. Another case involved the sheriff of Philadelphia, Mississippi, who turned two young white civil rights workers, Andrew Goodman and Michael Henry Schwerner, and their Black compatriot, James Earl Chaney, over to Klansmen who shot all three in June 1964. Other whites brutally murdered as race traitors include Reverend James Reeb, a Unitarian minister from Boston who joined the Selma marchers and was beaten to death, and Vernon Ferdinand Dahmer, who died of severe burns after his house was firebombed following his offer to pay poll taxes for those who couldn't afford to pay them (see Southern Poverty Law Center, 2021, for all examples cited here).

There are also recent incidents that target so-called race traitors (St-Esprit, 2018). Starting in 2017, for example, white women in Pittsburgh who were part of multiracial families and spoke out about diversity and racial justice were being targeted by a white man in the Pittsburgh chapter of the Church of Creativity, a group the Southern Poverty Law Center classifies as a hate group. Policing the boundaries of whiteness today rarely amounts to murder of other whites; however, whites who digress from white group norms continue to be policed, threatened, or pathologized. Policing other whites to maintain white dominance and advantages is what Angelique M. Davis and Rose Ernst (2019) call racial gaslighting; "the political, social, economic and cultural process that perpetuates and normalizes a white supremacist reality through pathologizing those who resist" (p. 763). These are a few examples of the boundaries of whiteness, the ways in which whites who are following the group's norms and moral codes surveil, police, threaten, and sometimes kill those who step outside of group norms.

To avoid psychological, social, and sometimes physical negative consequences, most whites avoid stepping outside of white social norms. Through this choice they not only avoid negative consequences but also maintain material advantage. In the United States, to be white is to have and use the wages of whiteness; it comes with social approval, praise from other whites, and status. In the words of Du Bois (1966):

> It must be remembered that the white group of laborers, while they received a low wage, were compensated in part by a sort of public and psychological wage. They were given public deference and titles of courtesy because they were white. . . . The police were drawn from their ranks, and the courts, dependent upon their votes, treated them with such leniency. . . . Their vote selected public officials, and while this had small effect upon the economic situation, it had great effect upon their personal treatment and the deference shown them. (pp. 700–701)

Slave patrols had given way to the lynch mob; the role of the white working class was to serve as a buffer between white elites and Black Americans, and it remains so (Allen, 2012; Roediger, 2007). The average white was poor and thus had more in common with working-class African Americans than with white elites; they were inducted into the white race to disrupt this natural affinity. This whiteness provided psychological wages of whiteness but brought no economic benefits to the white working class writ large. As Eula Biss (2015) clarifies, as a result whites "entertain the delusion that we're business partners with power, not its minions." Non-elite whites do the *work* to maintain white supremacy, maintaining white elites' monopoly on power and capital by continuing to oppose policies that would otherwise even the playing field among differently positioned racialized groups. As a result, white Americans continue to vote for candidates and policies that go against their economic self-interest simply to maintain white supremacy. This is achieved through perpetuating myths such as the welfare queen (Hancock, 2004), such that the average white American associates government spending with non-white Americans and immigrants and either do not recognize or choose to deny how they too personally benefit from some of the programs they vehemently oppose (Cramer, 2016; Gilens, 1999; Mettler, 2011), or how much they lose by opposing such programs (McGhee, 2021).

I theorize at the intersection of whiteness and immigration through a race, ethnicity, and politics lens, which seriously investigates and engages with questions of power vis-à-vis race and ethnic relations; absent this lens white identity politics remains uncomplicated and underexamined in political science. By merging role identity theory and social identity theory, I offer a better understanding of white identity politics, as I will illustrate by examining immigration attitudes. White identity is both an identity and something that goes beyond an identity. Being white and placing meaning on being white can be a social identity in and of itself, but whiteness in the United States stems from an understanding of whiteness as race-less and "normal." Political scientists, and social scientists generally, cannot understand white identity as strictly about whites being able to name it, recognize it, or deem it important to their identity, because being white involves a role. The role comes with a set of norms, beliefs, values, and behaviors that mean white people are part of the group of other whites who chose to *do* whiteness. However, the role does not require being able to identify as white or admit to its importance. On the contrary, to be white in the United States meant to be race-less. The phenomenon of whites talking about being white is recent, but many whites continue to be socialized and to socialize their children as race-less.

White Socialization and Predispositions

White socialization teaches whites how to be part of the white club, what is expected of them (their role), and how to maintain the exclusivity of the club. Embedded in these teachings are values and morally based justifications for group norms and rules. I argue that predispositions serve as a key mechanism for understanding whites' heterogenous political behavior as learned through socialization. Predispositions are inherently tied to the values we were taught as children and values that many continue to hold onto. Predispositions are individual-level traits that influence the communication and information that people encounter and the extent to which the information is received. As John R. Zaller (1992) explains, they "are the critical intervening variable between the communications people encounter . . . and their statements of political preferences" (p. 23). Predispositions are learned in early life, and some work suggests that they are "attitudes [that] become highly crystallized and serve as 'predispositions' for responses to new attitude objects" (Sears & Funk, 1999, p. 1). Predispositions are often, though not always, relatively stable through the life course (Sears & Funk, 1999). However, other work suggests that personality traits, in particular, are not as stable as previously conceived and that they can be activated (Winter, 2008). It is through socialization that children and young adults learn particular attitudes, and these attitudes are crystallized and reinforced by parents, friends, teachers, and communities, especially homogenous communities and spaces.

In her autobiography, Lillian Smith (1949), a Southern white woman, details this kind of socialization, the contradiction between principles and praxis, and the inherent moral choices available to whites:

> The mother who taught me what I know of tenderness and love and compassion taught me also the bleak rituals of keeping Negroes in their "place." . . . [A] terrifying disaster would befall the South if ever I treated a Negro as my social equal. . . . [T]he deep respect I felt for [my black nurse], the tenderness, the love, was a childish thing which every normal child outgrows. . . . I, too, must outgrow these feelings. . . . From the day I was born, I began to learn my lessons. . . . I learned it is possible . . . to pray at night and ride a Jim Crow car the next morning and to feel comfortable in doing both. I learned to believe in freedom, to glow when the word *democracy* was used, and to practice slavery from morning to night. I learned it the way all of my southern people learn it: by closing door after door until one's mind and heart and conscience are blocked off from each other and from reality. (pp. 17–20)[7]

Smith details how she learned to be white (Thandeka, 1999), which she attributes not only to her mother, as in this passage, but also to other whites, such as those in her white women's club. She and others have written about the (white) norms and moral codes they were taught, further indicating that not only is being white socially constructed (i.e., taught), it is also more than just indicating being white on a government form. Moreover, it is often unrelated to whether one feels it is important to one's own identity. Being white is connected to behavior and norms that either work to dismantle white supremacy or perpetuate it. Race, as Charles Mills (1998) argues, "influences the socialization one receives, the life-world in which one moves, the experiences one has, the worldview one develops . . . one's *being and consciousness*" (p. xv; italics in original).

Whites' predispositions toward beliefs about structural racism, equality, morality, and authority should condition WRI and how they *do* whiteness. In other words, certain predispositions should condition white racial identity as an identity. Because not all whites in the United States deem being white an integral part of their racial identity, predispositions should then proxy levels of racialized socialization, the learned attitudes that influence how one sees the world. If whites' predispositions are strong, in many instances, I contend that WRI will be less significant. Generally, predispositions tell us something about the underlying norms attached to the social identity of the individual and its accompanying role(s). Moreover, I argue that partisanship shapes these norms and roles.

On Partisanship and Morality

One of the key interventions of this book is an examination of partisanship undergirded by whites' political choices, which, I argue, are moral choices. Partisanship predicts individual opinion more closely than most other factors (Stimson, 2004). To understand whites' heterogenous political behavior on immigration, this book examines numerous predispositions, including partisanship (Campbell et al., 1960; Zaller, 1992). Furthermore, partisanship and ideas about morality, and the moral choices both the parties and the partisans make regarding equality and justice, are intimately tied together.

Political parties represent social groups with which individuals can share a sense of belonging and membership (Green, Palmquist, & Schickler, 2002). This sense of belonging and membership in a party comes with partisan norms about expected behavior (Freeman, 1986; Grossman & Hopkins, 2016) and a value system that undergirds the norms and behavior (Fiorina, Abrams, & Pope, 2006; Lipset, Lazarsfeld, Barton, & Linz, 1954; Matos, 2020; McClosky & Zaller, 1984; Scammon & Wattenberg, 1970). These norms stem from a history shaped by race. The racial identities or racial worldview of Democrats/liberals and Republicans/conservatives are often associated with their party affiliation (Abrajano & Hajnal, 2015; Mason, 2018).

As David Courtwright (2013) notes, the Southern strategy has depended on "New Right operatives, media savvy religious conservatives, and a well-funded conservative counter-establishment, exploited moral outrage, racial resentment, and disenchantment with taxes and liberal social experiments to pry away moral traditionalists and Southern voters from the Democratic Party" since Richard Nixon's candidacy (p. 5). The Republican Party is known as the party of whites, in particular Southern whites (Heersink & Jenkins, 2020a, 2020b, 2020c), but more recently also whites across the Midwest and in rural spaces (Jardina, 2019). Carmines and Stimson's (1989) theory of issue evolution posits that racial policy issues have structured the partisan divide since the 1960s when the Democratic Party decided, however tepidly, to support civil rights and the Republican Party decided to oppose them. Boris Heersink and Jeffery A. Jenkins (2020b) demonstrate that this decision was deliberate, a conscious choice that allowed them to dominate Southern politics for decades (Heersink & Jenkins, 2020a), which ensured the Democratic Party would receive the Black vote. As White and Laird (2020) argue, racialized social constraints of Black group norms also dictate their party affiliation. However, white Americans had and still have a choice of party affiliation, unlike other non-white groups who feel that their only "good" or decent choice is the Democratic Party. Whites' status enables a choice of party identification; this choice is a moral choice. Through the choice to back the Republican Party, whites remain complicit in their own racialized privilege. Partisanship determines the (im)moral choices of partisans.

In 2016, Trump received 155 electoral votes. He won every former Confederate state except Virginia. Since 1972, Republicans have carried and won the South, particularly white, Southern voters (Heersink & Jenkins, 2020a; Lassiter, 2006; Maxwell & Shields, 2019). Today, the "Solid South" has reemerged as the base of Republican Party support; as White and Laird (2020) note, "white Southerners vote for Republican presidential candidates at about the same rate that blacks vote for Democratic candidates" (p. 204). Unique to recent times, the Republican Party's identity politics strategy is working outside the South as well. Although most people racialized as non-white or people of color in the United States are Democrats, there is variation among these groups, especially U.S. Latinos and Asians, while African Americans have very little variation and the group constrains even African American conservatives (White & Laird, 2020). The sorting of partisanship with other identities, including race (Mason, 2018), has driven Republicans' restrictionist stance on immigration policies and Democratic association with more liberal policies (Nevins, 2010; Newton, 2008).

Not only does partisanship coincide with racial identity, partisanship has differential effects by racial group (Masuoka & Junn, 2013). For example, white Democrats/liberals and Republicans/conservatives have substantially different values from Latinos and African Americans (Ciuk, 2017). Whites' value preferences affect their partisanship and ideology far more than Latinos', and for African Americans such effects are statistically indistinguishable from zero. To examine this heterogeneity among whites, I run models by partisanship to examine the differential effects of socialization (predispositions) on immigration attitudes as well as white identity. I expect to find that white Democrats and Republicans view their choices and evaluate values differently but both groups have values they care about and then use to make political decisions. Hence, by considering the influence of such values and how they differ for white Democrats and white Republicans, these models will shed light on how U.S. principles and values, such as equality, individualism, and egalitarianism, are understood. Whiteness is intricately tied to the U.S. political system. It is in this vein that the current project is intentional about focusing on white Americans, not because the theoretical framework does not transfer to other groups but because this is a story about how whiteness structures immigration and the connection between white being, party, and morality.

The Moral and Political Project of Whiteness—Theory and Praxis

According to Gunnar Myrdal (1962), the great moral and political project of the nation is to align the United States' ideals with its practices. Myrdal argued that the status accorded to Black Americans represents "nothing more and nothing less than a century-lag of public morals" (p. 24). Furthermore, for Myrdal, if whites were only more aware of the contradiction between U.S. ideals and Black subordination, they would act to eliminate the gap. The problem with this argument, however, is twofold. First, whites have been and continue to be aware of the contradiction and gap, and second, whites have historically consented to the gap.

The 2003 American Mosaic Project Survey found that a majority of white respondents acknowledged factors such as "prejudice and discrimination" (62%) and "access to schools and other social connections" (83%) as factors contributing to their own advantage (Hartmann, Gerteis, & Edgell, 2010). In the 2016 Cooperative Congressional Election Study (CCES), a little under 23% of whites strongly agreed that "white people in the US have certain advantages because of the color of their skin," while 24% only somewhat agreed. Taken together, 47% of whites somewhat to strongly agreed that whites have racial advantage. A slightly higher percentage characterizes millennial whites (those born between 1981 and 1996) who at 59% somewhat to strongly agree that whites have advantages due to their whiteness. A majority of whites (55%) expressed strong agreement with the statement, "I am angry that racism exists" (DeSante & Smith, 2020). Hence, in present day U.S. society and politics, a substantial percentage of whites are aware of white privilege and most whites are even angry that racism exists. These facts have not lessened the gap between U.S. ideals and practices. On the contrary, scholarship points to a widened gap instead (Abrajano & Hajnal, 2015; Alexander, 2012; Cramer, 2016; Hernández, 2017; Hochschild, 2016; Kinder & Kam, 2009; Shapiro, 2017; Sides, Tesler, & Vavreck, 2019; Tesler, 2012a, 2016b). Myrdal's belief in whites' moral choice to choose to work to lessen the gap if only they are made aware is unrealized. This is the case, I argue, as well as many others, because whites not only benefit from the gap, but most are active participants and complicit in its existence.

The American Mosaic Project researchers also found that about 54% of whites were unwilling to believe that laws and institutions contribute significantly to their own advantage over non-white groups (Hartmann et al., 2010). On the contrary, the study shows that 81% of non-white respondents believe that laws and institutions contribute to white advantage. In the 2016 American National Election Studies (ANES) study, only about 26% of whites said whites have too much influence in U.S. politics and only 30% said the government treats whites better than Blacks (American National Election Studies, University of Michigan, & Stanford University, 2017). U.S. institutions were designed to confer and normalize such white privilege. Thus, admitting that laws and institutions privilege whites is to also admit that most laws and U.S. institutions were created to do just that (Beltrán, 2020; Olson, 2004). Furthermore, it requires an admission by whites that they themselves are a party to such a system, a system of white supremacy. Joel Olson's (2004) argument about the implications of this refusal to recognize these facts is worth quoting at length here:

> Racial oppression makes full democracy impossible, but it has also made American democracy possible. Conversely, American democracy has made racial oppression possible, for neither slavery nor segregation nor any other form of racial domination could have survived without the tacit or explicit consent of the white majority. American democracy is a white democracy, a polity ruled in the interests of a white citizenry. (p. xv)

Political scientists Donald Kinder and Lynn Sanders (1996) find that Myrdal's predictions do not hold. Kinder and Sanders find that, whereas most whites adhere to liberal and inclusive ideals in theory, they distinguish the principles from the application of them by opposing policies, like affirmative action, aimed at realizing those liberal ideals. Most whites defend the "wages of whiteness" (Du Bois, 1966; Roediger, 2007). Some whites, however, have in the past as well as in contemporary politics worked to actively dismantle the system of white supremacy (Chappell, 1994; Dillon, 1969; Garrison, 1995), or what Olson (2004) calls "white democracy." Because whiteness is a choice, whites can also choose to do differently. Choosing to do differently or "undoing [the choice of whiteness] does not mean simply refusing to classify people by race; it means abandoning a politics in which the standing of one section of the population is premised on the debasement of another" (p. xviii). Non-Hispanic white Americans can choose to identify with their white racial identity or not or can choose to deem it an important aspect of their identity or not. However, unless whites are actively working to reject white supremacy through discourse *and* action, they continue to be complicit in the system from which they themselves benefit.[8] The decision to deviate from this system and their group, which a small percentage of whites do, is a political *and* moral choice, as is the decision to actively perpetuate the system or remain complicit.

To be clear, in describing whites' immigration political policy choices as moral choices, I am making a larger argument that whites' political behavior has always also been rooted in morality, often regardless of the actual behavior or universal definition of what is "moral." Exemplary of this are debates about the slave trade and colonial slavery between colonists and British abolitionists over the nature of liberty (Brown, 2012). Historian Christopher L. Brown, in his book *Moral capital*, argues that at some point in the 18th century it became a political virtue among British people to espouse anti-slavery and anti-slave trade attitudes and that we should understand British abolitionism as the result of moral capital. In other words, much like many U.S. abolitionists, their British counterparts did not reject slavery and the slave trade out of humanitarianism and a belief in the equality of all men and women, a moral choice; they did so out of their own selfish need for imperial rule, what Brown calls moral capital. In other words, to gain morality points (capital) to use later to justify British expansion. U.S. politics, generally, point to historical and contemporary tensions between deeply moral conceptions, such as liberty, freedom, and equality—the very values on which the United States claims to be founded—and policymaking in practice. As such, white identity politics is both political and moral.

This book employs morality as a conceptual framing device. Often, white individuals use discourses of colorblindness, meritocracy, individualism, and egalitarianism to engage in anti-racist work. These discourses are grounded in traditional concepts of morality and moral responsibilities, which help maintain white innocence and complicity. This signals an understanding of morality that is deeply invested in misunderstanding structural inequalities and race-based violence. The uses of moral values have always been part of the ideology of whiteness. Historically, concepts such as manifest destiny point to the foundational use of morality for self-interested behavior, in particular, the political decisions and actions that place white-identified people in positions of political, economic, and social supremacy over those who are racialized as non-white.

The notable contribution of this book to the field of immigration is that it uniquely argues that not only does whiteness structure immigration but that immigration attitudes are inherently moral choices—choices that are learned through the socialization of group norms. Partisanship and whiteness dictate group norms. White identity, identification, and whiteness undergird these moral narratives in varying ways. Whites' immigration choices either reproduce whiteness or repudiate it within the continuum of white supremacy.

Outline of the Book

In Chapter 1, I delineate the theoretical underpinnings of the book. I focus on the framework of moral and immoral whiteness to make three interrelated arguments about whites' attitudes on immigration. Grounding my theory in the history of immigration in the United States, I argue that whiteness structures immigration and thus immigration attitudes are moral choices. Since whiteness is about an understanding of race and power and thus moral culpability, whites' political attitudes and behavior should be understood via this lens. The final aspect of my argument is that whites' moral norms, the values, beliefs, and roles that dictate ingroup behavior, are intimately connected to whites' socialization and in turn their political and psychological predispositions. One of the contributions of this book in the burgeoning scholarship on white identity politics in political science is my argument that white racial identity is not as consequential to whites' attitudes and political behavior as a deeper understanding of how whiteness is embedded in whites' moral choices and behavior outside of group identification. The remaining chapters address key elements of my theory.

Chapter 2 tackles the connection between whiteness, immigration, and morality. I argue for the importance of predispositions as manifestations of whites' moral compass. Predispositions, as byproducts of socialization, either perpetuate whites' restrictive and punitive attitudes and beliefs about immigration or help attenuate these beliefs. Focusing on moral traditionalism, authoritarianism, racial resentment, egalitarianism, and partisanship, I argue that whiteness moderates the strength of whites' predispositions. The chapter goes through each predisposition at length and connects each to morality, to whites' moral understanding of "right" and "wrong." I also take the reader though the different levels of white identity that are addressed throughout the text and pinpoint the differences and the importance of understanding whiteness as something beyond an identity. Through descriptive data examination, I analyze how different measures and levels of whiteness influence whites' attitudes toward immigration, as well as a variety of other issues. I find that white racial identity is not as consequential to whites' attitudes as other levels of identification, namely ingroup favoritism and white group consciousness. I then test the relationship between whiteness and predispositions and find that whiteness informs the varying levels of predispositions.

Chapter 3 uses survey data to focus on whites' restrictive immigration attitudes. Most white Americans express restrictive immigration attitudes. I first show how these attitudes are related to the maintenance of the group, i.e., whiteness. I then test the relationship between white identity, white group consciousness, and predispositions on immigration attitudes. An examination of both white identity and white group consciousness reveals that the former very seldomly influences restrictive immigration attitudes, while the latter sporadically does. Once predispositions are considered, however, they are found to be stronger predictors of restrictive immigration attitudes. The chapter finds that white identity and whiteness do inform when predispositions are most important, and that moral traditionalism is one of the most consistent and strongest predictors of restrictive immigration attitudes. Chapter 4 is the flip side of Chapter 3, examining the minority of whites who hold progressive immigration attitudes. This chapter argues that since whiteness structures immigration, an admission of white advantages and privilege should diminish restrictive immigration attitudes and influence progressive immigration attitudes among whites. In essence,

Chapter 4 asks why some whites perpetuate the system of white supremacy while others reject it. I argue that the choice of race cognizance is a moral choice with deep political consequences. This chapter leaves the reader with four important findings. First, awareness of white racial advantages among whites pushes whites toward more progressive attitudes. Second, predispositions, byproducts of socialization, are associated with whether whites are pushed toward awareness or away from it. Third, patriotism is an important factor in determining white racial awareness. Finally, the influence of white racial awareness and predispositions are particularly telling for white Democrats. The reader will find references to Appendix B in Chapter 2–4. Appendix B is an online only appendix that can be found at: https://bit.ly/Matos_MoralWhiteness_AppendixB

Chapter 5 uses original roll call data to examine the consequences of whites' decision-making in electing state-level representatives who make decisions about how immigration is enforced in their state. Beginning in the 1970s, U.S. states started to pass or attempt to pass state-level restrictive (anti-sanctuary) and/or progressive (sanctuary) immigration legislation. However, not until the 1990s did a few states succeed in passing state-level immigration policies. These policies have detrimental consequences on immigrant communities, and those perceived as foreigners, in that they dictate daily life and mobility with (anti-sanctuary) or without (sanctuary) fear of punishment. I link white Americans' individual moral choice to elect certain representatives over others, who then vote on immigration legislation structured by white supremacy and party norms. I ground Chapter 5 in the historical link between the Fugitive Slave Law of 1850 and Northern Liberty Laws and anti- and pro-sanctuary legislation to further argue how whiteness structures (im)migration legislation aimed at controlling and surveilling non-white mobility to maintain the racial status quo. Ultimately, I find that representatives who served more non-Hispanic whites were more likely to vote against sanctuary. Chapter 5 is the culmination of the breadth and depth of how whiteness operates in immigration politics and the tangible consequences of whites' moral and immoral choices.

In sum, this book provides a much-needed lens for our understanding of white Americans' attitudes toward immigration as well as a host of other social policies. After the Civil Rights Movement, white elites and organizations worked hard to disentangle white identity from whiteness. This has resulted in scholarship that also divorces whites' attitudes and behavior from the political decisions they continue to make. Whites continue to oppose social policies that aim to level the playing field across racialized and minoritized groups and policies like immigration, which continue to perpetuate a pre-civil rights idea of white supremacy. Without an understanding of how immigration as well as other regimes and institutions continue to perpetuate white supremacy, imagining anything different is almost impossible. There is a link between whiteness and American-ness—between whiteness and the very institutions that define the United States—that continues to be important to write about and examine. The United States of America has chosen whiteness as its modal category, and this has been and continues to be a moral choice; a choice that white Americans do not have to make, but most continue to do so.

1

Moral and Immoral Whiteness
in Immigration Politics

In this book, I offer a theoretical framework that pushes our current understanding of whites' immigration attitudes, that of moral and immoral whiteness. My theory rests on three primary arguments. First, whiteness structures immigration attitudes. Second, immigration attitudes are moral choices. Finally, political and psychological predispositions give meaning to the moral foundation undergirding immigration attitudes.

My theory enriches our current understanding of immigration public opinion and policymaking in the United States in at least three ways. First, the current literature, especially in political science, is almost ahistorical. It treats white identity as completely disassociated from whiteness and from a history of white supremacy, empire, settler colonialism, slavery, and power (Bonilla-Silva, 1997, 2014; Frankenberg, 1993; Harris, 1993; Lewis, 2004; Lipsitz, 1998; Lopez, 1997; Omi & Winant, 2015; Roediger, 2007). To understand how whiteness works for white people is to understand how the U.S. racial hierarchy and U.S. institutions not only structure whites' understanding of their own group but also affirm their privileged position. Relatedly, the literature on immigration public opinion focuses on either whites' outgroup attitudes or, more recently, whites' ingroup attitudes. However, race is relational and outgroup and ingroup attitudes cannot be separated, especially for whites, whose definition as whites was born out of its purported antithesis, blackness. Hence, the argument made that there is a distinction between ingroup favoritism and outgroup hostility (Jardina, 2019) undermines the relationality of race and, quite frankly, how whiteness was socially constructed from its inception. To define white identity as unrelated to outgroups is to perpetuate a definition of white identity, or race, as color, an essential component to the norm of colorblindness. The new—post–civil rights—definition of race "denies the real linkage between race and oppression under systemic white supremacy" (Harris, 1993, p. 1768).

Moral and Immoral Whiteness in Immigration Politics. Yalidy Matos, Oxford University Press.
© Oxford University Press 2023. DOI: 10.1093/oso/9780197656259.003.0002

Second, I argue that the project of whiteness is political *and* moral, a narrative missing in the current scholarship. An examination of white racial attitudes should dismiss modern understandings of race, what Gotanda (1991) describes as "formal-race," where racial classifications are neutral and apolitical "descriptions reflecting merely 'skin color' or country of ancestral origin" (p. 4). This understanding of race should be dismissed precisely because it is defined as "unrelated to ability, disadvantage, or moral culpability . . . [and] unconnected to social attributes such as culture, education, wealth or language" (p. 4). If we are to understand immigration as a project grounded in whiteness, whites' moral psychology, a racialized understanding of right and wrong, is deeply related to white attitudes. Immigration attitudes are structured by whiteness and are thus moral in nature. A conceptualization of whites' immigration attitudes as moral invites a different kind of attention beyond the centrality of being white to whites and toward a politics of accountability and moral responsibility.

Finally, current work on immigration attitudes overlooks the significance and role of political and psychological predispositions—such as partisanship, authoritarianism, moral traditionalism, egalitarianism, racial resentment, and power-cognizance—in how whiteness functions. For example, the meaning of whiteness post–civil rights should be understood along a political continuum (Winant, 2004b). In the post-Obama era, scholars have shown empirically two sides of racialization due to the increased effects of racial attitudes on partisan attachments (Tesler, 2016b; Tesler & Sears, 2010). White racial liberals became increasingly more Democratic while white racial conservatives became more Republican. A kind of white racial dualism (Winant, 2004b) arose that is attached to the political projects of whiteness, on both the left and the right. These political projects, ranging from the far right to liberal to abolitionist projects aimed at abolishing whiteness, give meaning to whiteness. A disaffiliation between white supremacy and white identity is the common denominator among all of the white racial projects (Wiegman, 2012; Winant, 2004b). I argue that predispositions help frame whites' political and moral choices.

This book places race center stage, framing immigration policies as structured by whiteness, and a moral and political project committed to white supremacy. I will use a race and ethnic politics lens to understand the group centeredness of white immigration attitudes. In doing so, I argue that race for white Americans matters in ways that have gone previously understudied in political science even as it is vastly studied in other fields. Identity for white Americans is advantageous, as the historically dominant group in the United States. To "be white" has utility that is sometimes economic and sometimes psychological but always profitable (Akerlof & Kranton, 2010; Harris, 1993). Identity politics for whites is necessarily distinct from identity politics for non-white groups, given the distinct historical avenue of whiteness in U.S. politics and society.[1]

Theories of White Public Opinion on Immigration

We know a lot about immigration attitudes, especially the attitudes of non-Hispanic white Americans. White Americans are generally more opposed to immigration than other racial and ethnic groups in the United States (Abrajano & Hajnal, 2015; Espenshade & Hempstead, 1996; Kinder & Sanders, 1996; Schuman, Steeh, & Bobo, 1985). There is considerably less attention to white support of immigration and/or immigrants. The literature on immigration generally tries to understand the determinants of the public's views on immigration-related policy and immigrants at the individual level. Two broad categories are often put forward to understand opposition to immigration. One focuses on personal economic concerns, such as labor market competition (Hainmueller & Hiscox, 2010; Mayda, 2006; Scheve & Slaughter, 2001) and fiscal burdens (Dustmann & Preston, 2007; Facchini, Mayda, & Puglisi, 2017; Hanson, Scheve, & Slaughter, 2007). Overall, investigations of the impact of economic factors have yielded mixed results. The other category focuses on symbolic factors: Theories of symbolic politics posit that political attitudes and behaviors are motivated primarily by emotionally fraught predispositions such as partisanship and racial attitudes, which has produced much more consistent results (Burns & Gimpel, 2000).

Symbolic politics (Sears, Sidanius, & Bobo, 2000) show that affective and long-standing beliefs about particular groups or people within the political environment drive mass opinion and policy preferences. Scholars examining the impact of symbolic factors have investigated racial prejudice or race more broadly (Ayers, Hofstetter, Schnakenberg, & Kolody, 2009; Kinder & Sanders, 1996), as well as ideology/partisanship (Abrajano & Hajnal, 2015; Chandler & Tsai, 2001), nativism/cultural threat (Citrin, Reingold, & Green, 1990; Citrin & Sides, 2008; Knoll, 2013), and social context (Hero & Tolbert, 1996;

Hopkins, 2010; Rocha & Espino, 2009; Tolbert & Grummel, 2003). More recent work suggests there is a third camp operating as well, that of white identity politics (Chudy, Piston, & Shipper, 2019; Jardina, 2019; Jardina, Kalmoe, & Gross, 2021; Schildkraut, 2019). This section goes through these three categories and the following section delves deeper into what is missing from our current understanding of white immigration attitudes.

Economic Concerns

Economic concerns as a predictor of immigration attitudes deliver mixed results. A few studies argue that economic concerns are at the heart of anti-immigrant sentiment and anti-immigration policy preferences. Some scholars argue that individual attitudes toward immigration come from a fear about labor market competition—fear that immigrants will take away jobs from natives, contribute to higher unemployment, and reduce wages and working conditions of certain occupations (Hainmueller & Hiscox, 2010; Scheve & Slaughter, 2001). Fiscal burden on public services and general beliefs about the status of the welfare state is another manifestation of economic concerns (Facchini et al., 2017; Hainmueller & Hiscox, 2010). Both are about personal self-interest. Hainmueller and Hiscox (2010) find that a more national sociotropic view of the economy plays a role. This view is less about personal concerns and more a concern about the national outlook of the economy. Citrin, Green, Muste, and Wong (1997) and other scholars (Espenshade & Hempstead, 1996; Lee & Ottati, 2002) find that national economic concerns and anxiety over taxes play a role in immigration preferences. However, Burns and Gimpel (2000) find that these effects disappear once prejudicial stereotypes about immigrants are considered.

Evident in the findings is that there is no consistent answer as to whether economic concerns, whether personal or more sociotropic, play a definite role in individual attitudes toward immigration policy. However, economic concerns, whether personal or sociotropic, play a major role in how immigration is framed to the public as coded language for racial threat. Consider, for example, California's 1994 Proposition 187, the Save Our State initiative. This ballot initiative was established to prohibit or curtail undocumented immigrants' use of state-funded public services such as health care and public education (Campbell, Wong, & Citrin, 2006; Chong & Druckman, 2011; Garcia, 1995; Jacobson, 2008; Valentino, Brader, & Jardina, 2013).

Symbolic Politics

Much of the scholarship on white attitudes toward immigration focuses on outgroup attitudes. The literature on symbolic attitudes is clear that racial prejudice is a key predictor of white public opinion on immigration (Brader, Valentino, & Jardina, 2009; Burns & Gimpel, 2000; Hutchings & Wong, 2014; Kinder & Kam, 2009). In the field of white public opinion on immigration, there is a dearth of scholarship on the role of white ingroup identity and attitudes. In fact, prior work has mostly claimed that white ingroup attitudes are not particularly relevant to politics (Kinder & Winter, 2001; Sears & Savalei, 2006; Wong & Cho, 2005).[2] New work in white identity politics remedies this gap; however, I argue that whites' outgroup hostility or prejudice is necessarily connected to their ingroup attitudes.

Symbolic politics, namely racial prejudice, influence attitudes toward immigration as it concerns non-white immigrants, such as Latinos, Asians, and immigrants from African countries (Burns & Gimpel, 2000). Brader and colleagues (2009) find that negative stereotypes about Latinos in particular have dominated white attitudes toward immigration. In other words, when white Americans think about immigration, they are generally thinking of Latino immigrants (also see Pérez, 2016).

Scholars have also pointed to a general predisposition of ethnocentrism and whites' position in society as important determinants (Kinder & Kam, 2009).[3] Ethnocentrism refers to a "relatively consistent frame of mind concerning 'aliens' generally" (Adorno, Frenkel-Brunswik, Levinson, & Sanford, 1950, p. 102; as qtd in Kinder & Kam, 2009, p. 16) which predisposes most Americans to want immigration to be restricted, to withhold government benefits from immigrants, to require immigrant children to learn English, and to establish English as the official language of the United States.

Blumer's theory of group position comes close to theorizing about whites' understanding of their own positioning vis-à-vis non-white outgroups, but the theory stakes out no claim about whites' racial identity saliency. In Blumer's theory, it is almost a given that whites understand their position as white people in relation to non-white groups. Hutchings and Wong (2014) examine the influence of prejudice and group position on attitudes toward immigration among non-Hispanic whites and African Americans. They find that group position (Blumer, 1958)[4] accounts for immigration attitudes after controlling for other key variables, such as classical prejudice, racial resentment, and racial threat.

White Identity Politics

Newer work in political science focuses on the influence of white identity politics on immigration attitudes (Chudy et al., 2019; Jardina, 2019; Jardina et al., 2021; Metzl, 2019; Mutz, 2018; Pérez et al., 2021; Schildkraut, 2019). Recent work argues that white ingroup attitudes have been much more prevalent since the election of the United States' first Black president. According to Ashley Jardina (2019), white identity remains invisible when whites remain at the top of the racial hierarchy but gets activated when whites fear status loss. Once activated, white identity becomes increasingly relevant and accessible in shaping white attitudes and behavior, especially policies aimed at the collective interests of whites. In a study measuring white identity by asking whites how important being white is to their identity, Jardina finds that about 30%–40% of the sample indicate that being white is very or extremely important to their identity. She also taps into white consciousness by asking whites if they agree that whites should work together toward changing laws that are unfair to whites and the likelihood that whites are unable to find jobs because employers are hiring minorities. In her examination of policy attitudes, Jardina finds that white identity is negatively associated with pro-immigration attitudes, which she frames as a policy that threatens whites' status.

Whiteness allows white Americans choices vis-à-vis their identity (Masuoka & Junn, 2013) and these micro-level choices have macro-level behavioral consequences. White identity, I argue, really is more than just asking whites about identity centrality; it is also, and more importantly, a series of moral choices. How one chooses to identify oneself racially matters for self-image and belonging, and also for politics (Dawson, 1994; Jardina, 2019). That is, racial identity influences how people view themselves and others, as well as the world and issues, influencing the political behavior and choices individuals make. However, when only 30%–40% of the white American population suggests being white is important to them, it raises the question as to why so many more of them are voting against their economic interests in ways that seem to be based in racial identity. While exact figures for white non–college graduates, who, like all non–college graduates, stood to lose through Republican policies, are not available, 64% of non–college graduates and 54% of whites voted Republican in 2016 (Pew Research Center, 2018). How do we theorize about whites who have anti-immigration attitudes but who express that being white is not important to them? I argue that an examination of whiteness is necessary when examining white racial identity in ways that necessitate a different strategy precisely because of whites' group position in the United States. This project examines how both whiteness and racial identity matter for immigration policy preferences among white Americans.

I argue that identity is not separate from the historical context that helped create it. White racial identity (white racialization) cannot be detached from white supremacy, empire, settler colonialism, slavery, and power (Bonilla-Silva, 1997, 2014; Frankenberg, 1993; Harris, 1993; Lewis, 2004; Lipsitz, 1998; Lopez, 1997; Omi & Winant, 2015; Roediger, 2007). Furthermore, throughout U.S. history, movements and ideologies have also run counter to white supremacy, such as the abolitionist movement, progressivism, and liberal theology (Brewer Stewart, 1976; Garrison, 1995; Harrold, 2001; Moreno, 2013; Oshatz, 2008, 2011). Racialization is the process by which a group of people are defined by "race" and that race is given meaning. Michael Omi and Howard Winant (2015) define racialization as "the extension of racial meaning to a previously racially unclassified relationship, social practice, or group" (p. 111). Legal racialization is the process of racialization institutionalized or made legal by federal, state, or local policies and laws. White racialization depends "on a context forged by historical circumstances that have simultaneously influenced and structured political institutional practices" (Weller & Junn, 2018, p. 439; also see Acharya, Blackwell, & Sen, 2018). White identity is formed through racialization and maintained through socialization—this assumption exists a priori within my theoretical specification—which ultimately result in the predispositions human beings carry, which are in line with the norms and values they hold to be true (Zaller, 1992) and that ultimately influence political behavior.

Whiteness Structures Immigration Attitudes

Immigration is one of the most enduring and significant forces shaping the United States. As is whiteness. An examination of white identity without attention to white racialization and how U.S.-American white identity is born out of violence and "othering" misses a crucial point that "racial identity is not just an individualized process but involves the formation of social groups organized around material interest with their roots in social structure, not just individual consciousness" (Andersen, 2003, pp. 29–30).[5] As Baldwin

(1998) argues, "America became white—the people who, as they claim, 'settled' the country became white—because of the necessity of denying the Black presence, and justifying the Black subjugation" (p. 178).

To understand whites' attitudes toward immigration is to understand how whiteness structures immigration attitudes and policymaking, both past and present. One gap in the current literature on white identity politics in political science is the ahistorical and contextually fragile nature of white identity. That is, it has erroneously disassociated white racial identity with the history and meaning of whiteness as a racial classification and as a system of white supremacy and its ever-evolving processes.

Pre–Civil Rights Era

As a social construction, race is not stagnant. It is shaped and molded by context (time and place). The meaning of whiteness and how it operates is no different. Prior to the Civil Rights Movement and during de jure segregation and discrimination, white identity and white supremacy were intimately linked and for many were one and the same. It is easy to argue that whiteness structured immigration policymaking and attitudes prior to the 1960s, and many scholars have done so (Das, 2020; Haney Lopez, 2006; Higham, 1958; Ngai, 2004; Parker, 2015; Schrag, 2010; Takaki, 1989).

During the 19th century and the first half of the 20th century, the nation was imagined in racial terms. Immigration can lead to a path to citizenship, and because of this immigration policy shapes "Americans' understanding of national membership and citizenship, drawing lines of inclusion and exclusion" (Ngai, 2004, p. 5). Hence, restrictive immigration policies and laws created and recreated racial difference during this time, namely the "legal racialization" of non-white groups, which casts them as permanently foreign and unassimilable. As Harris (1993) makes clear, "Whiteness conferred on its owners aspects of citizenship that were all the more valued because they were denied to others. Indeed, the very fact of citizenship itself was linked to white racial identity" institutionalized and normalized by the Naturalization Act of 1790 (p. 1744). Furthermore, Harris notes, the trajectory of expanding democratic rights for whites since 1790 coincides with the contraction of the same rights for Blacks (p. 1744). The production of racial difference did not happen absent of the production of whiteness. Whiteness had to be defined if racial others were to also be defined.

Alien land laws exemplify the production and reproduction of whiteness vis-à-vis other groups. Beginning in 1913, several U.S. states, including California and Arizona, started to pass laws to limit land ownership by non-citizens.[6] They were written as race-neutral, but they primarily targeted Asian immigrants, who were already barred from obtaining citizenship as a result of immigration laws, namely the Chinese Exclusion Act and the 1917 Immigration Act, and by default barred from land ownership.[7] In practice white non-citizen immigrants were not seen as foreign and thus they could migrate from state to state, own land, and accumulate wealth through property ownership.

Indeed, the purpose of earlier alien land laws, which explicitly permitted non-citizens to own land, was to increase white dominance (Lazarus, 1989), such as the 1864 law passed in Washington territory. In this case, displacing Native peoples was a priority. Such laws had been in essence homestead acts[8] designed to encourage white immigration to turn the land from "Indian country" to "white man's land" by giving any alien the right to "acquire and hold lands . . . as if such alien were a native citizen of this Territory, or of the United States."[9] Oregon territory passed such a law in 1854 and then passed the later type of alien land law, barring non-citizens from land ownership, in 1923. They all had the same implication: Whites—even those who were first-generation immigrants, unnaturalized, and undocumented—were rightful inhabitants, rightful landowners, while Native peoples and Asians were not considered legitimate members of an expanding society. When the landscape of the United States and its territories started to change, when non-white bodies either started to migrate or were *recruited* to migrate for labor, the second wave of land laws became exclusionary. But like the earlier laws they were a tool used to empower whiteness.

Intrinsic to any analysis of race are concepts of nationalism and patriotism, which in the United States are intricately threaded. National citizenship has been and continues to be, especially vis-à-vis immigration, a major way by which race and racialization take place (Ngai, 2004). According to Yeatman (2003), "Westphalian interstate order necessarily entails constructing strangers, outsiders, aliens, foreigners and so on, in order to differentiate selves and others on national scales" (as qtd in Calcutt, Woodward, & Skrbis, 2009, p. 171). The Naturalization Law of 1790, the first attempt to define U.S. citizenship, proclaimed "That any alien, being a free white person, who shall have resided within the limits and under the jurisdiction of the United States for the term of two years, may be admitted to become a citizen thereof . . . making proof to the satisfaction of such court, that he is a person of good character."[10] Such constructions of strangers is attached not only to nation-building and national sovereignty but to patriotism as well. In fact, Robert S. Chang (1999) argues that in the United States the exclusion of foreigners is an expression of patriotism (as qtd in Harvey, 2007, p. 13). By definition, immigration delimits U.S. national identity; however, it does so by defining American-ness as a cultural identity that is explicitly descriptive about who belongs and who does not belong.

The invocation of "good character" conflated citizenship and nationality with heteronormativity (Brandzel, 2016) and was used to exclude some women, indentured servants, enslaved persons, and non-whites.[11] Without citizenship, non-whites were denied the right to vote and own property, among other things. The conflation of citizenship, race, and morally infused ideas about who belongs to the nation-state (i.e., good character) continued with amendments to immigration legislation.

Post–Civil Rights Era

Whiteness in the post–civil rights era has necessarily changed. As Winant writes (2004b), "white identity has been reinterpreted, rearticulated in a dualistic fashion: on the one hand, egalitarian, on the other hand, privileged; on the one hand, individualistic and 'color-blind,' on the other hand, 'normalized' and besieged" (p. 52). The post–civil rights era generated a split in the national white subject "between disaffiliation from white supremacist practices and disavowal of the structural reformation of white power and white investments in it" (Wiegman, 2012, pp. 150–151). In other words, once the white supremacist practice of segregation was legally abolished, so too was white power and investment in it. White supremacy was linked to segregation and overt racist practices; once those were deemed unconstitutional, so too was white supremacy. Wiegman (2012) argues that "coherent public discourse" about white power has been made impossible since the 1980s by the claim that the ending of official segregation constituted the ending of all institutionalized race inequality.

The seeming disconnection between white supremacist practices and white identity, what Howard Winant calls "white racial dualism," is the experience of division for whites. After the Civil Rights Movement, whites have to contend with the legacy of white supremacy, their inheritance of the benefits

of white supremacy (Biss, 2015), *and* are also "subject to the moral and political challenges posed to that inheritance by the partial but real successes
of the black movement. . . . As a result, white identities have been displaced
and refigured: They are now contradictory, as well as confused and anxiety-
ridden, to an unprecedented extent" (Winant, 2004a, p. 4).

In the 1960s, amid the African American Civil Rights Movement, as well
as the Chicano Movement in the Southwest, U.S. immigration law stood
out as incongruent to U.S. values of equality. The Civil Rights Movement
opposed racially discriminatory laws, including the 1952 Immigration and
Nationality Act's (INA) national origins quota restricting the immigration of
Southern Europeans and non-Europeans to the United States. This exclusion
was framed as protecting the United States' image in the world.

The 1965 Immigration Act placed the U.S. immigration system within the
same spirit as the Civil Rights Movement of a "new global egalitarianism"
(Hing, 1993). U.S. immigration policies are a byproduct of containment,
repression, and rearticulation strategies that were implemented during the
Civil Rights Movement (see Anderson, 2003). These were the same tactics
used by the new right, neoconservatists, and neoliberalists to maintain white
supremacy.

The 1965 Act was supposed to keep the country a *white* nation (Gjelten,
2015; Jacobson, 1998, 2006). Specifically, it prioritized family reunification
instead of skilled labor due to a nativist Democratic member of Congress,
Representative Michael Feighan of Ohio. Feighan was chairman of the House
Immigration subcommittee, and he demanded the change. While it would be
key to the dramatic demographic changes that followed,[12] Feighan saw it as
a way to effectively continue the national origins quota and Asian exclusion.
Conservative groups were persuaded by this logic, including the American
Legion, whose members said that Feighan had "devised a naturally operating
national-origin system." They wrote cheerfully, "Nobody is quite so apt to be
of the same national origins of our present citizens as are members of their
immediate families" (Gjelten, 2015, p. 126).

After the civil rights era, one can track a moral crisis of whiteness. Policy
can be used as the foundation to track such crisis, including the battle over
affirmative action (Kinder & Sanders, 1996; Sears, Sidanius, and Bobo, 2000;
Steinberg, 1995), welfare (Hancock, 2004; Quadagno, 1996), and immigration.
Starting in the 1970s, colorblindness emerged as a hegemonic racial project
(Omi & Winant, 2015, p. 205), which led to the emergence of a new type of
racism. Immigration, I argue, is a policy in which we can track the moral crisis

of whiteness, especially through racially coded language, seemingly race-neutral language, and in the 1980s and 1990s—as we see conservativism ramp up—an immigration regime focused on control, detention, and deportation.

Both civil rights and immigration legislation succumbed to race neutrality, and as a result the substance and extent of the rights attained were constrained. The white racial dualism theorized by Winant (2004a) is indicative of how a post–civil rights immigration system started to emerge. On the one hand, immigration policy needed to appear to conform to U.S. values and democracy and, on the other hand, immigration policy was never intended to change the demographic mosaic of the country.

In the aftermath of civil rights reform, there is a liberalizing demand that all white racial projects inherit. Amid this demand, "that white identity be differentiated in discourse and image from white racist self-fashionings" (Wiegman, 2012, p. 153), the country had to deal with the unanticipated consequences of the 1965 Act, including the dramatic increase in Asian and Latino immigrants and decrease in white immigration. The 1980s and 1990s saw a resurgence of reactionary politics, or what scholars call white backlash (Abrajano & Hajnal, 2015), along various policy avenues. It is in the post-segregationist era, the era where all white racial projects were trying to disentangle white identity and white supremacy, that we start to witness policies that, in fact, are aimed at maintaining the racial status quo through colorblind ideology and race neutrality in the name of U.S. democracy and values.

Manifestations included the "War on Drugs" and the ramping up of incarceration of Black bodies (Alexander, 2010), as well as welfare and immigration reforms. The Immigration Reform and Control Act (IRCA) of 1986, signed by President Reagan, and the 1996 Illegal Immigration Reform and Immigrant Responsibility Act (IIRIRA), signed by President Clinton, reflected the role of immigration in the backlash. There was a ramping up of criminalizing immigrant behavior and detaining immigrants. IRCA marked a shift in how the United States approached immigration enforcement. More resources were channeled to border enforcement as well as detention and removal activities. Between 1985 and 2002, for example, detention and removal/intelligence activities multiplied, with an increase in appropriations of over 751% (Dixon & Gelatt, 2005). In 1980, immigrant detention centers had the capacity to hold over 4,000 detainees; by 1994 this number had increased to 6,785 and by 2009 to 33,400 (Juarez, Gomez-Aguinaga, & Bettez, 2018). While IRCA provided a pathway to citizenship for *some*, it also ramped up apprehensions. The number of apprehensions peaked at 1.7 million in 1986 (Massey & Pren, 2012).

In the years prior to IRCA, a new wave of Irish immigrants had entered America, largely settling in Boston. The rhetoric surrounding Irish immigrants was quite distinct from the rhetoric of the "Latino threat" (Chavez, 2013) that attended Latin American immigration.[13] *Time* hailed the approximately 100,000 Irish newcomers that had come beginning in 1982 and overstayed their visas, thus becoming undocumented immigrants, as the "Re-Greening of America" (Magnuson & Painton, 1989). "[U]nlike the flood of Third World immigrants, the Irish come with advantages: white skin, good education, a knowledge of the language and a talent for politics," the article stated (Magnuson & Painton, 1989). A *New York Times* headline called these "new Irish" "illegal but not alien," manifested in both rhetoric and experience as these new immigrants were met with direct services in Boston (Gold, 1989). Rather than a painful disruption to the landscape of Boston, *Times* journalist Allan Gold explained that Boston "wholeheartedly embraces these new Irish, despite their illegal status, largely because so many people of Irish descent live [in Boston] and have fond feelings for their ancestral home" (Gold, 1989).

These Irish newcomers represented the immigrant narrative,[14] the kind that is assimilable, not perpetually foreign, regardless of legal status. The response contrasted sharply with another *Time* article that ran about a year later, which referenced the "browning of America." It bemoaned the shrinking number of towns in the country "where English and Irish and German surnames will predominate, where a traditional (some will wistfully say 'real') America will still be seen on almost every street corner" (Henry, 1990). These towns, the article says, "will be only the vestiges of an earlier nation." The difference in tone and message regarding the greening and browning of the United States work to create completely different fates for immigrants who are treated as forever foreign, while others are seen as almost unequivocally belonging—this is the politics of belonging—even though they lack the same documents. The Irish's undocumented presence was not "alien," it was quite normalized, seen as natural, while Mexican presence, for example, was seen as unnatural and transgressing. These differences are inherently about how whiteness has been (and continues to be) defined.

Another example of how whiteness continued to structure immigration politics is the creation of the Diversity Visa Lottery through the Immigration Act of 1990. The Diversity Visa Lottery Program was designed to help admit those immigrants from low-admittance countries, defined as any country with fewer than 50,000 natives admitted to the United States in the previous five years. At the end of a successful lottery process, individuals are granted lawful permanent resident status (or green card status), which is different than individuals who come to the United States on a non-immigrant tourist visa and overstay their visa, who are not counted as being admitted in the United States. Advocates, including Irish American lawmakers such as Senator Edward Kennedy (D-MA), specifically advocated for the measures as a means to help Irish and Italian immigrants after the demographic shifts due to the 1965 Immigration Act (Alvarez, 2017; Law, 2017). While the Immigration Act of 1990, through the Diversity Visa Lottery program, provided immigrants from Ireland, Italy, and some other primarily white countries an easier (and legal) way to enter the United States, it also increased border enforcement, limited the legal rights of "criminal aliens," and led to two Southern border operations, Operation Blockade in El Paso (1993; later renamed Operation Hold the Line) and Operation Gatekeeper in San Diego (1994).[15] White immigrants who came by airplane were would-be Americans, while immigrants who come over land, are "criminal aliens," always and in all ways un-American.

The decade of the 1990s saw a resurgence of the militia movement[16] and conservative media outlets, as well as the revival of anti-immigration initiatives and hysteria that focused on racial/ethnic distinctions. It is not a coincidence that it all happened in tandem. Anti-immigration initiatives included IIRIRA and the Antiterrorism and Effective Death Penalty Act (AEDPA) also signed in 1996. Through these laws thousands who had been legal residents became deportable, and immigrants were furthered criminalized by an expanded list of crimes that made them eligible for deportation. For example, prior to AEDPA and IIRIRA, non-citizen immigrants, including legal residents, had to receive a sentence of five years or more for the crime to be considered an aggravated felony. After 1996, sentences (or the possibility of a sentence) of one year can be considered an aggravated felony. Aggravated felonies are deportable offenses that preclude immigrants from asking for discretionary relief and in many cases expedite removal without the right to a hearing before a judge (Johnson, 2001). After the 1993 World Trade Center attack and Oklahoma City bombing, immigration was conflated with terrorism (Massey, 2009, p. 20). The impact was the permanent creation of a racialized underclass of non-white bodies, mainly but not entirely Mexican immigrants (Hing, 2009).[17] The legislation generally conflated Latinos with crime, danger, terrorism, and creating a drag on society by collecting unde-served public benefits (Cacho, 2012).[18] The AEDPA also conflates Muslims and Americans perceived as Muslim (and thus all Arabs, other Middle Easterners, and Southeast Asians) with terrorists (Corbin, 2017).

The significance of whiteness in the development of restrictive immi-gration policies, alongside restrictive drug and counterterrorism policies, cannot be overstated. Whiteness has been and continues to be *the* protected status; whiteness is what these policies aimed to protect, not the economy or national security. The language in IIRIRA and AEDPA may have been race-neutral, but their outcomes were not, including the militarization of the U.S.–Mexico border; the mass incarceration of Black people, including Black immigrants; the mass detention of Latino, mainly Mexican, immigrants; and the sharp reduction of the rights of such detainees. The conflation of the U.S.–Mexico border with criminality, drugs, and terrorism simulta-neously conflates these things with racial others. However, racial others—whether Mexican or not—cannot be understood without their counterpart. Whiteness is inherently embedded in the U.S. immigration regime, in-cluding immigration law, defining belonging in racial terms. IIRIRA only cemented these ideas, and, ultimately, became the legal foundation of a post-9/11 world.

Following the terrorist attacks of 2001, the War on Terror and the subse-quent discourse of national security gave way to the ideological rationale behind anti-immigration legislation and unprecedented levels of deportations and U.S. Immigration and Customs Enforcement (ICE) raids (Chacón, 2006). Even though immigration was actually on the decline between 2001 and 2003, immi-gration prosecutions increased from 16,300 to 38,000 (Chacón, 2006). In line with the "new penology" of criminality, the state deploys immigration law, sur-veillance, and detention against non-white immigrants by framing these meas-ures as a means to prevent terrorism even though there is a scarcity of terrorist operations linked to Mexican nationals or individuals of Mexican descent (De Genova, 2007, p. 434). The conflation of the U.S.–Mexico border with terrorism led to the passage of the Secure Fence Act of 2006, which provided authoriza-tion for the construction of hundreds of miles of additional fencing along the southern U.S. border; more vehicle barriers, checkpoints, and lighting; and increased use of advanced technology for enforcement at the border. In a con-tinuation of the "Latino threat" narrative of the 1990s, terrorism provided the pretext to describe immigrants, who had previously been seen as a threat prima-rily to national *identity* (Kaplan, 2003), as a threat to national *security*.

The new race-neutral policies, much like the family reunification provision, were designed to suppress changes in the racial status quo and they did so successfully. By marginalizing groups as "others," they maintained the racial hierarchy. As Patricia Hill Collins (2000) argues, "strangers threaten the moral and social order of society. But they are simultaneously essential for its survival because those individuals who stand at the margins of society clarify its boundaries. . . . [B]y not belonging, [they] emphasize the significance of belonging" (p. 70). Understanding this is essential to an understanding of how the colorblind racism that emerged in the 1970s, took hold in the 1980s, and came into full force in the 1990s influenced U.S. immigration policies.

Immigration policy attitudes and white political behavior tie into the long history of race in the United States, the use of policy for exclusionary purposes, and the morally infused ways in which inclusion, exclusion, and *othering* happens under a veneer of (white) American values, norms, and concepts—for instance, "citizenship," "Americanism," and "nationalism"— which are themselves racialized projects that mask the moral and political work of whiteness.

The production of the *other* is part of what articulates what it means to be white in the United States; thus, the presence of *otherness* necessitates the presence of whiteness and white racial identity. White racial identity is inescapable given that being white is socially recognizable and politically advantageous, and it is made real through relational interactions. White ingroup identity cannot exist outside of outgroups; it necessarily implicates outgroups. The constitution of whiteness as a racial group identity happens through *othering*, whether through violence or state-sanctioned policies. Policies work to produce and create white selves and the continuation of a white dominant privileged group. The link between "(Im)moral and political agency [give] 'white' (and White!) meaning" (Harvey, 2007, p. 31).[19] In essence, policy preferences (among many other forces) work to make legible white racial identity. White Americans could and should be confronted with the ways their policy preferences reveal their (im)moral choices and own moral standing.

Immigration Attitudes as Moral Choices

Being white in the United States is bound up with state violence, economics, nation-building, and other social realities with which those who have white identities must wrestle. "The fault lines of white identity," to quote Harvey (2007), "exist precisely because the relations of production by which white comes to be are fundamentally immoral" (p. 35). To be white is "a moral crisis" (p. 36). White Americans' political attitudes and behaviors are but one realm in which the moral crisis of whiteness gets realized. Political choices over policies become one way we can measure this crisis, and the inherently (im)moral choices that whites make.

The framing of white public opinion as a moral choice is scant in the field of political science. Morals are a set of principles that are derived from ideas about what is "good" or "right" and what is "bad" or "wrong." Put another way, morals conform to a standard of right that is localized and fluid and is often used for expediency (Bierce, 2000, p. 87). The standard of right can be derived from one's religion, culture, or group; or it can derive from universal beliefs about the standards humanity should follow. Morals have three important aspects. First, they depend on group, not just individual, conformity. The idea that one must conform necessitates a contract of sorts that delineates what these standards are, and individuals have to sign on, either consciously or unconsciously, to the standards. Whites do so through the racial contract (Mills, 1997). Second, morals are mutable, liable to change. In other words, what was "moral" in the 1800s and what is "moral" in the 2020s are likely to differ, at least in ways that signal the process of race and other constructions that define U.S. society. Finally, morals have a disposition of expediency—that is, the quality of being suitable for a particular end in mind. In other words, morals are subjective and often used toward an outcome that is suitable for those defining what is moral.

There is morality embedded in the choices or non-choices of whites, I argue, not because there are no white people, as Baldwin (1998) suggests, but because white people have been given and use unwarranted advantages due to their whiteness. Further, whites cannot escape whiteness, regardless of how they feel about it (Mills, 1997; Wiegman, 2012). Race, then, is a social construct *and* a real concept with tangible and often deadly consequences (Alexander, 2010; Omi & Winant, 2015). The racial categories are constructed, but there are material and psychological benefits to being white, just as there are to being of a particular class, sexuality, gender, and religion (Du Bois, 1966; McIntosh, 1989; Roediger, 2007). However, whites can make *choices* precisely because of their racialized, privileged standing in U.S. society. Whites' privilege is what allows for choices in ways that other non-white groups' choices are constrained.

Both moral and immoral whiteness are defined by how white people respond to whiteness, white privilege, and white supremacy. That is, "moral whiteness" involves recognizing whiteness (and not just white identity) and white privilege and actively defying the norms of white supremacy. Immoral whiteness involves making choices that are complicit with or that double down on the norms of white supremacy, denying white privilege, and failing to recognize whiteness or taking a colorblind approach to race. The moral choice is not in the expression of the importance of whiteness to one's identity but rather in the political and social behavior that follows from a white person's understanding of whiteness, white privilege, and white supremacy.[20]

The difference between being "white" and being "White" (Mills, 1997, p. 106) is the difference between understanding whiteness as a racial classification and understanding whiteness as a system of racialized standing intricately connected to white supremacy. This difference exists within a racial polity that defines whiteness by way of non-white racial subjugation. Hence to be white meant to live in a white supremacist state "for which white racial entitlement and non-white racial subordination were defining, thus inevitably molding white moral psychology and moral theorizing" (Mills, 1997, p. 106). This moral psychology frames white attitudes, so white attitudes must be and should be explicated in moral terms. But being white does not necessarily mean being White; the separation of the two opens the possibility for white repudiation of whiteness, of the system rather than themselves as white people. It is worth quoting Mills at length here:

> There *is* a real choice for whites, though admittedly a difficult one. . . .
> And in fact there have always been praiseworthy whites—anticolonialists,
> abolitionists, opponents of imperialism, civil rights activists, resisters
> of apartheid—who have recognized the existence and immorality of
> Whiteness as a political system, challenged its legitimacy, and insofar as
> possible, refused the Contract.[21] (p. 107)

History does not support the broad view of slavery abolitionists as people whose moral compass led them to advocate for the immediate emancipation of slaves and equality for African Americans (Harrold, 2001). First, this broad view ignores the plurality of views among white abolitionists of the day, some of whom sought to end slavery gradually and some of whom merely wanted to prevent slavery from extending into other territories.[22] Second, it ignores the presence of slave rebels and free Black Southerners who sought the end of slavery as a moral issue, for their own well-being, and for removal of the constant threat of re-enslavement. These differences, then and now, however, point to variation in white identity formation, and subsequently, variation in policy preferences and choices.

Abolitionists by definition desired the same outcome, that slavery should end, but the factors that led to this differed widely among white abolitionists, who held myriad belief systems, values, rules, and norms. Scholars have described abolitionism as a movement among Northerners that used Southerners as a negative reference group. For some abolitionists, their reasons for opposing slavery were outside of moral bounds, such as the North's need for social control. The Northern concept and value of family life, for example, served as a reason for some abolitionists to denounce slavery for its disruption of the white family unit.[23] For others, religion served as the foundation for their stance on slavery. It seemed that for some, abolitionism was a way to "absolve themselves from a morally corrupting proslavery culture," not a prompt for actual political and cultural change (Harrold, 2001, p. 7; also see Brewer Stewart, 1983; Huston, 1990).

The different pathways that prompted whites to avow support for abolition exemplify the different ways in which white identity can form, whether consciously or not, and the psychological, social, and political underpinnings of the choices white abolitionists made. More generally, we all form predispositions that are directly related to our racialization and socialization. Socialization becomes what informs personal values. Personal and group values then become the basis for "a way of living with characteristic codes and beliefs, standards and 'enemies' " (Allport, 1954, p. 39). However, they are not static. These sets of codes, beliefs, and standards can be measured and found in individual predispositions, which, in turn, have social and political consequences for attitudes and behavior.

The Politics of Belonging as Moral

Toni Morrison wrote in 1992:

> It is no accident and no mistake that immigrant populations (and much immigrant literature) understood their Americanness as an opposition to the resident black population. Race in fact now functions as a metaphor so necessary to the construction of Americanness that it rivals the old

pseudo-scientific and class-informed racisms whose dynamics we are more used to deciphering. . . . Deep within the word "American" is its association with race. . . . American means white. . . . (p. 47)

Immigrant populations, especially white ethnic immigrants of the 20th century (Jacobson, 1998, 2006; Roediger, 2005) but even recent immigrants including Latinos (Alamillo, 2019; Hickel, Alamillo, Oskooii, & Collingwood, 2021; Waters, 1994), have understood their standing as Americans in racial terms. They understand an American identity in opposition to the native Black population.

One way to understand the fundamental connection between immigration, American identity, and morality is to look to the point of origin for restricting migration to the United States, the Naturalization Act of 1790. The Naturalization Act of 1790 was the first immigration legislation to require that naturalized migrants have "good character."[24] Later in 1795, when the 1790 law was repealed, the word "moral" was added to the language of the replacement act and the long-standing requirement of "good moral character" (GMC) was introduced and institutionalized. Prospective immigrants were, and continue to be, prohibited from engaging in what the state deemed "immoral."[25] In essence, the boundaries of an American identity, starting in the late 1700s, are policed in terms of "good moral character"; moral character and racial purity were intricately linked through the Naturalization Acts of 1790 and 1795 as part of immigration attitudes formed during that time.[26]

Section 101(f) of the INA provides for the denial of naturalization to "habitual drunkard[s]," people convicted of two or more gambling offenses, polygamists, and people who have an extramarital affair that destroys an existing marriage, as well as people who violate laws against prostitution,[27] murder, illegal drugs, and all people convicted of an aggravated felony. All immigration laws since 1795 reference GMC. The U.S. Citizenship and Immigration Services (USCIS) Policy Manual in force today references GMC, stating that it is measured by the "standards of the average citizens of the community in which the applicant resides" (USCIS, 2022, volume 12, part f, chapter 1). GMC is used to deny U.S. citizenship, and at times admission to the United States, to non-citizens, as well as in asylum cases; women who have experienced violence or abuse must show it when applying for lawful immigration status under the Violence Against Women Act of 1994. The U.S. government has denied naturalization to individuals who were deemed to have given "false testimony," did not pass FBI clearance, or had criminal records, among other factors. The process of evaluating moral standards became a process of evaluating racial permissibility. Immigration and naturalization law police the borders of race alongside other factors like sexuality and marriage.

While nominally race-neutral, the charge that particular immigrant groups are immoral has long been cited as a rationale for legal racial exclusions. Whiteness was associated with "moral maturity, self-assurance, personal independence, and political sophistication" and racial others were considered to have "a certain degeneracy of intellect, morals, self-restraint, and political values" that made them unsuitable for citizenship (Haney Lopez, 2006, pp. 11–12). It is the meaning attached to racial categories that is most important, not the racial categories themselves; this is what Omi and Winant (2015) call the process of racialization. In the context of immigration, "The notion of heritable physical traits becomes an abbreviation for heritable moral and cultural qualities" (Lee & Appiah, 1994, p. 762).[28] This strong linking of the heritability of moral and cultural qualities with the heritability of physical traits is what becomes most important to one's experience in society, to how one is treated. Whiteness still affords advantages, and among its many advantages is the "moral certainty regarding one's civic belonging and fundamental goodness" (Haney Lopez, 2006, pp. 149–150). The physical trait of being non-white does not afford the same advantages of belonging. The meaning attached to the moral agency of whites and the moral degeneracy of non-whites lives on through GMC, which is still an integral aspect of how immigration law is practiced. The politics of immigration are the politics of belonging. The politics of belonging are a moral politics. To belong as an American is to embody a moral character worthy of full inclusion and rights.

Another way immigration attitudes are at bottom undergirded by (im)morality is through an understanding (historic and contemporary) that immigration is about the freedom to move, about mobility. Movement is governed by how "moral" we think a group of people is (Bashford, 2014; Cresswell, 2006; Soss, Fording, & Schram, 2011). In other words, if society deems your physical traits to be attributed to a moral standing, movement is easier, smoother, without racial profiling.[29] People barred through immigration restriction are prevented from moving into particular spaces. Historically, the United States made clear that movement without fear of death or retaliation was a right only reserved for whites, due to whites' racialized and moral standing. This understanding of citizenship as white, moral, and able to move freely was reaffirmed by the 1857 Supreme Court ruling of *Dred Scott v. Sandford*. Scott's case was based on his movement from a slave state, Missouri, to Illinois, where slavery was illegal, and back to Missouri. His movement into a "free" state held no bearing on his freedom and his freedom was ultimately tied to his status and not his movement into a slave-free state. Chief Justice Roger Taney's decision, which six of his colleagues signed, returning Scott to bondage, stated, "The only two clauses in the Constitution which point to this race [meaning Black people], treat them as persons whom it was morally lawful to deal in as articles of property and to hold as slaves." It said, further:

> They had for more than a century before been regarded as beings of an in-
> ferior order, and altogether unfit to associate with the white race, either in
> social or political relations; and so far inferior, that they had no rights. . . .
> This opinion was at that time fixed and universal in the civilized portion
> of the white race. It was regarded as an axiom in morals as well as in poli-
> tics, which no one thought of disputing, or supposed to be open to dispute.
> (*Dred Scott v. Sandford*, 1857)

The upshot of the opinion was that Dred Scott could not be a citizen because of his race. As Taney's language suggests, this understanding was based on moral understandings of the racial hierarchy and the humans and non-humans that make up the hierarchy. During this time the mores of mobility were understood in racial terms. The conscious and (im)moral choice Taney and the Supreme Court justices made was affected by a sense of what Mills (1998) calls "white right." That is, choices the justices made about Scott's racialized standing, citizenship, and freedom (ultimately, about whether he belongs and where he belongs) were actually immoral choices. Dred Scott's case is an illustration of what Susan Opotow (1990) calls "moral exclusion," which "not only relies on moral flexibility [the same standards do not apply to everyone], but also on the appearance of moral legitimacy (also see Smith, 2003). Moral reasoning in the service of moral exclusion is typically self-serving, utilizes trivial criteria to justify harm, and implicitly asserts that particular moral boundaries are correct" (p. 8). The exclusion of Dred Scott from morality and thus the freedom to move freely is in direct connection with Taney's comparison to the white race in his opinion. Moral exclusion and inclusion are happening simultaneously.

Although the 13th, 14th, and 15th Amendments essentially negated Taney's assertions, the movement of Black, Latino, and non-white bodies

continued and continue to be surveilled and controlled through policy, social norms, moral codes, and de facto discriminatory and racist practices
(Alexander, 2010; *Corrigan v. Buckley*, 1926; Fair Housing Administration,
1936; Gerster & Cords, 1989; Loewen, 2005; Shapiro, 1988; Wilderson,
2015). At the same time immigration policy remained de jure discriminatory and racist, restricting the rights and citizenship of non-white migrants
(Johnson, 2004), including the right to move freely without fear.

I have laid out my arguments about how whiteness structures immigration. Moreover, how immigration is connected to an understanding of race
as less about the categories themselves and more about the meaning given to
the categories of whiteness and non-whiteness, and thus, the people under
those umbrella categories. The legal system in the United States defined
being white as having moral authority. Judge Taney's "moral" authority was
to reject Scott's freedom on the basis of white supremacy. The Naturalization
Act of 1790, the 1917 Asiatic Barred Zone Act, and the 1924 National Origins
quota all institutionalized and legalized a discourse around immigrants'
moral character and whites' fitness for citizenship.

To be white meant to have moral authority and to *use* moral language and
mores to understand their own racial positioning vis-a-vis the position of
non-white others.[30] This understanding, I argue, is borne out in whites' political behavior—their policy preferences, candidate choices, jury decisions,
and most generally their attitudes. As Winant (2004b) writes:

> To interpret the meaning of race in a particular way at a given time is at least
> implicitly, but more often explicitly, to propose or defend a certain social
> policy, a particular racialized social structure, a racial order. The reverse
> is also true: in a highly racialized society, to put in place a particular social
> policy, or to mobilize for social or political action, is at least implicitly, but
> more often explicitly, to articulate a particular set of racial meanings, to sig-
> nify race in certain ways. (p. 53)

There is no way around it. Whites base their decision-making as white
people who live in a racial polity that is structured by race. When whites
make decisions about immigration policies and interpret immigrants in a
racialized way, they are putting in place a social policy that gives meaning to
race. And in so doing they are making decisions about the racial meanings of
themselves (as white) and others (as non-white).

At bottom, when whites make decisions about immigration, they
are proposing a moral understanding of themselves as white and others

as non-white. One group deserves to belong (Devos & Banaji, 2005), to move freely without fear of being picked up by ICE, to be able to punish outgroups for transgressing or asking for equality, while the other group does not belong and thus should not be able to move freely and should be detained and deported and punished (Brewer, 1999; Mills, 1997). Whites are making (im)moral choices because choices about immigration are intricately entangled with whiteness and the racial status quo, both of which are defined and justified morally. Immigration confronts white identity with whiteness, what the post–civil rights era, the project of whiteness, worked so hard to disentangle. What characterizes the contemporary period in relation to immigration is the ways in which immigration brings to the fore the tension between de facto white privilege and the formal extension of rights to non-whites (Beltrán, 2020; Mills, 1997, p. 73). This book is interested in racial making, how whites make and reproduce whiteness through policy preferences and behavior. The production and reproduction of whiteness as privileged, as moral, is the product of human decision-making. In essence, policy preferences (among many other things) work to make legible white racial identity. Policy preferences, the act of having choices when it comes to policy preferences, confront white Americans with (im)moral choices.

Moral Norms: The Importance of Predispositions to Moral Choices

Being white in America, like any other social category, comes with a set of norms and social/racial scripts to be followed. These norms can often be assessed in individual-level predispositions, which then manifest themselves in group-level political behavior. Predispositions include personality traits that predispose individuals to have a particular attitude or behavior (e.g., authoritarianism). Predispositions can also be broader attitudinal and behavioral dispositions, such as racial resentment. One's predisposition on egalitarianism, for example, means that the norm for white Americans post–civil rights is to believe in equality of opportunity, but the political choices on varied policies may not align. Norms evolve to maintain a sense of belonging to one's socialization, one's identity, and thus, one's group (Horst, Kirman, & Teschl, 2007). These norms influence choices. This is where we can witness moral and immoral choices that operate within whiteness. In essence, racialized norms are moral norms (Mills, 1997).

White Americans who are aware of their white privilege are less likely to hold anti-immigrant and anti-immigration policy preferences, while the inverse is also true. This section broadly theorizes how predispositions, generally, are connected to social identity, the learned norms and rules of groups, and the consequences of nonconformity. I focus on well-studied predispositions: partisanship, moral traditionalism, authoritarianism, racial resentment, egalitarianism, and power-cognizance (awareness of white privilege). The following chapters detail how these individual predispositions affect immigration attitudes and how they influence white attitudes. All but power-cognizance have been shown to influence political attitudes and behavior and are essential aspects of how people think about and behave toward groups. In essence, those high on levels of racial resentment, authoritarianism, and moral traditionalism and low on egalitarianism are more likely to have anti-immigrant and anti-immigration policy preferences. This section furthers a theoretical understanding of how individual-level choices are, in fact, group-oriented and have group-level outcomes.

What it means to be white in the United States is not just a question about individual white selves. As Jennifer Harvey (2007) argues:

> It is a question about the formation of a group, the creation of a public consciousness. Identity here is an organizing principle: our sense of "who we are" deeply shapes how we see the world, and how we make sense of our position in and experience of it. These, in turn, inform our behavior. (p. 100)

In essence, regardless of how conscious individual whites are about their white racial identity, it still informs their political behavior, and this behavior has group-level motivations and implications. White racialization produced white Americans, not just individual whites, but a *group* of people who, due to their skin color, were privileged. For some the privilege is in the form of materiality (wealth), for others it is merely psychological. Behavior, then, is connected to this privileged identity in ways that are not deterministic and in ways that are not devoid of the production of "white" as a racial category.

A combination of social identity theory (SIT; Turner et al., 1987), group position theory (Blumer, 1958), and role identity theory (RIT; Burke & Reitzes, 1991; Hogg et al., 1995; McCall & Simmons, 1966; Stryker,

1968) dictates how predispositions/norms interact with collective group political and moral behavior. Social categories and norms are tied together (Akerlof & Kranton, 2010). "First, there are social categories. . . Second, there are norms for how someone in those social categories should or should not behave. Third, norms affect behavior" (Akerlof & Kranton, 2010, p. 13). In a society that is stratified by the meta-category of race, norms specify how groups relate within and among themselves.

People gain or lose privilege, standing, status, or materiality by either conforming to behavior or differentiating from the normative behavior. Generally, individuals want to belong and are more incentivized to conform to group norms that they have learned through socialization to maintain a sense of belonging. Whiteness, and those enrolled in it whether consensually or not, has rules, norms, and scripts that members of the group must follow (Mills, 1997). There are consequences to nonconformity, sometimes deadly; breaking the rules may sever a person from their family and the protection of the group (Ignatiev & Garvey, 1996; Segrest, 2019). Thandeka (1999) calls this "racial exile" (p. 9).

The adoption of norms and rules cements the adoption of the appropriate social identity, the one that has the most benefits and carries the most positive weight. Social identity links the individual to the group. It provides the link between the self and the structure and process by which social groups become important for the self (Brewer, 2001). An individual's self-concept is derived from social relationships and groups. Social identity is "that part of the individual's self-concept which derives from [their] knowledge of [their] membership of a social group (or groups) together with the value and emotional significance attached to that membership" (Tajfel, 1981, p. 251).

According to Brewer (2001), group-based social identity influences individuals in two ways. First, when a group identity is engaged, the self moves beyond being an individual to being part of a larger social unit. Second, "the attributes and behaviors of the individual self are assimilated to the representation of the group as a whole, enhancing those features that make the group distinctive from other social categories and at the same time enhancing uniformity and cohesion within the group" (p. 119). Collective identity involves a shared representation of a group based on commonalities and the active process of shaping and reshaping the ideology of the group (Brewer, 2001). Collective identity represents the norms, values, and ideologies that form identification with a collective group. Collective identity, as Brewer describes it, links social identity (whether individual or group-based) to the political arena.

The literature suggests that group membership is distinct from group identity and group consciousness. People who are racially white have a person-based social identity, which may be ascriptive by external factors (group membership), such as the courts (Lopez, 1997) and the Census (Nobles, 2000), or by oneself (group identity). Collective social identity requires group consciousness, which McClain and colleagues define as "[i]n-group identification *politicized* by a set of ideological beliefs about one's group's social standing, as well as a view that collective action is the best means by which the group can improve its status and realize its interests" (McClain, Carew, Walton, & Watts, 2009, p. 476; italics in original). Thus, group identity requires conscious awareness of belonging to a certain group and having a psychological attachment to that group. SIT is helpful in linking individual-level traits and behavior and group-level social identities and politicized consequences.

Group position theory (Blumer, 1958) helps us think about group-level policy outcomes as a collective and relational process. Theoretically, Blumer's *the sense of group position* understands individual-level policy preferences as part of a collective process by racial groups precisely because racial groups are defined and maintained by relating to each other. Thus, whites' political behavior is grounded in a collective process that either maintains their dominant position or helps to destroy it. Blumer helps us move away from individual feelings to a concern about the relationship between (and within) groups. Thinking relationally shifts our attention from individual experiences, attitudes, and behavior to the collective process by which groups define and redefine themselves and other racial groups (Blumer, 1958, p. 3). Normative ideas about the appropriate relation between groups underlie individual behaviors and attitudes (Bobo, Kluegel, & Smith, 1997). Individuals understand their identity in relation to other groups (Kim, 2000). Policy preferences become a representation of whether individuals see their group as benefitting from a policy or being harmed by it precisely because another group is gaining (Weller & Junn, 2018).

Social context plus group-based imperatives leads to political behavior and attitudes (Key, 1949), and because there is a utility to being white in the United States and socialization and context vary, political behavior by whites is a key variable in determining whites' (im)moral choices. The utility of being white can be material (wealth) and/or psychological (Du Bois, 1966), thus the motivation to adhere to or deviate from the norms of whiteness in any particular context *is* the (im)moral choice. In other words, the norms of my social identity dictate I say or do X and I am either following them because there are material and/or psychological benefits to conforming or I am deviating and saying and doing Y, not because there are material benefits, but because there is a different kind of psychological benefit, one that is aligned with a moral compass that alleviates white guilt, shame, and cognitive and moral dissonance.

White supremacy hurts white people. White group membership above all else is costly: deep shame (Thandeka, 1999), guilt (Biss, 2015), internal psychological moral dilemmas (Pettigrew, 1981), and negative health outcomes (Metzl, 2019). Thandeka's white participants wept recalling the memories of enacting whiteness toward Black individuals. For example, one of his participants, Dan, cried retelling the story of expelling a Black fraternity brother from the fraternity house. Thandeka argues that white shame is at the root of these tears. For some whites there is a daily moral dilemma, a deep understanding that they have failed morally, that they have compromised too much of themselves to live in accordance with the strictures of whiteness. Though there are "wages of whiteness" (Du Bois, 1966), there are also "wages for whiteness" (Thandeka, 1999). Although all whites benefit from race privilege, some are plagued by the recognition that they have traded on race privilege for economic gains. The wages for whiteness are economic as well as moral. For many poor whites, it is the illusion of whiteness that keeps them in the cycle of poverty because whiteness necessitates choosing the psychological wages of whiteness rather than actual wages. As Dr. Martin Luther King, Jr. (2010 [1967]) explained, "White supremacy can feed their egos but not their stomachs" (p. 161). By contrast white Americans who, "through a deep moral compulsion" (p. 73), fight for racial justice are morally compensated.[31]

2

Immigration Attitudes as a Racialized "Morality of Exclusion"

Lillian Smith (1949), a Southern white woman, describes in her autobiography the moral choices whites made daily in the Jim Crow South, the lessons, the white norms, and the moral codes of her childhood. How she could choose to "pray at night and ride a Jim Crow car the next morning and to feel comfortable in doing both" (p. 17). She describes the "tenderness and love and compassion" she was taught by her mother. She was socialized, against her own moral tendencies, not to show her "black nurse" compassion in order to continue the "bleak rituals of keeping Negroes in their 'place'" (p. 17). She was taught that it is impossible to show compassion to both ingroups and outgroups. Like praying to God, choosing whiteness, choosing your family, your group was "good," a way to stave off a "terrifying disaster [that] would befall the South" if Smith treated a Black person as her social equal (p. 17). The kind of (white) socialization she describes teaches white children and young adults a kind of moral psychology that is constricted by whiteness, that can only be understood through the veneer of whiteness and embeds in young people a set of dispositions that later influence political attitudes and behavior.

In *White backlash*, Marisa Abrajano and Zoltan L. Hajnal (2015) note the significance of immigration to white Americans, that "there is something significant about immigration itself that matters to white Americans when they make basic political decisions" (p. 51). This work explains this significance theoretically through the relationship between immigration and whiteness: the potential of immigration politics to unravel the ways in which white identity and white supremacy continue to be knotted even in a post–civil rights United States and to hold whites accountable for their immoral choices and moral exclusions.

Anti-immigration attitudes involve viewing (non-white) immigrants as outside the boundaries of moral values, rules, and norms of fairness. Under

Moral and Immoral Whiteness in Immigration Politics. Yalidy Matos, Oxford University Press.
© Oxford University Press 2023. DOI: 10.1093/oso/9780197656259.003.0003

this form of "moral exclusion," those outside "are perceived as nonentities, ex-
pendable, or undeserving; consequently, harming them appears acceptable,
appropriate, or just" (Opotow, 1990, p. 1). These exclusions happen by way
of individual acts and more broadly policy and candidate preferences that
dictate the fate of many immigrants. Under the belief that most immigrants
in the United States are undocumented (Flores & Schachter, 2018),[1] whites
roam free in oppressing them (Beltrán, 2020). Immigrants are oppressed in
both the figurative sense, as whiteness as a system is everywhere all of the
time, and the literal sense, as immigrants are caged and children are separated
from their families (Shear, Benner, & Schmidt, 2020; Southern Poverty Law
Center, 2020) and immigrants experience civilian acts of violence (Mathias,
2019; Rogers & Fandos, 2019; Staff, 2020). Immigration and immigrants
pose an opportunity for U.S. society to choose whiteness or repudiate it precisely *because* policymakers have perceived immigration as colorblind and
race-neutral. White Americans can be complicit in a system that maintains
the racial status quo without acknowledging it as part of a larger system of
white supremacy. Immigration as a colorblind policy issue depends on the
enactment of racial spectacles (Davis & Ernst, 2011, 2019), "narratives that
obfuscate the existence of a white supremacist state power structure" (2019,
p. 763). Racial spectacles about immigration deemphasize the effect of
U.S. imperialism on migration patterns, for example, and place the attention
on voluntary immigration. They lay blame on non-white immigrants, who
are profiled as undocumented, for not migrating the "right" way, and thus
undeserving of being included in the polity in any way.

Immigration poses a rare opportunity for white Americans to make
decisions based on a policy that is supposedly colorblind and a group of
people, immigrants, who are perceived to be outside of U.S. moral bounds.
While immigrants are excluded, ingroup members, other non-Hispanic
whites, are included in ways that ground the inclusion of ingroup members
in moral understandings of worth. To be morally included is to believe that
considerations of fairness apply to the individual or the group, to have a willingness to share resources, and to make sacrifices for the well-being of the
group (Opotow, 1990, p. 4). To exclude others and include some (ingroup
members), a moral reasoning must occur in the service of exclusion; this is
often for the protection of the ingroup (the boundaries of the group and its
group members), the morally included. This kind of moral psychology, an
internal, psychological understanding of "right" and "wrong," of "good' and
"bad," is omnipresent when immigration is the topic.

Immigration is important to whites because their moral psychology is at stake; immigration has the potential to illuminate for whites and for the rest of the population what Mills (1997) calls the "epistemology of ignorance" (p. 93)—the morally constricted ways in which white Americans think about policies that have dire and deathly consequences for people and groups that fall outside of their moral boundaries. White morality or ethics, Mills' idea of a "white right" that is convoluted because race structures what is moral, disallows some whites from seeing immigration as a political and moral issue that is intricately connected to whiteness and the maintenance of whiteness. In this chapter, I argue that predispositions, tendencies to hold particular attitudes or behave in certain ways, are manifestations of whites' (im)moral compass and what underlies whites' (im)moral choices. Focusing on the predispositions of moral traditionalism, authoritarianism, racial resentment, egalitarianism, and partisanship, I argue that whites' whiteness informs their predispositions, and that predispositions are morally derived. Predispositions allow for a measure of the morally infused justifications white Americans use about immigration politics and policy, which is the topic of Chapter 3. This chapter connects whiteness and morality with predispositions and shows the limits of just focusing on white racial identity (WRI) to explain whites' immigration attitudes and white identity politics.

Whiteness, Predispositions, and Morality

Historical accounts of the use of morality for immoral behavior abound. The nativist American Party of the 1850s and the second Ku Klux Klan (KKK), which gained momentum in the 1920s, were both rooted in the preservation of "traditional" morality and moral codes. The KKK saw itself as the "moral police force" (Parker & Barreto, 2013, p. 26). The American Party, whose proponents were commonly called the Know-Nothings, saw themselves as protectors of Protestantism and the attending work ethic as well as proponents of temperance (Boissoneault, 2017; Volle, 2019). By name alone, they articulated a moral understanding of who are "real Americans": descendants of colonists and of Protestant European immigrants. In the defense of Protestant religious and political values, they opposed Roman Catholic and Irish immigration, but generally spewed an anti-immigration and anti-immigrant discourse.[2]

Contemporary accounts of right-wing movements, in particular, New Right movements, like the Tea Party, have many commonalities with these older nativist movements. Contemporary New Right movements originate from resistance to the Black Civil Rights Movement of the 1950s and 1960s and from the Wallace nativist and populist presidential campaign. The resistance of the New Right was national and focused on making electoral gains by way of selecting their own candidates to run for elected offices. New Right movements, and Wallace's campaign, were threatened by real Black progress and what racial equality could mean for their envisioned nation-state and society (Edsall & Edsall, 1991). New Right movements, according to Winant (2004b), understand something important about the United States and this knowledge is what gave way to these movements. New Right movements "grasp a deep truth: that white supremacy was not an excrescence on the basically egalitarian and democratic 'American creed' but a fundamental component of U.S. society. To destroy it meant reinventing the country, the social order, the government" (p. 55). The "terrifying disaster [that] would befall the South," as Lillian Smith recognized, would be the dismantling of whiteness, which is deeply and intimately intertwined with the U.S. nation-state; the reinvention of one necessitates the reckoning and reinvention of the other.

In the same vein as the Know-Nothings, the New Right seeks to legitimate the privilege of whiteness. Citing W. E. B. Du Bois, Winant (2004b) identifies the "covert" effort "to legitimate the 'psychological wage'" that white supremacy gave to all white people (p. 56). Much as the Know-Nothings associated whiteness with capitalist virtues, according to Winant, the New Right decries Latinos and to some extent Asians as lacking "productivity, thrift, obedience to law, self-denial, and [obedience to sexual mores]. This in turn permits the crucial articulation of corporate and white working-class interests—the cross-class racial alliance—that endows New Right positions with such strategic advantage today" (p. 56). The New Right understands its base as white and presents itself as a champion of disenfranchised whites and uses seemingly colorblind code words to promote white supremacy and racism.

New Right movements continue a tradition of using morality and moral language to justify their political agenda. The Know-Nothings and the second KKK, like these contemporary movements, constructed the world in morally absolute terms.[3] They articulate their movement as one of moral traditionalism and support the construction of moral, social, and political arrangements that maintain their dominance (Barreto, Cooper, Gonzalez,

Parker, & Towler, 2011). Moral traditionalists prefer the racial status quo, condemn alternative lifestyles, and are resistant to change (Conover, 1988). Moral traditionalists often use the moral language of "right" and "wrong" when expressing and justifying their attitudes, thus engaging in a kind of moral absolutism. Furthermore, moral traditionalists often claim that members of outgroups—those who exist outside of the moral boundaries— have a culture that creates moral decay and represents a threat to the morality of the ingroup.

Moral traditionalism, as Conover and Feldman (1986) define it, refers to people's underlying beliefs about family and social organization. Moral traditionalists believe in the hetero-normative nuclear family, and thus often oppose policies that protect gay rights (Brewer, 2003; Parker & Barreto, 2013), for example. Moral traditionalists have a reverence for tradition (which is highly associated with conservatism) rather than modernism (highly associated with liberalism). Moral traditionalism taps into an understanding of partisanship and ideology as rooted in morality, resulting in a strong association between higher levels of moral traditionalism and conservative ideology (Ciuk, 2017; Lipset et al., 1954). In essence, moral traditionalism, partisanship, and ideology are intricately connected, both historically and in present-day politics. In the past as well as now, moral social policies and stances play a role in contemporary partisan polarization. Liberals and conservatives base their views on different configurations of moral values (Graham, Haidt, & Nosek, 2009). Republican strategy has been to graft "moral traditionalism onto the patriotic and racial traditionalism" that has helped them win elections throughout U.S. history (Gregory, 2005, p. 316). They have done this through opposition to feminism, gay rights, sex education, and abortion, and won the allegiance of economically disadvantaged whites who were once consistent Democrats (p. 316). Yet in fact moral traditionalists who win public office are often less concerned about tradition itself than about having the power to define the traditions, to label them as moral, and then to suggest they should be adhered to. Thus, the tradition can change—for example, the differences between Anglo Saxon whites and white ethnics are no longer important—but who gets to make these moral decisions does not.

Research on political socialization, values, and traditionalism suggests that morality, traditionalism, and political values work differently for white Americans than for other racial groups. Furthermore, among whites, moral values or ideas about traditionalism differ. For example, while Democrats generally prioritize equality and Republicans prioritize values of social order and traditionalism, the disagreement between people who identify with each party is largest between white members (Ciuk, 2017). In other words, the disagreement between Black Democrats and Black Republicans and Latino Democrats and Latino Republicans is not as large as that for whites. In fact, white conservatives, who tend to be Republican, tend to link morality, social order, and patriotism far more than Black conservatives (p. 491). Similarly, white evangelicals behave politically differently from Black evangelicals, even though they all have strong traditionalist beliefs. In line with wide agreement that evangelical beliefs, conservative views on social issues, and identification with the Republican Party are strongly linked (Brooks & Manza, 1997; Langer & Cohen, 2005; Wilcox & Robinson, 2010), white evangelicals heavily identify with the Republican Party but Black evangelicals do not.[4]

The connection between the usage of moral social policies and moral codes to maintain dominant arrangements for white Americans makes morality, and moral traditionalism in particular, an important explanatory factor of immigration policy preferences (Kinder & Sanders, 1996). Regina Branton and colleagues (2011), for example, find that since the 9/11 attacks, white Americans who adhere to moral traditional beliefs have tended to favor restrictive immigration policy preferences.[5] Bradford Jones and Danielle Martin (2017) likewise find moral traditionalism to be a significant and consistent predictor of restrictive immigration policy. Moral traditionalists exhibit a stronger likelihood of preferring deportation policy over a path-to-citizenship policy.

Researchers often examine authoritarianism and moral traditionalism as mechanisms that drive racial prejudice (Brandt & Reyna, 2014; Duckitt, Bizumic, Krauss, & Heled, 2010). Authoritarianism is a predisposition that reflects a belief in absolute obedience or submission to authority figures, as well as the administration of that belief through the oppression and punishments of individuals or groups considered violators of conventional values (see Adorno et al., 1950). High authoritarians often make behavioral justifications based on morality; they see their actions as morally justified especially if also approved by ingroup authority figures. According to Adorno and colleagues, authoritarian individuals rigidly adhere to conventional values (conventionalism), submit to and obey the proponents of these values (authoritarian submission), and advocate punishment for those who violate conventional values (authoritarian aggression). Furthermore, authoritarians are likely to exhibit an extreme negative view of humankind (e.g., human beings are inherently evil, greedy, selfish), oppose all reliance on subjective feelings, and readily accept supernatural determinants of behavior and categorical thinking (superstition and stereotypes) (Adorno et al., 1950).

Authoritarians are preoccupied with power relationships and exaggerate assertions of strength (power) and toughness toward those they perceive as subordinate and weaker. They are preoccupied with sexuality and project their own sexual and aggressive motives on those around them. Those persons high in authoritarianism with personality characteristics such as submissiveness (prone to submit to authorities) and conventionalism (belief in traditional lifestyles and conventions) are often more prejudiced against minority groups than persons low in authoritarianism (Adorno et al., 1950; Cohrs & Stelzl, 2010; Esses, Dovidio, & Hodson, 2002; Esses, Dovidio, Jackson, & Armstrong, 2001; Esses, Jackson, & Armstrong, 1998; Pettigrew, Wagner, & Christ, 2007). Furthermore, because authoritarians are preoccupied with power relationships, examining the role authoritarianism plays vis-à-vis white racial identity makes theoretical sense, as white identity and whiteness are connected, and the latter is ultimately about power and the maintenance of it. In line with the scholarship on authoritarianism, those high on authoritarian personality are more likely to have anti-immigration policy preferences as well as high white racial identity or colorblind ideology, which maintain current power relations.

Racial resentment, a post–civil rights form of prejudice among whites consisting of anti-Black sentiments and a sense that Blacks violate U.S. values (Kinder & Sanders, 1996), is one way researchers have conceptualized colorblind ideology. Racial resentment provides whites a socially desirable way to resist changes to the racial status quo based on moral feelings wrapped up in traditional U.S. values such as individualism, self-reliance, Protestant work ethic, and law and order (Kinder & Sears, 1981). After the Civil Rights Movement, most whites in the United States endorsed the *idea* of school integration, but not the necessary *solutions* needed to integrate schools (Kinder & Sanders, 1996). Prior to 1965, blatant or explicit racism was the norm, but after 1965 a more subtle but insidious expression of racism emerged, a symbolic kind. The symbolism appears in the dissonance between a belief in equality and the practical application of it among whites (and those invested in whiteness).[6] It is symbolic because it is racism nonetheless. Racial resentment influences white racial attitudes on numerous race-related and non-race-related policy issues, including immigration (Valentino, Brader, &

Jardina, 2013). In general terms, racial resentment is a survey measurement of symbolic racism, a subtle, implicit kind of colorblind racism that sprang up post–civil rights as it was no longer appropriate to be outwardly racist.

The traditional racial resentment measure focuses exclusively on attitudes toward Black Americans. This project uses the traditional racial resentment scale as well as other measures of prejudice. The traditional racial resentment scale "is rooted in deep-seated feelings of social morality and propriety and in early-learned racial fears and stereotypes"; thus, it falls in line with the examination of morality in which this book is interested. The root of symbolic racism can be traced to a process of socialization (Kinder & Sears, 1981, p. 416; also see Ward, 1985), a key component of this book's theoretical framework. Predispositions generally are acquired through socialization, a conditioning in early life that is often stable in adult years (Sears, 1986; Sears & Funk, 1999; Sears & Valentino, 1997). However, predispositions should not be thought of as completely immovable and static (Winter, 2003). Like moral traditionalism, there is a moral foundation to being predisposed to varying levels of racial resentment because racial predispositions, like racial resentment, are intimately tied to white socialization, and thus, whiteness.

Although racial resentment focuses on attitudes toward Black Americans, I argue that it captures whites' belief in long-standing and entrenched U.S. values of racial individualism—the belief that the problems experienced by non-white people of color are due to their own individual choices rather than structural racism—and deservingness that have been adopted by whites as values that define belonging, and thus, whiteness. In other words, the moral boundaries of deservingness are defined by whites' belief that to be a "good" American, you must work hard and if you are poor, low-income, or struggling, it is your fault. Embedded in the measurement of racial resentment is a belief in the Protestant work ethic, which can be traced as a primary component of the story of U.S. whiteness and how whiteness has come to be defined in relationship to racialized others (Baker, 2011).

White Americans who score high on the racial resentment scale tend to explain racial inequality in terms of individual behavior (racial individualism), while white Americans who score lower on the scale focus on structural forces (Kam & Burge, 2018). Beliefs about why racial inequality exists are rooted in racial resentment.[7] In the 21st century, racial resentment remains a significant predictor of policy attitudes (Tuch & Hughes, 2011). There is no theoretical reason why racial resentment should be excluded from whites' attitudes toward immigration policies. If immigration is a racialized issue (Parker & Barreto, 2013) and whites' racial resentment can spill over to seemingly non-racial policies that target Black Americans (Tesler, 2012b, 2016b), then racial resentment can signal more than just anti-Black sentiments; in fact, I argue, it signals just as much if not more about whiteness.

Racial resentment is intricately tied to white socialization, as it provides white Americans moral justifications to support restrictive policies and to do so without thinking of their desire to maintain the racial hierarchy. Immigration activates whites' racial attitudes toward outgroups and the ingroup (Jardina, 2019), generating a correlation between racial resentment and whites' attitudes about their own race and position. Furthermore, higher levels of racial resentment are significantly correlated with whites' denying they have racial advantages (DeSante & Smith, 2018, 2020).

The fear of difference and of change defines, in part, moral traditionalism, authoritarianism, and racial resentment. Individuals whose scores on these predispositions are high fear disruption to the status quo, to what they see as white "purified spaces," because "living with the other, with the foreigner, confronts us with the possibility, or not, of being an other" (Sibley, 1995, p. 112). This confrontation gets embodied as a moral dilemma in that any disruption leads to a crumbling of the moral justifications for immoral behavior. Consequently, we see a realization on the part of white Americans that suggests that the foundation on which whiteness stands is shaky and movable.

Egalitarianism helps make sense of the subjective moral compass some whites use to make political decisions. At the root of egalitarianism lies the belief that equality of opportunity exists for everyone, and those that do not work hard are to blame for their own misfortunes. Hence, egalitarianism, generally, is strongly related to racial resentment. Americans understand equality as equality of opportunity, political equality, rather than equality of results (Feldman, 1988); indeed, most white Americans believe that equality of results would indicate an underlying injustice to their own ingroup (Sears, Henry, & Kosterman, 2000). Different outcomes, then, occur because individuals do not capitalize on the opportunities they have. Egalitarianism is a racialized concept precisely because it denies the existence of structural racism. African Americans, like Americans generally, endorse U.S. values of individualism and equality (they, too, are egalitarians in this way), but they are far more likely to support policies such as

affirmative action that are designed around an understanding that egalitarianism without practical solutions is insufficient (Kinder & Sanders, 1996;
Myrdal, 1962). Most white Americans believe in equality of opportunity,
but they are less willing to support policies to ameliorate structural barriers
to opportunities. Egalitarianism, in other words, is a colorblind ideology
that can be used to both disrupt and maintain hierarchy. Egalitarianism can
disrupt the hierarchy if white Americans with high levels of egalitarianism
also have low levels of racial resentment, a belief that structural racism
exists. Egalitarianism can also maintain the hierarchy by doubling down
on a belief that the United States has already reached an egalitarian state
where programs and policies are no longer needed to alleviate inequality
(see Bonilla-Silva, 2014; Matos, 2020).

Egalitarianism exists on a spectrum. High egalitarians believe that
the United States should continue to work on equality and that an equal
country does not yet exist, while high anti-egalitarians wrongly assume that
the United States has already reached an equal society status and that any
more work on equalizing society is preferential treatment (Matos, 2020).
Because egalitarianism is rooted in a U.S., and thus racialized, understanding of equality, even egalitarians can have a threshold of supporting
race-based or progressive policies that they deem help minoritized groups
unequally or unfairly. Generally, those with high levels of egalitarianism
have positive feelings toward minorities, including immigrants, and tend
to have pro-immigration attitudes (Espenshade & Calhoun, 1993; Pantoja,
2006). Those whites who believe in egalitarian ideals *and* support social
policies to that end are morally aligned, while those who believe in egalitarian ideals in theory *and* still oppose policies that would help equal the
playing field for minoritized racial and ethnic groups are not. The interaction of levels of egalitarianism and levels of racial resentment explains
these differences.

Finally, partisanship identification, one of the most political
predispositions (Zaller, 1992), shapes whites' attitudes in ways that perpetuate their (im)moral choices. Throughout this work, I assume that white
Americans self-select into party affiliations and have at least a rudimen-
tary understanding of the major policies the two major parties support.
Identification with one party or the other has real-world consequences for
attitudes, public opinion, and ultimately political behavior. With this understanding, I argue throughout this book that partisanship shapes the norms
and rules for white Americans and generates moral narratives for policy

and political issues. I focus on the two major parties as well as independents and measure the strength of party identification among those who have one (weak or strong Democrats/Republicans) to understand how party explains white identity and how party identification influences white consciousness and immigration attitudes.

Party affiliation offers individuals a group of which to be a part. Partisan membership allows individuals, especially those who are strong Democrats and strong Republicans, to feel a sense of belonging (Green, Palmquist, & Schickler, 2002). Party identification is measured in two ways. First, I use a seven-point scale that runs from strong Democrat to strong Republican; the middle is "pure" independents. Second, I use a three-point scale that collapses all Democrats (strong, weak, and leaners) and Republicans (strong, weak, and leaners), and maintains independents as the middle category. This sense of belonging to a group is important psychologically and politically. When collective identities are primed and salient, ingroup–outgroup categorizations become the basis for evaluating others (Brewer & Gardner, 1996). Ingroups provide the frame of reference for self-evaluation at the individual level and the frame of reference for self-evaluation at the group level. The frame of reference is also relevant for evaluations of outgroups as they relate to the ingroup. However, ingroup bias does not necessarily lead to outgroup derogation or outgroup hate (Allport, 1954; Brewer, 1999). The conditions under which ingroup love can lead to outgroup hate include moral superiority, perceived threat, common goals, common values, social comparison, and power politics. Moral superiority is the belief that the ingroup, the "we," is morally superior to the outgroup, "they"; perceived threat is the understanding that an outgroup threatens the well-being and status of the ingroup; common goals and common values are undergirded by the idea that ingroup members all have common (superordinate) goals and values, which are in direct opposition to the goals and values of outgroups; social comparison seeks ingroup–outgroup comparisons that enhance the ingroup; finally, power politics is when ingroup leaders manipulate and exacerbate ingroup goals and values to secure and maintain power (Brewer, 1999).

I argue that ingroup love and outgroup derogation or denigration cannot be separated for whites as a group. Precisely because of moral superiority and power politics, whiteness is political and moral, and thus, when whites make decisions about immigration as well as numerous other policies, they are making decisions from their position in society, which cannot be disassociated from whiteness (Masuoka & Junn, 2013). Moral superiority, Brewer (1999) states, stems from

[a] sense universally true that "we" are more peaceful, trustworthy, friendly, and honest than "they." . . . As ingroups become larger and more depersonalized, the institutions, rules, and customs that maintain ingroup loyalty and cooperation take on the character of moral authority. When the moral order is seen as absolute rather than relative, moral superiority is incompatible with tolerance for difference. To the extent that outgroups do not subscribe to the same moral rules, indifference is replaced by denigration and contempt. (p. 435)

Moral superiority can also lead to what seem to be "moral" justifications for domination of outgroups (Sidanius, 1993). Hence, groups that feel morally superior will make political decisions based on that feeling, which has detrimental consequences to outgroups. Party affiliation and party politics discourse can provide such narratives around moral superiority and power politics.

Power politics is basically what happens when ingroup love and outgroup derogation or conflict involve political entities or groups. When this is the case, processes of moral superiority, fear, and mistrust of outgroups and social comparison are exacerbated through manipulation by group leaders "in the interests of mobilizing collective action to secure or maintain political power" (Brewer, 1999, p. 437). In other words, group leaders (political party elites) can exploit differences for political reasons, and one way they do so is through framing issues for their constituencies. As previously stated, research on U.S. core values describes Democratic/liberal Americans as caring about equality and Republicans/conservatives as caring about the values of moral traditionalism and social order (Fiorina, Abrams, & Pope, 2006; Lipset et al., 1954; McClosky & Zaller, 1984; Scammon & Wattenberg, 1970). Thus, party politics are an important mechanism through which the moral choices of white Americans are decided. Party politics provide moral rules for the group.

Levels of White Identity and Measuring Whiteness

Using social identity theory (SIT) tenets, I make use of five measures of white social identity to explain its significance to immigration attitudes.

SIT seeks to explain how an individual's social identity is formed and how it influences evaluations of not only an outgroup, but also an ingroup. Tajfel and Turner (1979) establish three core theoretical principles. First, individuals attempt to achieve and maintain a positive social identity. Second, positive social identity is based on comparisons to relevant outgroups; ingroup members must perceive themselves as positively different than outgroups. Finally, when social identity is negative or unsatisfactory, individuals will leave their group and join another group and/or attempt to make their current group more positive and satisfactory. I detail below the five levels of social identity, which range from a basic level of group membership (ascribed identification) to being conscious about one's membership in the group and believing in collective action for the group to an awareness of white privilege, which necessitates an awareness of being implicated in the group.

Whiteness affords whites the flexibility to identify with or disidentify from their group, a choice that remains constricted for many racialized and minoritized members. Whites have choices due to their position in the racial system (Masuoka & Junn, 2013). Whites' political behavior is driven to varying degrees by the recognition of their positionality as a *group* (Dawson, 1994; Fraga et al., 2010; Masuoka, 2006; Masuoka & Junn, 2013).

The first, most basic, level of social identity that affects attitudes and behavior is self-identification as "white," following a question about one's race(s) (Gurin, Miller, & Gurin, 1980; McClain et al., 2009; Miller, Gurin, Gurin, & Malanchuk, 1981). These individuals understand that either they are white or they are perceived as such given the racial categories in the United States. In all statistical models in this book, I only examine self-identified non-Hispanic whites, hence these are all individuals who have chosen white as their race.

The next level, level two, asks, "How important is being White to your identity?" This is a five-category question with answers ranging from not at all important to extremely important. Level two asks whites to think about the centrality of being white to their identity. It goes beyond just choosing white and requires the respondent to think a bit more consciously. However, given the history of whites in the United States, some white Americans might have positive feelings about being white, while others might feel shame or guilt. This question does not really tell us much about white Americans' underlying attitudes or perceptions about being white.

Level three is a measurement of ethnocentrism, that is, ingroup favoritism: a preference for and positive affect toward the ingroup compared to outgroups. This level comes after white racial identity because it relates being white to other non-white groups. It is a measure of white identity as relational because it is an affective measure—one that considers an outward expression of feelings and emotion—that utilizes not only ingroup affect but also outgroup affect and calculates the difference.

Level four starts to move into a more conscious level. At this level, I argue, the intersection of white identity and whiteness is more present. Assessing level four involves asking the question, "How important is it that whites work together to change laws that are unfair to whites?" It is a measure of group consciousness. To answer this question, white respondents must have a sense that "white people" are a group of people who are either experiencing unfair treatment or not. This sits at the intersection of white identity and whiteness because it is implied that respondents understand that a white racial identity is a real thing *and* that behavior is necessary to *protect* the group (or not). There is a *choice* that happens when white respondents answer this question.

Finally, level five, which addresses their being aware of their own white racial privileges, power-cognizance, goes beyond an understanding of white identity. One measure from DeSante and Smith (2020), which is a direct and explicit measure, asks respondents to agree or disagree with the following statement: "White people in the U.S. have certain advantages because of the color of their skin." I also use other proxies, including asking whites whether discrimination against whites is just as big a problem as discrimination against racial minorities, and whether racial problems are rare and isolated in the United States. Understanding white privilege, I suggest, goes beyond knowing one is white or beyond whiteness being an important aspect of one's identity. Understanding that whites have advantages due to their skin color or race reveals a deeper understanding of whiteness and white supremacy. This awareness goes beyond the strength of white identity and examines identity formation. Whites who are aware of their privilege because of their skin color or race and who understand that white discrimination can never be the same as discrimination against Black people or other racialized minorities are power-cognizant (see Knowles & Peng, 2005; Perry, 2001, 2002).

Theoretically, power-cognizant individuals will have more progressive immigration policy preferences and generally progressive preferences due to their understanding of white privilege. A line of scholarship suggests that thinking about one's relative privilege might lead to higher levels of egalitarianism (Katz & Hass, 1988; Walster, Berscheid, & Walster, 1973). The reverse may also be true. If whites believe in egalitarianism, strong identification may also lead to power-cognizance and anti-racism (Eichstedt, 2001).

Being asked about racial privilege can also lead to feelings of guilt (Branscombe, Doosje, & McGarty, 2002; Powell, Branscombe, & Schmitt, 2005), anger, and other emotions (Huddy, Feldman, & Cassese, 2007; Nussbaum, 2016; Phoenix, 2019; Rogers & Prenticedunn, 1981; Williams, 2010), as well as disgust (Jardina, Kalmoe, & Gross, 2021). These negative emotions can lead to negative and conservative views on outgroups and outgroup-centered policies. However, given what we know about white identity politics, we may expect the level of white identity to predict differences in such reactions (Branscombe, Ellemers, Spears, & Doosje, 1999; Branscombe, Schmitt, & Schiffhauer, 2007). High white identifiers might have a defensive reaction and deny white racial privilege, while low white identifiers might be moved to agree due to feelings of guilt or desire for social desirability (Branscombe et al., 1999). Those who are ambivalent are harder to theorize about and can go either way, likely depending on the other levels of their predispositions.

Questions about white racial privilege threaten white people's social identity and therefore might elicit a morally infused reaction. That is, they may feel they themselves and their racial group are morally implicated by such questions. These kinds of questions about white racial privilege make it "difficult for Whites to maintain their 'innocence' about the unfairness of their racial group's favorable position [and] thoughts of privilege could imply that their group is immoral" (Branscombe et al., 2007, p. 204). Branscombe and colleagues (2007) find that for high white identifiers priming white privilege—showing them stimuli of white privilege—increases modern racism, but for low white identifiers it decreases modern racism. Modern racist beliefs involve denying that racial inequality results from discrimination and asserting that Blacks are making unwarranted demands for change (McConahay, 1986). Furthermore, Branscombe and colleagues found that low white identifiers may respond by seeking to rectify their immoral behavior by becoming more egalitarian while high white identifiers are more likely to exhibit defensive responses. For example, high white identifiers may question the deservingness of non-whites by suggesting that a poor work ethic, not racial privilege, prevents the equal prosperity of other groups (Henry & Sears, 2002). Examining whites' understanding of their own racial privilege is important to understand white racial attitudes about immigration.

Level One: Self-Identified White Americans

This book examines the immigration attitudes of self-identified non-Hispanic white Americans. On any governmental or other type of forms, like the Census or a job application, individuals are asked their race and ethnicity. All the respondents who chose non-Hispanic and white are included in all analyses.[8] This self-identification is the baseline for white racial identity. Respondents who choose white have at minimum a recognition that others perceive them as white individuals even if they do not see whiteness as a conscious social identity. Table 2.1 shows the sample sizes across public opinion surveys and year.

Level Two: White Racial Identity

The question of whether being white is important to the identity of white respondents is politically consequential, as it is grounded in SIT. The more a self-identity is seen as part of a larger group, the more the members of the group use group norms to make evaluations. Furthermore, saliency of a group identity influences the group members' loyalty to the group and their willingness to behave in such a way as to keep the group's positive identity.

Table 2.1 Sample Size of Self-Identified Whites

	Self-Identified Sample
American National Election Studies (ANES)	
2000	1,197
2004	710[a]
2008	1,002
2012	3,102
2016	3,007
Cooperative Congressional Election Study (CCES)	
2018	30,875
Collaborative Multiracial Post-Election Survey (CMPS)	
2020	1,620

[a] In 2004, only 1,212 respondents completed both a pre-election and a post-election survey, which greatly diminishes the number of non-Hispanic, third-generation white respondents. This is an anomaly, as participation was far higher in other years.

Self-categorization theory, an offshoot of SIT, posits that salient identification with a group makes the group a central aspect of one's identity (Oakes, Haslam, & Turner, 1994; Turner et al., 1987). However, asking whites whether being white is important to them may or may not provide information about how salient white identity is for that person, so the measure is incomplete in some ways (Leach et al., 2008). Research suggests that a recognition that being white is important does not automatically drive political attitudes.

Table 2A.1 in Appendix B provides an examination of the distribution of the importance of white racial identity using the 2016 ANES: extremely important, very important, a little important, and not at all important.[9] It shows that gender identity does not strongly predict responses ($\chi^2 = 3.56, p = 0.31$).[10] With respect to partisanship, Republicans are significantly more likely to indicate that WRI is important to them than a combination of independents and Democrats ($\chi^2 = 29.32, p = 0.000$), while Democrats are significantly less likely to indicate that WRI is important to them ($\chi^2 = 11.11, p = 0.01$) than independents and Republicans combined. Independents as a group do not differ from Democrats and Republicans combined ($\chi^2 = 5.95, p = 0.11$). There are also regional differences ($\chi^2 = 21.43, p = 0.001$). White Southerners appear to place more importance on their white identity compared to the other regions combined ($\chi^2 = 11.83, p = 0.01$). A Kruskal–Wallis equality-of-populations rank indicates that educational attainment is negatively correlated with the importance of white identity ($\chi^2 (3) = 49.96, p = 0.000$), as is income ($\chi^2 = 19.02, p = 0.000$). There is no statistically significant difference between evangelicals and non-evangelicals ($\chi^2 = 2.48, p = 0.48$). However, people who consider the Bible the literal word of God are more likely to indicate white identity is important to them ($\chi^2 = 55.36, p = 0.000$). Finally, people who voted for Trump in 2016 are more likely to indicate white identity is important to them ($\chi^2 = 47.64, p = 0.000$).

Level Three: Measuring Whiteness through Ethnocentrism

A measurement of affective white identity is ethnocentrism or ingroup favoritism,[11] defined as a preference for and positive affect toward the ingroup relative to outgroups (Yinger, 1985). William Graham Sumner (1913) defines ethnocentrism as "The sentiment of cohesion, internal comradeship, and devotion to the ingroup, which carries with it a sense of superiority to any outgroup and readiness to defend the interests of the ingroup against the outgroup" (p. 11). As a relational concept it measures ingroup centeredness in relation to other groups (Sumner, 1906). Used primarily as a psycholog- ical predisposition, ethnocentrism can also be conceptualized as measuring white group identity and consciousness. Ethnocentrism is measured by subtracting whites' affective feeling thermometer toward their own ingroup (whites) to whites' average feelings toward outgroups (Black Americans, Hispanics/Latinos, and Asians). ANES data from 2000 to 2016 show es- sentially steady rates of ethnocentrism over almost two decades (Kinder & Kam, 2009).

Research both in the United States and in Europe has shown ethnocen- trism predicts opposition to immigration (Kinder & Kam, 2009; Sniderman, Hagendoorn, & Prior, 2004). But examinations of it as a measure of identity that informs the distribution of white social identity and as a predictor of both restrictive and progressive immigration attitudes are scarce. Measuring ingroup favoritism is important because the measurement asks respondents to rate their own ingroup and outgroups in distinct questions. Using Janet Helms's (1990) definition, positive white identity is indicated by a high (warm) index toward whites.[12]

Level Four: Group-Centric White Consciousness

Racial identity among whites has utility precisely because agency is un- equal at the individual level. Poor and low-income white Americans have agency because of their group, not because of their individual political cap- ital. This is identity politics and economics at play; when group identifica- tion matters for white Americans, when whiteness trumps individual class status. The group-centric white consciousness items in the survey ask white respondents, "How important is it that whites work together to change laws that are unfair to whites?" and "How likely is it that many whites are unable to find a job because employers are hiring minorities instead?" These questions get at the importance of white consciousness as political and moral, be- cause the question asks explicitly about whites *working together as a group* to change the laws that are seemingly unfair *to the group* in the United States. Working together signals to whites that the group norm is to stick together to make policy changes. Moreover, the second item makes this measurement of white consciousness relational. Whites as a group matter in relation to other outgroups. Whites who indicate it is very important for whites to work together to change laws they see as unfair to whites and who believe that whites are unable to find jobs due to minority hiring are following group norms. They understand their identity as white individuals who are part of a larger group and who must work together for the group (Brewer, 1999; Brewer & Gardner, 1996).

Level Five: White Identity as White Awareness of Power

Finally, this study probes whiteness and whites' understanding of how whiteness works and their role in it through questions about white racial privilege. In the 2018 CCES, two questions ask whites the extent to which they agree or disagree with the following statements: "White people in the U.S. have certain advantages because of the color of their skin" and "Racial problems in the U.S. are rare, isolated situations." In the 2020 CMPS, the first question was reframed as follows: "White people in the U.S. have certain advantages because of their race." The 2020 CMPS also asks whites to agree or disagree with several other statements, including "White privilege is a major problem in the U.S. today" and "Discrimination against Whites has become as big a problem as discrimination against racial minorities." In all these indicators, numbers were assigned to the agree/disagree scale such that higher numbers indicate whites with awareness of white privilege, whereas lower numbers indicate racially unaware whites.

White Identity, Whiteness, and Immigration Attitudes

Do all measures of white identity affect politics? Table 2A.2 examines the distribution of white racial identity on ingroup-centered factors—including other measures of white identity—as well as factors that the literature tells us matter for political behavior and for immigration politics. Whites who attach very or extreme importance to whiteness are more likely to believe that to be truly American it is important to be born in the United States[13] than whites who claim their whiteness is not at all important to their identity ($z = 13.34$, $p = 0.000$). The same pattern holds for the belief that whites face discrimination in the United States. Whites whose whiteness is important to their identity believe whites face discrimination a little to a moderate amount more than whites whose whiteness is not at all important ($z = 13.34$, $p = 0.000$). Significant differences in frequencies are found for high white racial identifiers and low white racial identifiers in their responses to whether whites have a lot of influence in politics ($\chi^2 = 38.42$, $p = 0.000$). High white racial identifiers are more likely to feel warmly toward other whites ($t(1443) = 8.92$, $p = 0.000$) and are more likely to think of whites as hardworking ($z = 9.06$, $p = 0.000$). Finally, white racial identity engenders nationalistic ($z = 9.83$, $p = 0.000$) and patriotic ($z = 7.63$, $p = 0.000$) beliefs.

High white racial identifiers are also more prone to express group consciousness, which is a politicized form of group identity. High white racial identifiers are more likely to believe that whites need to work together to change unfair laws toward whites ($z = 12.38$, $p = 0.000$) and more likely to believe that whites have a hard time finding jobs because employers hire minorities instead ($z = 11.54$, $p = 0.000$). Substantively, high white racial identifiers are more likely to be ingroup centered and feel closer to their own group and they are more likely to express group consciousness in ways that are socially and politically meaningful (McClain et al., 2009). Low white racial identifiers are not necessarily the complete opposite as they tend to appear more ambivalent, less extreme one way or the other than their counterparts. Thus, whites whose whiteness is not important appear more ambivalent and confused about their own whiteness and what it may mean than those whose whiteness is important to them.

The data show that any assumption that indicates that awareness of white racial identification automatically leads to recognition of white privilege is inaccurate. The repudiation of the system of white supremacy involves awareness both that one is white and that it means something, recognition of the privilege that comes with being white. Additionally, social change in the racial status quo necessitates action after awareness and recognition of whiteness and the privileges bestowed upon the group members. As Croll (2007) makes clear, "[d]ecades ago, the power of whiteness was believed to be its invisibility. Now that the veil of invisibility is being slowly removed, the power of whiteness remains. Whiteness may be the luxury to choose when to see it and when to ignore it, an important shift from presumed unconsciousness" (p. 635). What makes those who see and recognize whiteness different than those who may or may not recognize whiteness but whose white identity is not important to their sense of self? What are the choices afforded to whites? What choice do they make, and who does it benefit? Table 2A.3 examines the distribution of white identity on attitudes and policies geared toward leveling the playing field depending on the importance (or lack thereof) of white racial identity. In essence, does the recognition of whiteness as important to their sense of self influence whites' willingness to support policies that level the playing field across racial and ethnic groups?

Table 2A.3 shows that neither group differs tremendously on race-related policy outcomes. For example, opposition to preferential hiring and promotion for Black Americans is high for both groups. Additionally, 50% or more of whites in both groups oppose affirmative action, while the share of neutral views is also about the same for both groups. More than 50% of whites in both groups hold positive (warm) affect toward Black Americans, Latinos, and Asians. Undocumented immigrants fare poorly affectively for both groups, while affect toward Muslims brings out the biggest difference between high and low white racial identifiers. High identifiers are far less likely to feel warmth toward Muslims. Finally, more than 50% of whites in both groups place Black Americans, Latinos, and Asians as having just about the right amount of influence in politics. Thus, identifying with being white does not automatically predict having negative outgroup affect. More importantly, neither perceiving being white as important nor perceiving it as not at all important to one's self-identity increases whites' willingness to support policies created to bring about equity.

What are the political consequences of high and low white racial identity for immigration politics? Table 2.2 examines the influence of the dual distribution of white racial identity on immigration-related attitudes and policy preferences. Whites with high white racial identity are more likely to agree that immigrants harm U.S. culture than their low identifier counterparts ($z = 10.33, p = 0.000$); however, the mean for high identifiers is between "disagree somewhat" and "neither agree or disagree." The same pattern holds for the belief that immigrants increase crime ($z = 9.92, p = 0.000$). Importantly, in both cases, a sizeable sample on both sides of racialization holds opposite views from the norm. For example, although high white identifiers are more likely to agree that immigration is a cultural and economic threat, some individuals still hold the opposite view. We often pool these individuals with the rest because they, too, identify with their white identity. The reverse is true for those who do not identify with being white as important to their identity; there is variation within the two subgroups. Pooling solely based on white identity measures does not reveal these differences.

Table 2.2 Distribution of Immigration Attitudes by Importance of White Identity

	Not at All Important (%)	Very or Extremely Important (%)
America's culture is generally harmed by immigrants (cultural threat)		
Agree strongly	2.59	7.82
Agree somewhat	11.99	24.86
Neither agree nor disagree	21.53	25.56
Disagree somewhat	27.66	25.42
Disagree strongly	36.24	16.34
Immigrants increase crime rates in the United States		
Agree strongly	3.96	12.03
Agree somewhat	20.33	32.73
Neither agree nor disagree	27.29	26.15
Disagree somewhat	21.56	19.02
Disagree strongly	26.88	10.07
U.S. government policy toward unauthorized immigrants		
Make felons and send them back to their country	17.01	25.63
Have a guest worker program in order to work	13.47	14.90
Allow them to remain and qualify for U.S. citizenship with requirements	58.50	53.76
Allow them to remain and qualify for U.S. citizenship without penalties	11.02	5.71
How likely it is immigration will take away jobs (realistic group threat)		
Extremely likely	14.56	23.09
Very likely	16.33	27.68
Somewhat likely	41.36	35.88
Not at all likely	27.76	13.35
Young people brought illegally as children sent back (i.e., DREAMers)		
Should be allowed to stay	80.39	74.37
Should be sent back	19.61	25.63
Country needs strong leader to take us back to true path		
Agree strongly	23.13	37.78
Agree somewhat	23.40	28.61
Neither agree nor disagree	20.14	15.97

(continued)

Table 2.2 Continued

	Not at All Important (%)	Very or Extremely Important (%)
Disagree somewhat	13.74	7.92
Disagree strongly	19.59	9.72

Data: 2016 ANES.

Note: Column percentages shown based on all five categories of identity. In other words, the percentages are based on all white respondents in the category of "not at all" across the rows.

Likewise, more than half of the sample in both groups indicated the United States should provide a path to citizenship with requirements. Many respondents in both groups believe immigration is likely to take away jobs, though the belief is more prevalent among high racial identifiers ($z = 8.30$, $p = 0.000$). A very large majority in both groups believe young people who were brought to the United States illegally (what some call DREAMers) should be allowed to stay. The final question, "Does the country need a strong leader to take the country back to its 'true' path?" is immigration-related because the 2016 Trump presidential campaign used this rhetoric to argue that Trump was such a leader and that he would do so by tightening immigration restrictions. High white identifiers are more likely to say yes ($z = 8.18$, $p = 0.000$).

Racial identity among whites has utility for whites precisely because agency is unequal at the individual level. One way to examine the distribution of whiteness is to cross-tabulate the importance of white identification with white group consciousness, which is more political and group-conscious in nature. Table 2.3 is evidence of the distribution of whiteness. It shows, for example, that the lack of importance some white Americans place on white identity does not necessarily mean all whites in this category behave the same way politically. Among whites whose white identity is not important to their own identity, we observe a split between those who do not think whites need to work together to change laws which they believe unfairly disadvantage whites (~35%) and those who think it is very or extremely important for whites to work together to change laws unfair toward their own group (~28%), with about 25% suggesting it is moderately important. For high white racial identifiers, more than half (~57%) think it is very or extremely

Table 2.3 Cross-Tabulation of White Racial Identity and White Group Consciousness

| White Identity | Unfair Laws | | | | |
	Not at All	A Little	Moderately	Very or Extremely	Total
Not at all important	253	95	179	203	730
A little	102	90	124	129	445
Moderately	116	82	241	226	665
Very or Extremely	76	52	183	405	716
Total	547	319	727	963	2,556

Data: 2016 ANES.
Note: Raw numbers.

important for whites to work together, while only about 11% do not think it is important at all.

Whiteness being seemingly irrelevant to self-identity does not mean individual-level behavior is solely self-motivated. In the case of both groups, but especially among non-identifiers, behavior is group motivated. More than half of whites who suggest that their white identity is not at all important to their own self-identity (52%) say that working together with other whites to change the unfair laws targeting whites is moderately, very, or extremely important.

Do politically consequential distinctions exist between those with high group consciousness and those with no group consciousness? Table 2.4 examines this question by comparing the groups on a selection of ingroup, outgroup, and immigration-related attitudes. Whites with high levels of group consciousness are more likely to believe that whites are unable to find jobs due to employers hiring minorities ($z = 20.23$, $p = 0.000$). In relation to nationalistic attitudes, both groups' means hover over the neutral category, though higher levels of group consciousness increase the mean to just over the neutral category ($z = 9.58$, $p = 0.000$).

Most individuals in both groups say discrimination against whites does not happen or only happens a little. A significant difference exists between the two groups ($z = 11.70$, $p = 0.000$): Those with high group consciousness have a higher likelihood of believing anti-white discrimination happens a little to a moderate amount. More than half of both groups agree that whites have just the right amount of influence in politics. Two noteworthy subsamples emerge when asking about whites' influence in politics: Approximately 18%

Table 2.4 Distribution of Attitudes and Preferences by Importance of White Consciousness

	Not at All Important (%)	Very or Extremely Important (%)
Ingroup Centered		
Discrimination in the United States against whites		
A great deal	1.30	4.78
A lot	2.60	6.91
A moderate amount	10.22	22.00
A little	38.10	46.23
None at all	47.77	20.09
How much influence do whites have in U.S. politics?		
Too much influence	45.52	18.48
Just about the right amount	52.10	70.35
Too little influence	2.38	11.17
Warm affect toward whites (0–100)		
Less than 50	6.00	2.39
50–59	28.00	13.74
More than 60	66.00	83.87
How likely are whites to be unable to find job because employers hire minorities?		
Extremely likely	0.91	15.46
Very likely	2.73	21.68
Moderately likely	13.30	30.29
Slightly likely	37.89	22.41
Not at all likely	45.17	10.17
Nationalism: Better if the rest of world was more like America		
Agree strongly	3.09	12.03
Agree somewhat	16.55	27.49
Neither agree nor disagree	34.36	33.92
Disagree somewhat	22.91	15.66
Disagree strongly	23.09	10.89
Outgroup Centered		
For or against preferential hiring/promotion of Blacks		
For	26.92	14.27
Against	73.08	85.73

(continued)

Table 2.4 Continued

	Not at All Important (%)	Very or Extremely Important (%)
Affirmative Action		
Favor	25.27	10.05
Neutral	33.70	33.61
Oppose	41.03	56.34
Immigration Preferences		
America's culture is generally harmed by immigrants (cultural threat)		
Agree strongly	2.73	7.82
Agree somewhat	6.91	18.77
Neither agree nor disagree	13.09	22.00
Disagree somewhat	30.55	29.93
Disagree strongly	46.73	21.48
Country needs strong leader to take us back to true path		
Agree strongly	12.55	39.63
Agree somewhat	21.27	26.66
Neither agree nor disagree	16.55	14.42
Disagree somewhat	15.27	10.27
Disagree strongly	34.36	9.02

Data: 2016 ANES.

of those with high group consciousness and about 46% of those with no group consciousness believe whites have too much influence in politics. This has two implications. First, high group consciousness among some whites does not necessarily mean that they are unaware of whites' privileges, in this case, disproportionate political influence. Second, having no group consciousness does not determine this group's willingness to see whites as a group and to accept whites' disproportionate advantage in politics. The questions about discrimination against whites and about whites' influence in politics are relational in that they ask participants to compare whites to other groups; hence they differ from the questions about outgroup policy preferences.

Whites' social identity on politically relevant policies that have the potential to level the playing field among groups, outgroup-centered attitudes, is important to examine. More than half of both whites with no group consciousness and whites with high group consciousness oppose preferential hiring of Black Americans. More whites with higher levels of group consciousness oppose affirmative action (χ^2 (2) = 67.67, p = 0.000). However, a sizeable number of members of this group chose the neutral category, while a substantial number of those without group consciousness oppose affirmative action. In essence, most whites, regardless of white consciousness, are hesitant to support affirmative action, which might even the playing field among themselves and other racial groups, indicating again that white individuals make group-level decisions and that white group consciousness alone is not enough to make systemic changes.

Finally, higher levels of group consciousness increase the belief that immigrants pose a cultural threat (z = 11.62, p = 0.000) and that the country needs a strong leader to take the United States back to its true path (z = 14.54, p = 0.000). Although higher levels of group consciousness increase the likelihood of agreeing with these two statements, a sizeable number of these group members disagree somewhat or strongly. Additionally, a sizeable number of whites who do not believe whites need to work together agree that the country needs a leader to take the United States back to its true path. A lack of group consciousness does not preclude whites from feeling nostalgic for a country that they feel used to be better, where whites were a broader majority and the perception that they held a greater monopoly on power was prevalent.[14]

An examination of the 2012 and 2016 ANES indicates that most white Americans have neutral to high levels of ingroup favoritism regardless of the importance they place on whiteness as an aspect of their identity. In 2012 (not shown), those with higher levels of white racial identity are more likely to have higher levels of ingroup favoritism (t(1497) = 16.46, p = 0.000). Table 2.5 depicts the cross-tabulation between the group-centric white identity measure and levels of ethnocentrism. In the 2016 ANES, there are a substantial number of whites who do not think whites need to work together to change the unfair laws toward whites and who exhibit low levels of ingroup favoritism (~32%). However, the largest percentage of whites in this group (~42%) express neutral affect toward white Americans. Whites who believe in working together to change the unfair laws targeting their group are more likely to have higher levels of ingroup favoritism (χ^2 (2) = 124.73, p = 0.0001), with no significant differences between the first (< 0.5) and second (= 0.5) categories. In 2000, whites who did not feel close to other whites (of whom there were only 157 out of 1,056 respondents) were more likely to hold neutral affect toward other whites, while about half of whites who felt close to

Table 2.5 Ethnocentrism by Group-Centric White Consciousness

	Outgroup Favoritism (< 0.5)	Neutral (= 0.5)	Ingroup Favoritism (> 0.5)
2016 ANES			
Not at all important (%)	31.88	41.89	26.23
A little (%)	18.61	39.75	41.64
Moderately (%)	16.18	36.12	47.70
Very or extremely (%)	15.52	28.23	56.25
2000 ANES			
Not close to whites (%)	15.38	53.85	30.77
Close to whites (%)	12.09	37.79	50.13

Data: 2000 ANES; 2016 ANES.

other whites were more likely to hold positive affect toward other whites. A substantial number of whites, however, held neutral affect toward their ingroup even though they felt close to other whites.

In 2000, ingroup favoritism was consequential to preferences that would help level the playing field, especially between white and Black Americans. A significant difference in proportions between the two groups exists for affirmative action ($z = 3.63$, $p = 0.000$), preferential hiring of Black Americans ($z = 2.18$, $p = 0.03$), and whether the government should have an active role in ensuring equal treatment toward Black Americans ($z = 4.53$, $p = 0.000$). Whites who hold higher than neutral affect toward whites are more likely to affirm the restrictive position on these policies. On immigration, there is a positive relationship between ethnocentrism and the likelihood of wanting to decrease legal immigration ($rho = 0.32$, $p = 0.000$) and increase federal spending for border security to prevent illegal immigration ($rho = 0.24$, $p = 0.000$). Thus, in 2000 levels of ingroup favoritism mattered for politics.

The same pattern holds for 2016; higher levels of ingroup favoritism influence politically relevant outcomes. Whites with ingroup favoritism are more likely to be against preferential hiring ($z = 8.26$, $p = 0.000$),[15] more likely to say the government treats Blacks and whites the same instead of treating whites better ($z = 9.70$, $p = 0.000$), and more likely to be against affirmative action ($z = 9.63$, $p = 0.000$). On immigration attitudes, whites with higher levels of ingroup favoritism are more likely to agree that immigration is a cultural threat to the United States ($rho = 0.36$, $p = 0.000$),[16] that immigrants increase crime rates ($rho = 0.38$, $p = 0.000$), and that immigration takes jobs away from those already in United States ($rho = 0.29$, $p = 0.000$). The likelihood of whites with higher levels of ingroup favoritism who favor the elimination of birthright citizenship is also proportionally higher ($z = 8.79$, $p = 0.000$). Ingroup favoritism (ethnocentrism) as a measurement of white racial identity is crucial in understanding whites' political behavior as inherently relational. Politically and normatively important is an examination of what makes whites who are aware of their whiteness and have a recognition of it *choose* to deviate from the norms of whiteness, while others *choose* to double down on white supremacy. I argue that the answer lies in understanding how white identity and whiteness are related to whites' predispositions.

The Relationship between Whiteness and Predispositions

As shown in Table 2.6, in general, whites who believe that their whiteness is very or extremely important to their identity have, compared to their counterparts, significantly higher levels of racial resentment, authoritarianism, and moral traditionalism and lower levels of egalitarianism.[17] The same pattern holds using the 2012 ANES as seen in Table 2A.4 in Appendix B. Using a seven-point party identification scale indicates that strong identifiers are also more likely to lean Republican than Democrat.[18] The biggest difference between the two groups pertains to levels of authoritarianism. Hence, the norms of whiteness, as learned through socialization and expressed through predispositions, are intricately connected to white racial identity. How whites are socialized and what they learn about whiteness, other groups, law and order, authority, equality, and family structure are intricately tied to who they are not just as individuals but also relationally.

Table 2.6 Predispositions by Importance of White Identity

	Not at All	Very or Extremely	Difference in Means
Predispositions			
Racial resentment	.556 (.300)	.669 (.255)	$t(1448) = 7.70, p = 0.000$
Authoritarianism	.477 (.324)	.615 (.300)	$t(1451) = 8.43, p = 0.000$
Moral traditionalism	.503 (.263)	.599 (.227)	$t(1451) = 7.46, p = 0.000$
Egalitarianism	.337 (.224)	.410 (.200)	$t(1449) = 6.49, p = 0.000$
Partisanship	.499 (.355)	.592 (.361)	$t(1451) = 4.95, p = 0.000$

Data: 2016 ANES. Cell values are mean responses with standard deviation in parentheses.

All the predispositions tap into relational factors, such as norms about how whiteness functions in the world vis-à-vis African Americans (racial resentment) and authorities (authoritarianism). Others address how whiteness functions in relation to norms around the nuclear family and the morality of different lifestyles (moral traditionalism) as well as conceptions of what is equal and equality in U.S. society (egalitarianism). White racial identity does not exist outside of white socialization.

Whites' choices are deeply connected to their predispositions, byproducts of white socialization. Table 2.7 depicts the difference in means among racial non-identifiers (those who said being white is not important to their identity) by group consciousness (*Unfair laws*). Racial non-identifiers display a substantial difference between those who say that it is not important at all to work together to change the unfair laws toward whites versus those who say it is very or extremely important to work together. Statistically significant differences exist among these two subsets in levels of racial resentment, authoritarianism, moral traditionalism, egalitarianism, and partisanship. Among racial non-identifiers, those with high group consciousness have higher levels of all predispositions, with the biggest differences involving racial resentment, authoritarianism, moral traditionalism, and partisanship, all of which have been shown to influence immigration-related and race-related policy preferences. In fact, we observe a bigger difference among racial non-identifiers than among high racial identifiers across levels of authoritarianism, partisanship, and to a lesser extent moral traditionalism, shown in Table 2.7 (non-identifiers) and Table 2.8 (high racial identifiers). In other words, among low white identifiers, levels of group consciousness affect predispositions more than for high white identifiers.

Table 2.7 Predispositions among Racial Non-identifiers, by White Group Consciousness

	Not at All	Very or Extremely	Difference in Means
Predispositions			
Racial resentment	.447 (.312)	.622 (.285)	$t(454) = 6.17, p = 0.000$
Authoritarianism	.376 (.311)	.555 (.316)	$t(453) = 6.06, p = 0.000$
Moral traditionalism	.417 (.272)	.589 (.255)	$t(453) = 6.87, p = 0.000$
Egalitarianism	.300 (.252)	.354 (.299)	$t(454) = 2.47, p = 0.014$
Partisanship	.416 (.358)	.559 (.362)	$t(453) = 4.21, p = 0.000$

Data: 2016 ANES. Cell values are mean responses with standard deviation in parentheses.

Table 2.8 Predispositions among High Racial Identifiers, by White Group Consciousness

	Not at All	Very or Extremely	Difference in Means
Predispositions			
Racial resentment	.522 (.328)	.704 (.238)	$t(475) = 5.72, p = 0.000$
Authoritarianism	.472 (.341)	.641 (.294)	$t(478) = 4.46, p = 0.000$
Moral traditionalism	.497 (.239)	.629 (.223)	$t(476) = 4.68, p = 0.000$
Egalitarianism	.322 (.237)	.416 (.198)	$t(476) = 3.65, p = 0.000$
Partisanship	.397 (.380)	.613 (.352)	$t(479) = 4.85, p = 0.000$

Data: 2016 ANES. Cell values are mean responses with standard deviation in parentheses.

Among high racial identifiers (Table 2.8), we also observe a difference between those who want to work with other whites to change perceived unfair laws toward whites and those who do not. In essence, this suggests that understanding your whiteness as important to your identity can have differing effects depending on the variation of predispositions, which help guide whites' internal compass when making political decisions. The same can be said of those whose whiteness is not important to their individual identity, but who nonetheless affirm group-centric, macro-level choices. Low white identifiers, those who said being white is not important to their identity but who want to work together with other whites to change the unfair laws toward whites, are driven by an understanding of whiteness as group centered. Individually, being white is not a salient identity marker, but they have an implicit understanding that they have something to lose if they do not conform to the norms of whiteness by supporting policies that maintain whites' position in the social and racial hierarchies. There are also those who do not conform, and whose lower levels of key political and psychological predispositions steer them in another direction. Key information about white identity politics can be found at the intersection of white group politics and the norms established through predispositions.

Underlying differences between those with high ingroup favoritism and those with low ingroup favoritism are significant differences in levels of predispositions. Table 2.9 shows the difference in means of levels of racial resentment, authoritarianism, moral traditionalism, egalitarianism, and partisanship. In 2000, those with higher levels of ingroup favoritism also have higher levels of racial resentment, authoritarianism, and moral

Table 2.9 Predispositions by Ethnocentrism, 2000

Predispositions	Outgroup Favoritism (< 0.5)	Ingroup Favoritism (> 0.51)	Difference in Means
Racial resentment	.529 (.255)	.706 (.203)	$t(546) = 7.89, p = 0.000$
Authoritarianism	.483 (.277)	.633 (.273)	$t(552) = 5.26, p = 0.000$
Moral traditionalism	.575 (.242)	.651 (.205)	$t(549) = 3.41, p = 0.001$
Egalitarianism	.372 (.216)	.445 (.187)	$t(547) = 3.61, p = 0.000$
Partisanship[*]	.465 (.424)	.558 (.412)	$t(486) = 2.00, p = 0.045$

Data: 2000 ANES. Cell values are mean responses with standard deviation in parentheses.
* This measure of partisanship only included a three-item scale.

traditionalism, lower levels of egalitarianism, and are more likely to lean Republican. Ingroup favoritism is related to the maintenance of the ingroup, as it is connected to increased levels of predispositions and norms about how outgroups should behave, what is appropriate behavior by children, the "right" and "moral" ways to live, and definitions of equality.

In 2016, the mean differences between whites with low ingroup favoritism and whites with high ingroup favoritism are stark. Table 2.10 depicts these differences alongside the difference of means t-tests. An examination of the distribution of whites across the ethnocentrism spectrum results in large differences in predispositions between whites with low ingroup favoritism and whites with high ingroup favoritism. In fact, the comparison of these two groups yields greater differences in predispositions than any other measurement of white racial identity. The social positioning of whites with low or high ingroup favoritism is significant in examining white political behavior.

Overall, ethnocentrism stands out as an important and implicit measurement of white group identity. Ethnocentrism is the only measurement used that does not ask whites about the importance of being white or working with whites or being close to other whites; it just asks about how warmly they feel toward white Americans. This measurement of ethnocentrism is relational in that it divides the world into "us" versus "them" for white Americans (Kinder & Kam, 2009). Across the board, white respondents have high levels of ingroup favoritism regardless of other measures of white identification. Even among low white racial identifiers, high levels of ethnocentrism were present. Ultimately, ingroup favoritism affects political

Table 2.10 Predispositions by Ethnocentrism, 2016

	Outgroup Favoritism (< 0.5)	Ingroup Favoritism (> 0.51)	Difference in Means
Predispositions			
Racial resentment	.414 (.295)	.674 (.233)	$t(1656) = 19.23, p = 0.000$
Authoritarianism	.366 (.314)	.607 (.296)	$t(1657) = 14.94, p = 0.000$
Moral traditionalism	.424 (.257)	.593 (.220)	$t(1655) = 13.62, p = 0.000$
Egalitarianism	.295 (.227)	.414 (.193)	$t(1657) = 10.87, p = 0.000$
Partisanship	.404 (.351)	.598 (.349)	$t(1657) = 10.38, p = 0.000$

Data: 2016 ANES. Cell values are mean responses with standard deviation in parentheses.

views, which is consistent with political scientists' work on ethnocentrism (Kinder & Kam, 2009). Finally, 2016 stands out as a year when levels of predispositions such as racial resentment and moral traditionalism varied hugely between low levels of ingroup favoritism and high levels of ingroup favoritism.

The ANES studies utilized do not include questions that measure power-cognizance. For this analysis, I turn to the 2020 CMPS, which addresses predispositions and identity using different questions from the ANES. Given its limitations, I utilized a measure of white linked fate as a proxy for white identity as well as questions that measure white racial advantages and privilege to measure power-cognizance. Whites with higher levels of linked fate are more likely to have higher levels of racial resentment ($t(842) = 5.25$, $p = 0.000$), to identify less strongly with the Republican Party, and to be closer to identifying as an independent ($t(804) = 4.38$, $p = 0.000$). Hence, the pattern holds even while using a proxy for white identification. See Table 2A.5 in Appendix B.

Using two different measures of power-cognizance,[19] Table 2.11 shows levels of racial resentment and partisanship by white advantages according to whether whites disagree or agree with the following statement: "White people in the U.S. have certain advantages because of their race." Whites who disagree with this statement have much higher levels of racial resentment and are stronger Republicans. The question on white discrimination asks whether respondents agree or disagree with this statement: "Discrimination against Whites has become as big a problem as discrimination against racial minorities." Whites who signal their lack of power-cognizance by agreeing with the statement have much higher levels of racial resentment than those

Table 2.11 Predispositions by Power-Cognizance, 2021

	Disagree	Agree	Difference in Means
White Advantages			
Racial resentment	.794 (.199)	.449 (.262)	$t(1718) = -29.42, p = 0.000$
Partisanship	.746 (.284)	.515 (.323)	$t(1558) = -14.23, p = 0.000$
White Discrimination			
Racial resentment	.440 (.199)	.720 (.262)	$t(1618) = -21.92, p = 0.000$
Partisanship	.706 (.310)	.499 (.314)	$t(1558) = -13.10, p = 0.000$

Data: 2020 CMPS. Cell values are mean responses with standard deviation in parentheses.

Table 2.12 Predispositions by Power-Cognizance, 2018

	Disagree	Agree	Difference in Means
White Advantages			
Racial resentment	.813 (.187)	.311 (.266)	$t(21943) = -160.00, p = 0.000$
Partisanship	.734 (.288)	.296 (.319)	$t(21737) = -100.00, p = 0.000$
Racism Is Rare			
Racial resentment	.439 (.326)	.797 (.195)	$t(21940) = -76.00, p = 0.000$
Partisanship	.397 (.361)	.753 (.361)	$t(21688) = -66.01, p = 0.000$

Data: 2018 CCES. Cell values are mean responses with standard deviation in parentheses.

who do not ($t(1618) = -21.92$, $p = 0.000$). They are also far more likely to identify as independents than as Republicans ($t(1558) = 13.10$, $p = 0.000$). This is a surprising finding, in that Republicans implicitly embrace policies that would seem to be based on the idea that discrimination against racial minorities does not exist.

I replicate Table 2.11 using the 2018 CCES, seen in Table 2.12, which has a much larger sample of non-Hispanic whites. The pattern holds: Whites who are unaware of power differentials and white advantages have higher levels of racial resentment and are more likely to identify as Republican. I used a third measure of white awareness that asks whether participants agree or disagree with the statement "Racial problems in the U.S. are rare, isolated situations." Whites who are racially aware disagree with this statement, while whites who are less aware agree. As the table shows, the influence of awareness of how whiteness works influences whites' predispositions. Whites who disagree with the statement have less racial resentment and identify with the

Democratic Party, while whites who agree that racism is a rare occurrence in the United States have more racial resentment and identify as Republicans.

Conclusion

Predispositions matter for white racial politics and whiteness studies. In fact, predispositions are foundational to white group racial politics; they are intricately connected to how whiteness is racialized and how whites are socialized. As George A. Akerlof and Rachel E. Kranton (2010) remind us, "[t]he norms of how to behave depend on people's position within their social context" (p. 11). Without an understanding of the normative behaviors of whiteness, which are learned by socialization in the home, neighborhood, and educational institutions, to name a few, we cannot understand white identity politics. From a very young age white Americans are taught how to behave, whether explicitly or by virtue of emulation, and these norms are directly related to the predispositions whites then come to hold. And these predispositions are the results of a series of (im)moral choices along the way. This chapter finds that whites' predispositions are influenced by how they see themselves as white people and how they understand whiteness but less by whether they see being white as important to their identity.

White identity is group-based. Regardless of whether individual whites said their whiteness was important to their identity or indicated that it is important that whites work together for policies that will benefit them, most whites expressed ingroup favoritism and are unable to support equitable policies that might result in leveling the playing field. More than 50% of whites who express white racial identity and those who do not express white racial identity oppose affirmative action and preferential hiring policies for African Americans. This is group-based political behavior. To oppose policies that might help another group, an outgroup, is to choose the maintenance of your own ingroup. Race-based policies are often framed and seen as zero-sum; thus whites' individual decisions do not affect just individual whites but the entire group. This group-based decision-making is most evident in cases of whites with high group consciousness and high ingroup favoritism. Whites with high levels of group consciousness and higher levels of ingroup favoritism are more likely than whites with lower levels of both to have higher levels of racial resentment, moral traditionalism, authoritarianism, and anti-egalitarianism. These findings are evidence of how

predispositions and whiteness work together to influence the group-based
nature of white political behavior. Predispositions are intricately connected
to white identity and whiteness. The extent to which whites have high levels
of group consciousness and ingroup favoritism and are aware of white power
molds whites' predispositions. Consequently, predispositions color whites'
political behavior, including their attitudes toward immigration.

3
How Whiteness Structures Restrictive Immigration Attitudes

Fiction and non-fiction alike provide examples of different kinds of embodied whiteness, different ways of choosing whiteness, and a window into what it may look and feel like to be white and choose to perpetuate white supremacy. They offer readers a way into the intimate moral struggles of white Americans in the choices they make and the political and social consequences of their choices.

James Baldwin's (1965b) short story "Going to Meet the Man," which was based on factual events of the time,[1] focuses on Jesse, a white deputy sheriff of a small Southern town. The reader finds him lying in bed with his wife, detailing the events of his day, which included arresting a Black civil rights leader and violently beating him in his jail cell. As he is talking, a childhood memory returns to him of his parents taking him to witness the lynching of a Black man when he was eight. He describes to his wife that it seemed like "millions" of white folks were expressing "their delight at what they saw" (p. 245). He describes his mother's face, her eyes "bright," her mouth open. Both excited and confused by the brutality he was witnessing, Jesse remembers thinking that his mother "was more beautiful than he had ever seen her" as she watched (p. 247). His father, he remembers, having lifted him to his shoulders, told him that he'd never forget *this* picnic. "At that moment, Jesse loved his father more than he had ever loved him," Baldwin writes (p. 248). Yet this love contradicts his own moral compass. He recalls shivering in terror, screaming. His love for his parents and his parents' love for him were wrapped up in anti-Black violence. Jesse also learned a type of citizenship, one that is upheld and sustained in the private sphere, in personal and intimate familial relations (Berlant, 1997).

As a child, Jesse chose his parents' love and his family—he chose "being white," as Baldwin would say—over his own moral compass. Like many of the people whose childhoods Thandeka describes in *Learning to be white*

Moral and Immoral Whiteness in Immigration Politics. Yalidy Matos, Oxford University Press.
© Oxford University Press 2023. DOI: 10.1093/oso/9780197656259.003.0004

(1999), Jessie was socialized by his parents and community to think that choosing anything other than whiteness implicitly meant giving up his family. He remembers having questions at the time of the lynching but that "he had no one to ask" (p. 243) and "could not ask his father" (p. 247). As an adult man in the story's present day, Jesse still grapples with this emotional and physical display of unresolved internal moral conflict, a moral conflict that is impeding his humanity.

In other writings and in live debates, Baldwin is clear about what he believed Jesse had suffered: one of the worst things that could happen to a human being. In a 1965 debate with conservative intellectual William F. Buckley Jr., Baldwin states that whites hold a helpless belief "that no matter how terrible some of their lives may be and no matter what disaster overtakes them, there is one consolation like a heavenly revelation—at least they are not black" (Baldwin, 1965a). Baldwin diagnosed this belief as a consequence of white supremacy for poor whites, and in particular, Southern whites. Baldwin states, "[W]hat has happened to the white Southerner is in some ways much worse than what has happened to the Negroes there," referencing the loss of white Southerners' moral lives (Baldwin, 1965a). In tracing genealogies of whiteness in "Going to Meet the Man," Baldwin sheds light on the lineage of whiteness, how it is passed on; the continued insistence of the past onto the present. Baldwin's decision to focus on a lynching, thought at the time to be part of a bygone era, emphasizes the ways in which the past informs the present; in particular, the ways in which the past informs white people's present-day beliefs and behavior. Baldwin's short story illustrates their impact of socialization on whites' predispositions and their learning of moral norms and the roles one ought to perform as a white person. Similarly, I argue these learned predispositions, norms, and roles influence white political attitudes and behavior.

A-Side: Restrictive Immigration Attitudes

Whiteness structures immigration attitudes and immigration is an avenue, a policy, where whites can *do* whiteness. That is, immigration provides white Americans with the ability to choose their group and follow group norms without the issue being explicitly about race. But it most certainly is all about race and thus power. Immigration is about the maintenance of the racial status quo because it threatens whites' position, and it threatens a social order that whites are comfortable with. Immigration can change group status in U.S. society. Whiteness also structures predispositions, which are a byproduct of socialization, a socialization that is raced. Hence, overall higher levels of racial resentment, authoritarianism, moral traditionalism, and anti-egalitarianism should influence restrictive immigration attitudes, while Republican Party identification should have the same outcome. However, whiteness will structure these results: Among white Americans with higher levels of group consciousness, predispositions will be the strongest and most significant. Furthermore, an examination of the main model by party will also dictate the influence of party on predispositions.

Commitment to one's group (Burke & Reitzes, 1991) is instrumental, affective, and moral (Kanter, 1968, 1972). Therefore, I expect that moral traditionalism will play an important and consistent role in influencing restrictive immigration attitudes. Furthermore, I expect whiteness to moderate the significance and strength of moral traditionalism. Moral traditionalism serves as one way to understand the role of moral politics in whites' attitudes toward immigration. Perceptions of societal instability and moral denigration are intimately related to perceptions of moral superiority, which Brewer (1999) has argued leads to ingroup love and outgroup derogation, it leads to prejudice and intolerance. Whites with higher levels of moral traditionalism inherently understand their beliefs about the right moral order to be right: superior to the beliefs of others whom they do not perceive to be ingroup members. Hence, higher levels of moral traditionalism are tied to perceptions of moral superiority. They frame and cloud whites' attitudes on immigration. These beliefs become the foundation of white immigration attitudes.

Immigration generally is likely to activate status threat for whites; because of this, immigration heightens perceptions of threat and thus group-like mentality. High levels of commitment to the group will result in political behavior that supports the group, especially because the individual's identification with the group is conflated. Individuals attain self-esteem and worth from the group (Tajfel, 1978; Tajfel & Turner, 1979, 1986). Moreover, people are motivated to improve their group position, especially when that position is heightened by perceptions of threat (Blumer, 1958; Bobo & Hutchings, 1996).

Immigration is also structured by whiteness. This leads to several expectations. First, I expect that immigration attitudes will be influenced more by predispositions and white group consciousness than white racial identity

(WRI). Second, I expect that predispositions, a byproduct of socialization, strongly influence immigration attitudes; higher levels of all predispositions will be associated with restrictive immigration preferences more than with WRI. Third, white consciousness will be associated with restrictive immigration attitudes. Fourth, white identity and white consciousness will moderate the strength of predispositions on immigration policy in that higher levels of predispositions will influence restrictive immigration attitudes among whites who express higher saliency of WRI and especially higher levels of white group consciousness. Finally, I expect that partisan identity will also moderate the significance and strength of predispositions.

The goal of this chapter is to explore the factors associated with restrictive immigration attitudes among white Americans, with special attention to the role of predispositions for white Americans and their heterogenous attachment to whiteness, not merely white racial identity. The next section tests how much immigration attitudes drive the racial status quo for white Americans.

Information on Data

This chapter utilizes the American National Election Studies (ANES) survey data to paint a correlational picture of whites' restrictive immigration attitudes and highlight the factors influencing their preferences. I draw primarily from the 2012 and 2016 ANES Time Series Studies and supplement some analyses using the 2000, 2004, and 2020 ANES studies. The ANES is a nationwide representative survey administered both face-to-face and through Internet surveys of U.S. citizens ages 18 and older. It is fielded before each election, in September through November of the election year, and after the election between November and January. Following prior work on immigration attitudes (Brader et al., 2008; Campbell et al., 2006; Hood & Morris, 1997, 1998, 2000) and because this project is interested in the heterogeneity of whiteness, I only utilize white non-Hispanic respondents with both parents born in the United States.

To measure restrictive immigration attitudes, I examine a variety of immigration attitudes and policy preferences that appear in all or some of the survey waves. *Police checks* (2012 only) refers to respondents' position on allowing the police to check documentation status if they have "reasonable doubt" that a person is in the country without proper documentation. *Immigration levels* refers to preferences for increasing, decreasing, or keeping the same the number of legal immigrants entering the country. *Immigration policy* preferences range from allowing undocumented immigrants to remain in the United States without penalties to making all undocumented immigrants felons and deporting them to their home countries in 2004, 2008, 2012, 2016, and 2020. The two earlier waves I use asked respondents whether controlling illegal immigration was a "very important," "somewhat important," or "not important at all" policy goal. *Border security spending*, asked in 2000, 2004, 2008, and 2020, refers to whether federal spending on tightening border security to prevent illegal immigration should be increased, kept the same, or decreased. *Border wall* refers to whether respondents favor, oppose, or neither building a wall on the U.S. border with Mexico, asked in 2016 and 2020. Finally, *Birthright citizenship* reflects whether respondents favor, oppose, or express no opinion on rescinding birthright citizenship for children of unauthorized immigrants to the United States in the U.S. Constitution, also asked in 2016 and 2020. All policy are coded to range from low to high restrictive immigration attitudes. All policy attitudes used in this chapter are ordinal and thus ordered logit models are employed (any deviation from this is noted in the text).

All predisposition scales are coded to range between zero and one, and higher numbers indicate higher levels of the respective predisposition. I also include an anti-egalitarianism measure, which is a scale that measures respondents' understanding of equality of opportunity and the need for the government to continue to push for equality. The egalitarianism measure is reverse coded, so higher levels indicate anti-egalitarianism. Information on these main predispositions by ANES year can be found in Table 3A.1, Table 3A.2, and Table 3A.3 in Appendix B.

Additionally, I include feeling thermometers toward Latinos, undocumented immigrants, Black Americans, and Asian Americans. Feeling thermometers elicit respondents' affective feelings toward a person, group, or issue using a numeric rating. Higher numbers (> 0.5) indicate warmer feelings toward a group and lower numbers (< 0.5) indicate colder feelings, while the middle (0.5) indicates neutrality. Finally, I consider perceptions of Latinos in politics (status threat), patriotism, the national economy, education, gender, age, income, party identification, and church attendance as additional indicators of restrictive immigration policy preferences.

Choosing the Group: The Relationship between Immigration Attitudes and Maintaining the Status Quo

Immigration is related to the racial status quo for white Americans and, I predict, most whites will choose to stick with group norms by choosing to maintain the status quo. This is a moral choice. The maintenance of the status quo is about the maintenance of whiteness. Figure 3.1 depicts the relationship between two ways of measuring the desire to maintain the status quo for whites and whites' immigration attitudes about appropriate immigration levels and policy, *Aid to Blacks* and *Preferential treatment*. *Aid to Blacks* refers to attitudes toward government aid to Black people, from (1) special effort in this regard to (7) Blacks should help themselves. *Preferential treatment* refers to support of (0) or opposition to (1) preferential hiring or promotion of Blacks in the workplace. All the correlations are positive and statistically significant. That is, restrictive immigration attitudes (decreasing legal immigration levels and punitive immigration policy) are positively related to higher

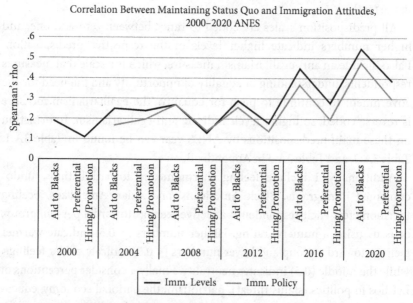

Figure 3.1 Weighted Correlation between Maintaining Status Quo and Immigration Attitudes
Source: 2000–2020 ANES.

levels of both opposing aid to Blacks and affirmative action for Blacks. Since 2000, the relationship between the two across both immigration questions has steadily increased, suggesting, in line with past research, that the 2016 and 2020 presidential elections heightened an explicit and emboldened kind of whiteness among the white population in the United States (Jardina, 2019; Lopez Bunyasi, 2019; Matos & Miller, 2021), but a whiteness that has always been present. Candidates reminded whites of the precarity of their dominance in the United States because of demographic changes due to immigration and, reputedly, discrimination against white Americans to the benefit of other groups.

The 2020 ANES, shown in Figure 3.2, shows that only 24% of respondents support preferential hiring or promotion of Blacks, suggesting a deep resistance to a policy that might offer redress for structural racism. I found a strong correlation between whites who do not want any systematic changes and whites who want decreased immigration levels, and who generally prefer more restrictive immigration policies. Among whites who chose the most restrictive immigration policy—to make all undocumented immigrants felons and deport them—90% also opposed the preferential treatment of Blacks in hiring and promotion. Likewise, most whites who want to decrease immigration levels a lot also reject preferential treatment (~92%). In fact, all the immigration policy attitudes are positively associated with a rejection of preferential treatment in ways that are statistically significant. As Figure 3.2 shows, a simple Spearman's correlation shows that immigration levels (rho = 0.39), immigration policy (rho = 0.30), birthright citizenship (rho = 0.29), border wall (rho = 0.39), and border spending (rho = 0.39) are all significant and weakly to moderately correlated.

Aid to Blacks shows similar patterns as *Preferential treatment*. Overall, whites' mean is at 4.08, which is about the middle of the scale. About 40% of whites chose between five and seven (maintain status quo), and 38% chose between one and three (disrupt status quo). Figure 3.2 indicates the Spearman correlation coefficients, which are positive and statistically significant moderate to strong correlations. In other words, whites who are closest to expressing that Blacks should help themselves (reject that the government should help level the playing field) also hold restrictive immigration attitudes.

One way to test whether whites' identity, consciousness, and feelings of precarity are related to the maintenance of the status quo is to examine the correlation between the two. As Figure 3.3 indicates, whites who place higher

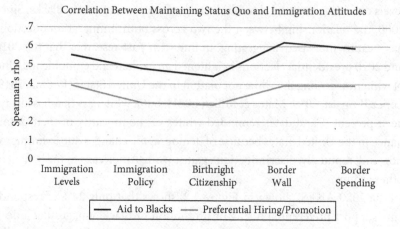

Figure 3.2 Weighted Correlation between Maintaining Status Quo and Immigration Attitudes
Source: 2020 ANES.

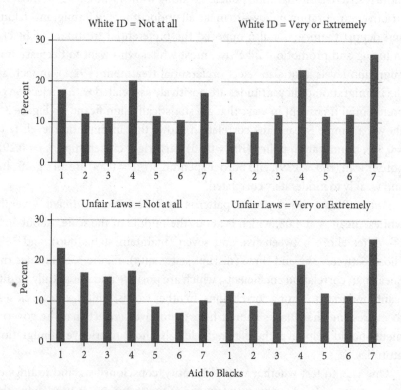

Figure 3.3 Aid to Blacks by White ID and Unfair Laws
Source: 2020 ANES.

levels of importance on being white are more likely to oppose aid to Blacks (4.66 versus 3.95 on a one and seven scale, higher numbers indicating more opposition or the belief that Blacks should help themselves, while four is the middle category) and whites who say that whites should work together to change the unfair laws toward whites have higher mean levels of rejecting aid to Blacks (4.46) compared to whites who disagree that whites should be working together for that reason (3.35). The difference between the mean levels of *Aid to Blacks* between whites with no group consciousness (those who say "not at all" when asked how important it is for whites to work together to change unfair laws toward whites) and whites with strong group consciousness (those who respond "very" or "extremely" to that question) are significantly different from one another ($t(1870) = 11.63$, $p = 0.000$). Differences with respect to importance of racial identity show the same pattern ($t(1771) = 7.11$, $p = 0.000$). Likewise, *Aid to Blacks* strongly correlates with beliefs about whether whites cannot find a job because employers are hiring minorities ($t(1353) = 22.80$, $p = 0.000$). This relationship is the strongest of all three, suggesting the relational nature of ingroup favoritism for whites. There is a strong relationship between white group membership and the maintenance of the group, and one way to maintain the group's position is to reject policies that aim at elevating an outgroup's position.

Support for or opposition to federal aid to Blacks is shaped by partisan identification. White Democrats are less likely to oppose aid to Blacks than Republicans, but higher levels of WRI and white group consciousness correlate with opposition to aid to Blacks for white members of both parties. For white Republicans whose white identity is very or extremely important to them, the mean opposing aid is higher (5.45) but not significantly different from white Republicans whose white identity is not at all important to them (5.31; $t(724) = -1.19$, $p = 0.23$). White Republicans who score high on *Unfair laws* (5.54) differ strongly and significantly from white Republicans who do not (5.10; $t(669) = -3.46$, $p = 0.001$) with respect to *Aid to Blacks*. In all cases, white Republicans are above the mean level for all whites (4.08). WRI does not predict opposition among Republicans—indicating that WRI and Republican identity align for whites in terms of this question—but white group consciousness does. This suggests there are real differences between racial identity saliency and measures that are closer to how whiteness operates. For white Democrats whose white identity is very or extremely important to them, the mean supporting aid is higher (3.01) and significantly different from white Democrats whose white identity is not at all important to them (2.35; $t(438) = -4.09$, $p = 0.000$). There is also a significant difference between white Democrats who chose very or extremely important in the *Unfair laws* measure (2.63) and white Democrats who did not (2.18; $t(557) = -3.56$, $p = 0.000$). All groups of white Democrats are below the mean and generally are more supportive of aid to Blacks than opposed to it, but WRI and white group consciousness make white Democrats less supportive.

The intersection of party and race defines whites' attitudes on the maintenance of the status quo. White Republicans and white Democrats follow the party norms to justify morally based support for policies. As theorized, party identification reinforces moral codes. The Republican Party reinforces the norms of white consciousness (Mason, 2018; Weller & Junn, 2018). Thus, Republican Party identification is a vehicle of the maintenance of the status quo, while Democratic Party identification helps to attenuate these norms and highlights some whites' choice of a partisan identification that they deem more aligned morally with their views.

Finally, to show the relationship between whites' predispositions (byproducts of their socialization as white people) and attitudes about maintaining the status quo, Figure 3.4 shows the association between the two. Whites' moral choice to remain complicit in the status quo is intimately associated with their predispositions. Figure 3.4 depicts the Spearman correlation coefficient between whites' predispositions and aid to Blacks and

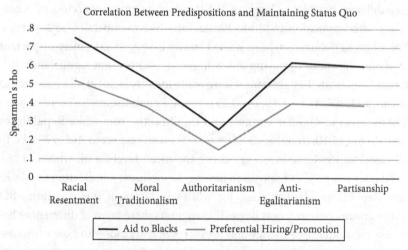

Figure 3.4 Weighted Correlation between Predispositions and Maintaining Status Quo

Source: 2020 ANES.

preferential treatment of Blacks in hiring and promotion. As expected, higher levels of racial resentment, moral traditionalism, authoritarianism, anti-egalitarianism, and Republican identification have positive connections to preferring to maintain the status quo by opposing government aid to Blacks and affirmative action as measured by *Preferential treatment*. The association is more pronounced with respect to *Aid to Blacks* than to *Preferential treatment*. Overall, there is a strong and positive relationship between higher levels of all predispositions and opposing aid to Blacks except for authoritarianism, which has a weak but significant relationship.

Empirically, by utilizing measures unrelated to immigration (*Aid to Blacks* and *Preferential treatment*), this section has shown that immigration attitudes are about the maintenance of the status quo. Both measures are significantly correlated with immigration attitudes, with *Aid to Blacks* being moderately to strongly correlated. Moreover, I provided evidence that whiteness structures *Aid to Blacks* (as well as *Preferential treatment*). In other words, white identification increases whites' moral choice to maintain the racial status quo by opposing government aid to Blacks and affirmative action, two policies that could substantially decrease racial inequality (Bobo & Smith, 1994; Gilens, 1996; Hughes, 1997; Kinder & Sanders, 1996). Furthermore, controlling for ideology, white consciousness and white racial identification both remain significant predictors of aid to Blacks. Finally, whites' predispositions are associated with complicity in a system that maintains the status quo.

I have argued that white identification alone does not predict whites' immigration attitudes and that measures of whiteness will do a better job at predicting immigration attitudes. The following section tests how important white identity is for immigration attitudes and whether measures of whiteness are more strongly associated with restrictive immigration attitudes.

What Influences Restrictive Immigration Attitudes

First, to get a broader sense of the immigration policy preferences of the full sample of white Americans, Figure 3.5 shows the percentage of whites with restrictive and progressive immigration attitudes across ANES studies.[2] Data for each question are reported for every year in which the question was asked; not all the questions were asked every year. As the figure shows, white Americans mostly hold restrictive immigration attitudes over progressive immigration attitudes, although ending birthright citizenship and building

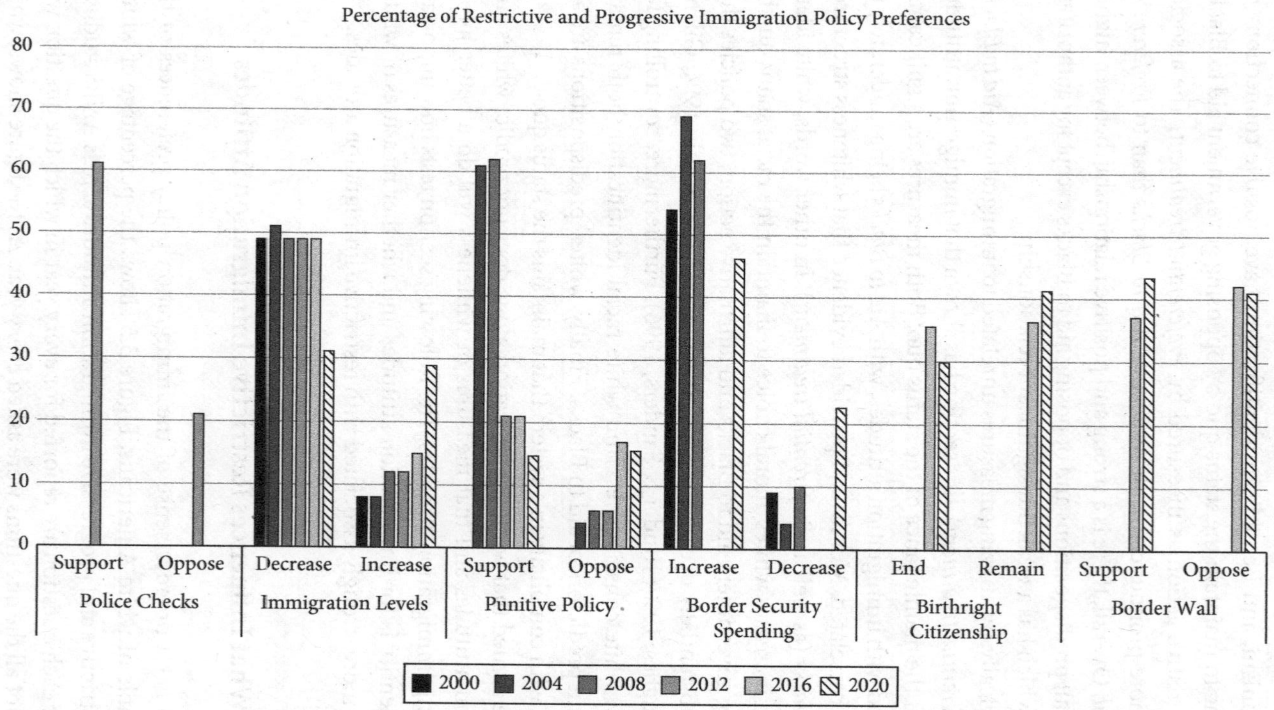

Figure 3.5 Weighted Percent Support and Opposition to Immigration Policies, by ANES Year

Source: 2000–2020 ANES.

a border wall in 2016 and deporting immigrants versus a pathway to citizenship without penalties in 2020 are exceptions. As the figure reflects, restrictive immigration policies did not start in 2008 with Obama's presidency or in 2016 after his presidency because of white backlash. Restrictive attitudes on immigration in the United States were strong across all years of the survey except for 2020. Almost the same percentage of white people, 61% and 62% respectively, believed that preventing illegal immigration is a very important policy goal in 2004 and 2008. Support for spending on border security was higher in 2004 and decreased slightly afterward.

Does White Identity Solely Predict Immigration Policy Preferences?

This section asks how important white identity and white group consciousness are in predicting immigration policy preferences. Table 3.1 shows the coefficients for white racial identity (full model shown in Table 3A.4 in Appendix B) and ethnocentrism (Table 3A.5), and Table 3.2 shows the

Table 3.1 Does White Identity Predict Immigration Policy Preferences, 2012

	Support Police Checks	Punitive Imm. Policy	Decrease Imm. Levels
Model 1: White Racial Identity	0.249*	0.121	0.489***
	(0.125)	(0.106)	(0.102)
N	2583	2592	2570
Pseudo R2	0.226	0.103	0.105
Log Likelihood	−1876.763	−2640.906	−3184.030
Model 2: Ethnocentrism	1.784**	1.404**	3.628***
	(0.640)	(0.479)	(0.495)
N	2585	2594	2572
Pseudo R2	0.227	0.104	0.107
Log Likelihood	−1877.246	−2639.453	−3178.919

Data: ANES 2012.

Note: *** p < .001 ** p < .01 * p < .05 + p < .10; standard error in parentheses.

The data are weighted. Table entries are ordered logit models. White Racial Identity and Ethnocentrism are part of two different models. Full models including controls can be found in Table 3A.4 for White Racial Identity and Table 3A.5 for Ethnocentrism in Appendix B.

results for white group consciousness measures (Tables 3A.6 and 3A.7 show an alternative model and a full model based on Table 3.2). The models control for various other factors that are known to influence immigration policy preferences, including demographic factors. All else equal, strength of identification with whiteness is associated with immigration policy attitudes among white Americans. As shown in Table 3.1 white racial identity, meaning how important being white is to one's identity, is positively associated with a preference to support police checks on those the police suspect of being in the country illegally and with a preference to decrease legal immigration levels, all else equal. Ethnocentrism or ingroup favoritism over outgroups in general is significantly and positively associated with all immigration policy attitudes, a preference to allow the police to check anyone they deem to be in the country illegally, more punitive immigration policies, and a preference to decrease legal immigration levels.

Table 3.2 uses two measures of white group consciousness and one measure of whites' belief in how much discrimination whites face in the United States. Table 3.2 reveals that *White group consciousness*, as measured by the belief that whites should work together to change the laws that are unfair to whites, is not directly associated with immigration policy preferences, all else equal. There is a slight significant and positive association as it relates to changing the Constitution to disallow birthright citizenship to children born in the United States of undocumented immigrants. However, *Unfair laws* is significant and positively associated with increased restrictive immigration attitudes without *White discrimination* and *Blame minorities*, as shown in Table 3A.6. *White discrimination* refers to belief that there is discrimination in the United States against whites. As whites increasingly believe that there is a lot to a great deal of discrimination against whites, the likelihood of whites preferring to build a border wall along the Mexican border and end birthright citizenship increases. *Blame minorities* is a measure of agreement with the idea that many whites are unable to find a job because employers are hiring minorities instead. Whites who personally feel an economic job threat due to the hiring of minorities generally favor more punitive immigration policies. Economic job threat is positively associated with all restrictive immigration attitudes. Whites who feel precarity and who blame minorities for this precarity are more likely to support decreasing legal immigration levels, more punitive federal immigration policy, building a wall along the U.S.–Mexico border, and ending birthright citizenship.

Other works on white identity politics have operationalized *Blame minorities* and *Unfair laws* as an index. I intentionally leave these two measurements separate because they are fundamentally asking different things, in two important ways. First, the jobs question rests on perceived economic insecurity. Second, it is relational in that it pits whites' economic difficulty with finding a job because employers are supposedly hiring minorities. In examining immigration, economic concerns must be kept separate from an explicit measure of white racial consciousness. Respondents may or may not consider the question *Blame minorities* to be about white consciousness, given its overwhelming economic aspect. Rhetoric suggesting that whites are unable to find a job because employers are hiring minorities instead is common in real-world media. However, the question references an economic threat to whites because of non-white minorities. Including non-white minorities adds a relational ingroup–outgroup aspect to it that makes a difference. In fact, the association between this question, *Blame minorities*, and *Immigration job threat*—another question that asks how likely is it that recent immigration levels will take jobs away from people already here—is only moderate but significant ($rho = 0.50, p = 0.000$). Therefore, I treat *Blame minorities* as a measurement that is inherently about economic threat, about the connection between whites' perceived economic status and positionality and those of minorities. More than *Unfair laws*, *Blame minorities* seems to tap into whites' sense of perceived material precarity because of minorities. Furthermore, the correlation between *Unfair laws* and *Blame minorities* is only moderate ($rho = 0.45, p = 0.000$). It has a Cronbach's alpha of 0.62, which is a moderate relationship but considered either a moderate reliability or unacceptable given the standards of reliability based on Cronbach's alpha (less than 0.60 is considered unreliable, 0.60–0.79 is considered acceptable and in some research questionable, and 0.80 and above are considered good and reliable) (Hair, Black, Black, Babin, & Anderson, 2010). The Cronbach's alpha of *Blame minorities* and *Immigration job threat* is higher at 0.66. A correlation clearly exists between *Unfair laws* and *Blame minorities*, but it lacks the strength that would warrant treating both items as part of the same scale.

Theoretically, whiteness is distinct from non-white group identity politics. Whiteness historically exists in relation to blackness and non-whiteness; a question about jobs and the effect of minorities on the availability of jobs for whites is a question that whites can answer more accurately given that they feel justified agreeing that minorities impact

Table 3.2 Does White Identity Predict Immigration Policy Preferences, 2016

	Decrease Imm. Levels	Punitive Imm. Policy	Build Border Wall	End Birthright
Unfair Laws (White Consciousness)	−0.029	0.153	0.123	0.239+
	(0.126)	(0.138)	(0.148)	(0.130)
White Discrimination	0.347+	0.337	0.617**	0.464*
	(0.207)	(0.215)	(0.226)	(0.205)
Blame Minorities	1.556***	0.727***	0.831***	0.452*
	(0.194)	(0.200)	(0.210)	(0.191)
N	2005	2001	2009	2010
Pseudo R2	0.188	0.167	0.250	0.106
Log Likelihood	−2333.454	−1894.759	−1589.959	−1957.879

Data: ANES 2016.

Note: *** $p < .001$ ** $p < .01$ * $p < .05$ + $p < .10$; standard error in parentheses.

Column labels indicate dependent variable. Table entries are ordered logit models. The data is weighted. Full model including controls can be found in Table 3A.7 in Appendix B.

job availability. The questions about discrimination and unfair laws out-side of an explicit relationship to non-white outgroups, however, do not give whites a socially acceptable way to perform whiteness without being perceived as racist or discriminatory. Thus, unlike other researchers, I consider it important to examine these questions separately. Moreover, in relation to immigration, it is clear which of the three dominates the scale: *Blame minorities.*

The literature on immigration suggests that other factors are also im-portant in influencing immigration policy attitudes, including economic factors, partisanship, and anti-immigrant sentiments. These factors are considered in Table 3.1 and Table 3.2, and after holding these alternative explanations constant, white racial identity and a measure of whites' group precarity are fairly consistent in increasing restrictive immigration attitudes among whites whose white identity is more salient and who feel more eco-nomic precarity.

In considering other factors, negative affect toward undocumented immigrants, for example, is a consistent predictor of immigration policy preferences in these models. Colder affect toward undocumented immigrants is associated with more restrictive immigration policy preferences, while warmer affect is associated with more progressive preferences. The same results persist when we consider whites' sociotropic views of the economy

(*National economy*). Partisanship functions as expected, though not as consistently as the economic factors shown in Tables 3.1 and 3.2. Another important and consistent factor is the positive and significant association between restrictive immigration attitudes and whites who believe that Hispanics have too much influence in politics.

Overall, white racial identity is positively associated with supporting police checks and decreasing legal levels of immigration. The belief that whites should work together to change the unfair laws toward whites is hardly predictive of immigration attitudes. Whites who feel that whites are being discriminated against are more likely to want a border wall and to end birthright citizenship. Finally, whites who believe that employers are not hiring whites because they are hiring minorities have more punitive immigration preferences; they support decreasing legal levels of immigration, passing more punitive immigration policy, building a border wall, and ending birthright citizenship. Prior work examining the influence of white identity on immigration policy preference has oversold the influence of white identity as a sole or even primary predictor of immigration policy. Holding education constant, the perception of both economic insecurity and whites' precarity seems to be the driving force in whites' punitive immigration policy preferences rather than the saliency of white racial identity on its own. This supports my expectation that WRI in and of itself is insufficient to examine how whiteness works in relation to immigration attitudes.

Ethnocentrism is one measurement of white identity that considers whites' affect toward outgroup members, and it shows a positive and significant association with restrictive immigration attitudes even after controlling for key independent factors. Whites with high levels of ingroup favoritism are more likely to hold punitive immigration policy preferences (Kinder & Kam, 2009). Ethnocentrism, of course, does not mean that whites also have negative outgroup sentiments; it just means they prefer their ingroup to Black Americans, Latinos, and Asian Americans. Even without knowledge of whites' sentiments toward outgroups, whites with higher levels of ingroup favoritism are associated with policy preferences that decrease the immigration of certain groups, in particular Asians and Latinos, both of which have increased since 1965.

My expectations are in line with the findings in this section. White identity on its own does not solely predict immigration policy preferences. The following section examines the role of predispositions without any measures of white racial identity or consciousness. My expectation, in line with prior literature, is that these predispositions will be significantly related to immigration attitudes.

Predispositions as Predictors of Immigration Policy Preferences

This section asks whether predispositions predict immigration policy preferences in the absence of white identity measures. Table 3.3 (full model can be found in Table 3A.8) presents these results using the 2012 ANES and shows strong associations between predispositions and immigration policy preferences, controlling for strong alternative explanations. Higher levels of racial resentment are associated with more punitive immigration policy preferences: allowing police to check the documentation status of those they perceive as undocumented, adopting a more punitive federal immigration policy, and decreasing legal levels of immigration. The association between egalitarianism and immigration attitudes is less consistent, but there is a strong association between anti-egalitarian levels and supporting police

Table 3.3 Predispositions as Predictors of Immigration Policy Attitudes, 2012

	Support Police Checks	Support Punitive Policy	Decrease Imm. Levels
Racial Resentment	1.826***	0.779***	1.615***
	(0.262)	(0.232)	(0.221)
Egalitarianism	1.104***	0.146	−0.679**
	(0.296)	(0.240)	(0.233)
Moral Traditionalism	1.388***	0.719**	0.692**
	(0.256)	(0.225)	(0.211)
Authoritarianism	0.072	0.611***	0.746***
	(0.174)	(0.152)	(0.144)
N	2559	2563	2544
Pseudo R2	0.257	0.113	0.119
Log Likelihood	−1785.025	−2575.674	−3098.461

Data: ANES 2012.

Note: *** p < .001 ** p < .01 * p < .05 + p < .10; standard error in parentheses.

Table entries are ordered logit models. The data is weighted. Full model including controls can be found in Table 3A.8 in Appendix B.

checks. However, higher levels of anti-egalitarianism are associated with less support for lower legal immigration levels. Beliefs about moral tradition-alism are also consistently associated with immigration policy preferences. Whites with high levels of moral traditionalism are more likely to support police checks, more punitive federal immigration policy, and decreased legal immigration levels. Finally, higher levels of authoritarianism are asso-ciated with more punitive federal policy preferences as well as decreasing legal levels of immigration. But they have no bearing on support for police checks.

An examination of the 2016 ANES reveals similar results (shown in Table 3.4), even after controlling for alternative explanations as seen in the full model (Table 3A.9, Appendix B). Table 3.4 does not include any of the white identity or white consciousness questions. These models, however, include concerns about the economy, affect toward undocumented immigrants, par-tisanship, and other alternative hypotheses. The relationship between higher levels of racial resentment, moral traditionalism, and authoritarianism are robust even after controlling for factors that are heavily associated with more punitive immigration policy preferences. Higher levels of racial resentment are associated with support for decreasing legal levels of immigration, more

Table 3.4 Predispositions as Predictors of Immigration Policy Attitudes, 2016

	Decrease Imm. Levels	Support Punitive Policy	Build Border Wall	End Birthright
Racial Resentment	1.851***	1.239***	1.721***	0.650**
	(0.235)	(0.248)	(0.259)	(0.232)
Egalitarianism	0.146	0.469+	0.544+	0.993***
	(0.258)	(0.272)	(0.292)	(0.262)
Moral Traditionalism	1.317***	0.474+	1.423***	0.875***
	(0.245)	(0.259)	(0.279)	(0.250)
Authoritarianism	0.617***	0.593**	0.345+	−0.122
	(0.169)	(0.182)	(0.189)	(0.172)
N	2029	2025	2032	2033
Pseudo R2	0.198	0.173	0.266	0.113
Log Likelihood	−2332.205	−1906.374	−1574.375	−1963.751

Data: ANES 2016.

Note: *** p < .001 ** p < .01 * p < .05 + p < .10; standard error in parentheses.

Table entries are ordered logit models. The data is weighted. Full model including controls can be found in Table 3A.9 in Appendix B.

punitive federal immigration policies, building a border wall, and ending birthright citizenship. The same is the case for higher levels of moral traditionalism. Increased levels of moral traditionalism, however, only have a slightly significant influence on federal immigration policy attitudes. Anti-egalitarianism is only significantly associated with ending birthright citizenship. Finally, higher levels of authoritarianism are associated with wanting to decrease legal levels of immigration and punitive immigration policy and only slightly associated with wanting a border wall.

An examination of the predictive power of these predispositions on immigration policy in 2000 (Table 3A.10) and 2008 (Table 3A.11) also reveals similar patterns, indicating that these relationships are not fleeting.[3] In 2000, higher levels of racial resentment increased the likelihood of support for decreased legal immigration levels and increased border security spending. Higher levels of moral traditionalism were only slightly significant for these two issues, while higher levels of authoritarianism influenced restrictive immigration attitudes for whites. In 2008, higher levels of racial resentment influences decreased support for legal levels of immigration and increased border security spending and controlling illegal immigration. Higher levels of moral traditionalism increase support for border security spending and controlling illegal immigration as a policy goal. Finally, higher levels of authoritarianism influence support for decreased immigration levels and increased border spending. Levels of anti-egalitarianism are insignificant on immigration attitudes. These results are consistent across numerous surveys conducted between 2000 and 2016, spanning both the Bush and Obama administrations.

Many of the other control variables/alternative explanations show inconsistent or weak relationships. However, concerns about the national economy are consistently and positively associated with more punitive immigration policy preferences. Colder affect toward undocumented immigrants is also consistently associated with more punitive immigration policies. In some instances, higher levels of patriotism are also associated with restrictive immigration policy preferences. Education is sporadically associated, in that higher education is associated with less restrictive immigration policy preferences. Partisanship functions as the literature suggests, in that independents and Republicans have more punitive immigration policy preferences. Personal income remains insignificant in all policy outcomes. Church attendance is associated with less restrictive policy preferences but largely insignificant in most models.

To summarize, using the 2012 data, whites with higher levels of racial resentment are associated with more punitive immigration policy preferences across the board. Levels of anti-egalitarianism are associated with supporting police checks. Higher levels of authoritarianism also influence preferences for more punitive immigration policies and decreased legal levels of immigration. Higher levels of moral traditionalism are associated with punitive immigration policy preferences across all three policies. Using the 2016 ANES, racial resentment remains consistently significant. Levels of anti-egalitarianism only influence birthright citizenship while higher levels of authoritarianism influence immigration levels and federal immigration policy attitudes. High levels of moral traditionalism are associated with decreasing immigration levels, building a border wall, and ending birthright citizenship. These results are not new; prior scholarship has examined these predispositions separately. An examination of these predispositions together, however, reveals their differential impact on different immigration outcomes.

The following section tests whether white identity and white consciousness hold up against predispositions on immigration attitudes. I expect that many of the white identity measures will become insignificant for two reasons. First, because predispositions are a byproduct of socialization, white identity is embedded within the predispositions of white Americans. Second, a salient WRI is not a condition for restrictive immigration attitudes. I expect group consciousness measures to become less significant, while predispositions will remain significant. Furthermore, the following section examines closely what happens to moral traditionalism, a belief in a "correct" or "right" moral, social, and political societal arrangement. I expect that this will be one of the strongest predispositions, alongside racial resentment.

The Influence of White ID/Consciousness Measures and Predispositions on Immigration Attitudes

Table 3.5 (full shown in Table 3A.12) tests how well WRI does once predispositions, as well as other alternative hypotheses, are controlled for in ordered logit models predicting restrictive immigration attitudes in 2012. Whereas Table 3.1 showed that WRI was significantly associated with support for police checks and decreasing legal levels of immigration, Table 3.5 shows that WRI is only significant when predicting decreasing legal levels

Table 3.5 White Identity and Predispositions as Predictors of Immigration Policy Attitudes, 2012

	Support Police Checks	Support Punitive Policy	Decrease Imm. Levels
White Racial ID	0.197	0.098	0.392***
	(0.130)	(0.108)	(0.103)
Racial Resentment	1.808***	0.764**	1.569***
	(0.263)	(0.233)	(0.221)
Egalitarianism	1.105***	0.161	−0.645**
	(0.296)	(0.240)	(0.233)
Moral Traditionalism	1.389***	0.726**	0.692**
	(0.257)	(0.225)	(0.211)
Authoritarianism	0.055	0.607***	0.725***
	(0.175)	(0.152)	(0.144)
N	2557	2561	2542
Pseudo R2	0.258	0.113	0.121
Log Likelihood	−1782.381	−2573.835	−3088.728

Data: ANES 2012.

Note: *** p < .001 ** p < .01 * p < .05 + p < .10; standard error in parentheses. Full model including controls can be found in Table 3A.12 in Appendix B.

of immigration. As the saliency of white identity increases, whites' support for decreasing legal levels of immigration also increases, as the positive and significant coefficient indicates (OR = 1.48, 95% CI [1.21, 1.81]).[4] Higher levels of moral traditionalism are positively associated with support for police checks (OR = 4.01, 95% CI [2.43, 6.63]), punitive immigration policy attitudes (OR = 2.07, 95% CI [1.33, 3.02]), and decreased levels of legal immigration (OR = 2.00, 95% CI [1.32, 3.02]). This is also the case for racial resentment: police checks (OR = 6.10, 95% CI [3.64, 10.21]); policy (OR = 2.15, 95% CI [1.36, 3.39]); immigration levels (OR = 4.80, 95% CI [3.11, 7.41]). Higher levels of anti-egalitarianism are positively associated with higher support for police checks (OR = 3.02, 95% CI [1.69, 5.39]) but seem to increase support for legal levels of immigration (OR = 0.52, 95% CI [0.33, 0.83]). Higher levels of authoritarianism increase support for punitive federal immigration policy (OR = 1.83, 95% CI [1.36, 2.47]) and decreased legal levels of immigration (OR = 2.06, 95% CI [1.56, 2.74]).

Compared to Table 3.1, where ethnocentrism was significant and positively associated with restrictive immigration attitudes, ethnocentrism is only significant in decreased support for legal levels of immigration (OR = 20.83, 95% CI [7.75, 55.95]), as shown in Table 3.6 (full model shown in Table 3A.13). Ethnocentrism's influence on support for punitive immigration policy just misses the significance mark (OR = 2.52, 95% CI [.964, 6.57], p = 0.056). However, the predispositions hold strong in their influence on restrictive immigration attitudes. Higher levels of moral traditionalism increase support for police checks (OR = 4.04, 95% CI [2.44, 6.68]), punitive immigration policy (OR = 2.05, 95% CI [1.32, 3.18]), and decreasing legal levels of immigration to the United States (OR = 1.99, 95% CI [1.31, 3.01]). This is also the case for higher levels of racial resentment (OR = 5.53, 95% CI [3.32, 9.23]; OR = 1.98, 95% CI [1.26, 3.12]; OR = 4.37, 95% CI [2.84, 6.74], respectively). Higher levels of anti-egalitarianism increase support for police checks (OR = 2.76, 95% CI [1.55, 4.91]) but have a negative relationship with support for decreased levels of legal immigration (OR = 0.53, 95% CI [0.334, 0.831]). Finally, higher levels of authoritarianism increase support for punitive immigration policy (OR = 1.84, 95% CI [1.37, 2.48]) and decreased levels of legal immigration (OR = 2.04, 95% CI [1.54, 2.71]).

Table 3.6 Ethnocentrism and Predispositions as Predictors of Immigration Policy Attitudes, 2012

	Support Police Checks	Support Punitive Policy	Decrease Imm. Levels
Ethnocentrism	0.799	0.923+	3.036***
	(0.651)	(0.490)	(0.504)
Racial Resentment	1.710***	0.682**	1.476***
	(0.261)	(0.232)	(0.221)
Egalitarianism	1.015***	0.150	−0.641**
	(0.294)	(0.239)	(0.233)
Moral Traditionalism	1.397***	0.717**	0.687**
	(0.256)	(0.225)	(0.212)
Authoritarianism	0.056	0.609***	0.712***
	(0.174)	(0.152)	(0.145)
N	2558	2562	2543
Pseudo R2	0.257	0.113	0.123
Log Likelihood	−1786.848	−2574.939	−3082.411

Data: ANES 2012.

Note: *** p < .001 ** p < .01 * p < .05 + p < .10; standard error in parentheses. Full model including controls can be found in Table 3A.13 in Appendix B.

Finally, Table 3.7 (full model shown in Table 3A.14) tests how well measures of white group consciousness do when also considering predispositions in the same models. Tables 3.7 and 3.2 are comparable. In Table 3.2, the belief that whites should work together against unfair laws against whites had no bearing on immigration attitudes, except slightly on ending birthright citizenship; the same is the case in Table 3.7. In fact, the slightly significant impact on ending birthright citizenship shown in Table 3.2 has disappeared completely. In Table 3.2, whites who believe there is discrimination against whites were more likely to support building a border wall and ending birthright citizenship. Only the positive relationship between discrimination against whites and building a wall remains in Table 3.7 (OR = 1.59, 95% CI [1.01, 2.50]). Finally, *Blame minorities* is

Table 3.7 White Consciousness and Predispositions as Predictors of Immigration Policy Attitudes, 2016

	Decrease Imm. Levels	Support Punitive Policy	Build Border Wall	End Birthright
Unfair Laws (White Consciousness)	−0.130 (0.128)	0.103 (0.139)	0.049 (0.153)	0.196 (0.132)
White Discrimination	0.122 (0.210)	0.181 (0.218)	0.462* (0.232)	0.322 (0.209)
Blame Minorities	1.265*** (0.198)	0.506* (0.204)	0.530* (0.217)	0.370+ (0.196)
Racial Resentment	1.543*** (0.242)	1.132*** (0.255)	1.577*** (0.267)	0.481* (0.238)
Egalitarianism	0.152 (0.264)	0.503+ (0.276)	0.524+ (0.297)	0.945*** (0.265)
Moral Traditionalism	1.222*** (0.250)	0.343 (0.263)	1.355*** (0.283)	0.746** (0.253)
Authoritarianism	0.561** (0.173)	0.520** (0.185)	0.273 (0.192)	−0.182 (0.175)
N	1985	1981	1989	1990
Pseudo R2	0.207	0.178	0.270	0.115
Log Likelihood	−2258.768	−1856.487	−1531.960	−1916.408

Data: ANES 2016.

Note: *** $p < .001$ ** $p < .01$ * $p < .05$ + $p < .10$; standard error in parentheses. Full model including controls can be found in Table 3A.14 in Appendix B.

positively associated with decreased legal immigration levels (OR = 3.54, 95% CI [2.40, 5.23]), support for punitive immigration policy (OR = 5.06, 95% CI [0.105, 0.906]) and building a border wall (OR = 1.70, 95% CI [1.11, 2.60]). The relationship between whites' economic precarity and ending birthright citizenship is only slightly significant, which is a change from Table 3.2.

Higher levels of moral traditionalism are positively associated with all immigration attitudes except for punitive immigration policy (which was only slightly significant in Table 3.4). The strength of moral traditionalism only diminished slightly comparing Table 3.4 and Table 3.7. Higher levels of racial resentment continue to be highly significant across all immigration attitudes. Higher levels of anti-egalitarianism are only significant at the 95% confidence interval in influencing support to end birthright citizenship. Finally, higher levels of authoritarianism are positively associated with decreasing legal levels of immigration and support for more punitive federal immigration policy. The strength of the predispositions seems to have diminished slightly compared to Table 3.4, but those that are significant remain strong predictors of restrictive immigration attitudes.

The belief among whites that it is very or extremely likely whites are unable to find a job due to minorities being hired is a strong predictor of restrictive immigration attitudes even after controlling for predispositions. This finding is important because it signals that when whites think about immigration, they also think about what immigration does to their ingroup, to people like themselves. Additionally, it seems that for whites, immigration solicits attitudes related to economic precarity or at least the perception of it. A deeper examination of the first model of Table 3.7, predicting decreased legal levels of immigration, shows that income is insignificant in influencing people's views, while education is significant and negatively associated with decreased levels of immigration. In other words, higher levels of education are associated with less support for decreased legal levels of immigration. More highly educated whites are less restrictive, all else equal. Unsurprisingly, an examination of immigration levels by employment status (see Table 3A.15) reveals that the perception of job precarity and its influence on immigration levels is significant among the employed but not the unemployed.[5] This reflects the fact that most whites are not interested in applying for the jobs in which minorities tend to predominate and these kinds of jobs do not personally affect most whites. The threat is not a real threat to participants' job security but rather a threat to social status, a threat to the position of the group, not themselves individually. This aligns with social identity theory and with my theory that whites' role within the ingroup is to protect and choose the group regardless of whether it makes sense to them personally.

How White Identity and White Group Consciousness Moderate the Strength and Significance of Predispositions on Decreasing Legal Levels of Immigration

This section focuses on how WRI and white group consciousness moderate the strength of predispositions. I argue that whiteness structures whites' predispositions, as shown in Chapter 2, precisely because whites' predispositions are associated with whites' immoral choice to be complicit in a system that maintains the racial status quo of white dominance in the United States.

For many of the models in the previous section, WRI was not a very strong predictor of restrictive immigration attitudes, while only whites' perceived economic threat to the group is significant in predicting several immigration attitudes. To test my expectations that varying levels of white group consciousness should moderate the significance and strength of predisposition, I run models based on the levels of WRI (Table 3A.16), ethnocentrism (Table 3A.17), and group consciousness (using *Blame minorities*; Table 3A.18). Additionally, this section only focuses on immigration levels as it was a consistent immigration outcome across 2012 and 2016. This section will focus primarily on moral traditionalism and racial resentment. I argue that moral traditionalism will be strongest among whites with higher levels of WRI and white group consciousness. Theoretically, I have argued that whiteness is intimately connected to whites' socialization as white people and that this socialization results in a "white right," a moral psychology that is undergirded by whiteness. Hence, higher saliency of white identity and a belief in white group consciousness and whites' precarity should influence levels of moral traditionalism. If moral traditionalists are invested in keeping a certain kind of social order, this social order, I argue, is raced. My expectation for racial resentment is that it in fact will influence all levels of white identity and consciousness except for whites with ethnocentric levels below the neutral 0.5 middle point. Whites with less than 0.5 levels of ethnocentrism technically feel more outgroup love than ingroup love. It makes sense that these whites might not have high levels of racial resentment or that racial resentment might be insignificant.

Support for Decreasing Legal Levels of Immigration

Table 3.8 (full model shown in Table 3A.16) replicates the third model of Table 3.5 by WRI. WRI was a significant predictor of decreasing legal levels of immigration in Table 3.5. Table 3.8 first shows that racial resentment is significant among whites who think their white identity is "a little," "moderately,"

Table 3.8 Predispositions and White Identity as Predictors of Decreasing Legal Immigration Levels, 2012

	White ID = Not at all	White ID = A little important	White ID = Moderately important	White ID = Very or extremely
Racial Resentment	0.830+	2.078***	1.724***	1.659***
	(0.466)	(0.547)	(0.434)	(0.392)
Egalitarianism	−1.076*	−0.896	−0.596	−0.191
	(0.488)	(0.548)	(0.475)	(0.419)
Moral Traditionalism	0.400	0.169	0.814*	1.135**
	(0.455)	(0.497)	(0.405)	(0.389)
Authoritarianism	1.244***	0.834*	0.344	0.694*
	(0.309)	(0.325)	(0.276)	(0.273)
Affect "Illegal"	−2.764***	−2.673***	−2.405***	−1.395***
	(0.407)	(0.490)	(0.378)	(0.347)
Affect Hispanics	−0.309	−0.708	−0.502	−0.551
	(0.660)	(0.830)	(0.588)	(0.429)
Affect Blacks	−0.341	0.911	0.012	−0.132
	(0.675)	(0.804)	(0.592)	(0.431)
Hispanics in Politics	−0.182	0.520	0.776**	1.034***
	(0.298)	(0.334)	(0.264)	(0.231)
N	554	511	703	774
Pseudo R2	0.128	0.126	0.115	0.111
Log Likelihood	−677.793	−617.546	−850.282	−907.166

Data: ANES 2012.

Note: *** p < .001 ** p < .01 * p < .05 + p < .10; standard error in parentheses. Full model including controls can be found in Table 3A.16 in Appendix B.

or "very or extremely" important. It is also slightly significant among whites whose white identity is "not at all" important ($p = 0.08$). For the most part my expectation that levels of racial resentment will supersede levels of WRI saliency is confirmed. As expected, levels of moral traditionalism are only significant among whites who say that being white is moderately important or very or extremely important but not among whites who say it is not at all or only a little important. Higher levels of moral traditionalism are positively associated with decreasing legal levels of immigration only among whites whose white identity is a stronger aspect of how they see themselves. Among these whites, moral traditionalism becomes an important predisposition that dictates immigration attitudes.

An examination of how different levels of ethnocentrism moderate the influence of predispositions for whites is shown in Table 3.9 (full model shown in Table 3A.17). In this table, racial resentment is only significant among whites with neutral levels of ethnocentrism and whites with higher than neutral levels of ethnocentrism; it is not significant among whites who rate whites lower than outgroups. Higher levels of racial resentment among

Table 3.9 Predispositions by Ethnocentrism as Predictors of Decreasing Legal Immigration Levels, 2012

	Ethnocentrism < 0.5 (Outgroup love)	Ethnocentrism = 0.5 (Neutral)	Ethnocentrism > 0.5 (Ingroup love)
Racial Resentment	0.681 (0.712)	1.749*** (0.374)	1.512*** (0.303)
Egalitarianism	−2.545** (0.921)	−0.585 (0.394)	−0.458 (0.313)
Moral Traditionalism	0.378 (0.753)	0.157 (0.357)	1.127*** (0.286)
Authoritarianism	1.492** (0.548)	0.834*** (0.244)	0.622** (0.193)
N	202	921	1420
Pseudo R2	0.132	0.095	0.102
Log Likelihood	−243.370	−1109.711	−1700.513

Data: ANES 2012.

Note: *** p < .001 ** p < .01 * p < .05 + p < .10; standard error in parentheses. Full model including controls can be found in Table 3A.17 in Appendix B.

the two former groups are associated with support for decreasing legal levels of immigration. Moral traditionalism, on the other hand, is only important among whites who rate whites higher than all outgroups, who have higher levels of ingroup love. Among these whites, higher levels of moral traditionalism influence support of decreased legal levels of immigration. Moral traditionalism seems to be an important aspect of how whites make attitudinal decisions about immigration.

Finally, Table 3.10 (full model shown in Table 3A.18) shows four models by level of white group consciousness. Higher levels of racial resentment are positively associated with decreased support for legal levels of immigration. This is the case across all four levels of white group consciousness. This

Table 3.10 Predispositions by Relational White Group Consciousness (*Blame Minorities*) as Predictors of Decreasing Legal Immigration Levels, 2016

	Minorities to blame for not finding job = Not at all likely	Minorities to blame for not finding job = Slightly likely	Minorities to blame for not finding job = Moderately likely	Minorities to blame for not finding job = Very or extremely likely
Unfair Laws (White Consciousness)	0.231 (0.257)	−0.174 (0.210)	−0.322 (0.272)	−0.135 (0.429)
White Discrimination	−0.790 (0.572)	1.011* (0.408)	−0.418 (0.383)	0.511 (0.426)
Racial Resentment	1.759** (0.606)	1.724*** (0.449)	1.972*** (0.450)	0.923+ (0.551)
Egalitarianism	0.320 (0.647)	0.913+ (0.495)	0.212 (0.508)	−0.543 (0.567)
Moral Traditionalism	0.716 (0.604)	0.914* (0.451)	1.352** (0.468)	1.668** (0.582)
Authoritarianism	1.520*** (0.433)	0.564+ (0.312)	0.247 (0.308)	0.075 (0.443)
N	396	636	551	402
Pseudo R2	0.192	0.162	0.132	0.136
Log Likelihood	−448.820	−740.098	−616.024	−405.857

Data: ANES 2016.

Note: *** p < .001 ** p < .01 * p < .05 + p < .10; standard error in parentheses. Full model including controls can be found in Table 3A.18 in Appendix B.

relationship is significant in three out of the four models and only slightly significant in the fourth model. In other words, among whites who range in their belief from not at all to moderate in the *Blame minorities* measure, levels of racial resentment are significant in their immigration attitudes. As for moral traditionalism, it is significant among whites who blame minorities from slightly to very or extremely, but not significant among whites who do not believe that it is at all likely whites cannot find a job due to employers hiring minorities. In both cases, my expectations are confirmed.

This section has shown that white identity politics is much more complicated than past research has suggested. WRI saliency does not predict most immigration attitudes among whites apart from whites' support for decreasing legal levels of immigration. In this case, increased saliency of WRI is important; it also moderates moral traditionalism in its influence on immigration attitudes. Overall, all measures of WRI and white group consciousness are weaker predictors than predispositions. That is to say, these predisposed beliefs that are a byproduct of whites' socialization are stronger predictors. However, whiteness itself is not insignificant. First, predispositions are raced. Second, white identity and whiteness do inform when predispositions are most important. One important finding from this section is that when whites have salient WRI and when their group consciousness is strongest, moral traditionalism is a significant and strong predictor of restrictive immigration attitudes.

What about Party Identification?

It is well known that party identification is one of the most salient and important factors influencing political attitudes and behavior in the United States. With this understanding, I have also hypothesized that party identification will also moderate levels of moral traditionalism, as well as other predispositions. This section focuses on how party identification among whites moderates the relationship between moral traditionalism and immigration attitudes. Figures 3.6 and 3.7 both show the predicted probabilities from two models, one focused on decreasing legal levels of immigration by a lot (Figure 3.6) and the other predicting support for building a border wall (Figure 3.7) in 2016 (full model in Table 3A.19).[6] Moral traditionalism is one of the Republican Party's most basic and integral values (Ciuk, 2017). Hence, I expect that moral traditionalism is important for white Republicans. However, given that Republican identity and beliefs about moral traditionalism are

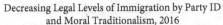

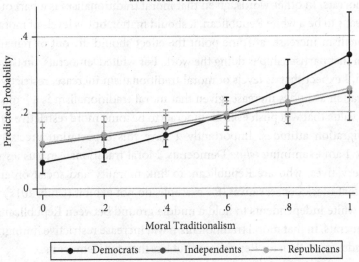

Figure 3.6 Predicted Probability of Decreasing Legal Levels of Immigration "A lot" by Party ID and Moral Traditionalism

Source: 2016 ANES.

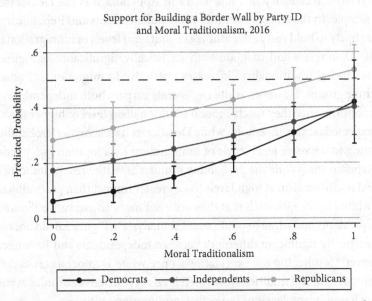

Figure 3.7 Predicted Probability of Building a Border Wall by Party ID and Moral Traditionalism

Source: 2016 ANES.

so intertwined, I expect that moral traditionalism is strongest among white Democrats. In other words, given that moral traditionalism is a part of what it means to be a white Republican, it should matter, but as levels of moral traditionalism increase, at some point the effect should die out or remain flat given that partisanship is doing the work. For white Democrats, on the other hand, I expect that as levels of moral traditionalism increase, restrictive immigration attitudes increase, given that moral traditionalism is a "conservative" value that will push even Democrats to become more restrictive in their immigration attitudes. Importantly, I have this expectation precisely because I am examining *white* Democrats. Moral traditionalism pushes white conservatives, who are Republican, to link morality and social order in a way that Black conservatives, for example, do not exhibit (Ciuk, 2017). I expect white independents to hold a middle ground between Republicans and Democrats, in that moral traditionalism will increase restrictive immigration attitudes more than for Republicans but less than for Democrats.

Figure 3.6 shows the predicted probability of decreasing legal levels of immigration by a lot, based on party identification and levels of moral traditionalism. I interacted party identification and moral traditionalism to test how party moderates moral traditionalism's influence on immigration attitudes. The reference category in Table 3A.19 in Appendix B is the Democrats in the sample. In the table, we see that white independents and Republicans are more likely to hold restrictive attitudes about legal levels of immigration than white Democrats and they are both statistically significant. As Figure 3.6 shows, moral traditionalism increases restrictive immigration attitudes for all three groups. However, white Democrats surpass both independents and Republicans once they reach a moral traditionalism level of higher than 0.6. As expected, at this threshold, white Democrats have a higher probability of wanting to decrease legal levels of immigration by a lot than independents or Republicans. While the probability is under 50%, the results indicate that moral traditionalism at high levels has a greater impact than party affiliation for white Democrats, such that they are even more conservative than white independents and white Republicans. The analysis in Figure 3.6 did not reveal a statistically significant difference between independents and Republicans, however. Confirming my expectations, once white Democrats cross the 0.6 threshold of moral traditionalism, their levels of restrictive attitudes bypasses white Republicans' levels of restrictive immigration attitudes.

During the 2016 elections, the Republican Party emphasized immigration and in particular rhetoric about building a border wall along the U.S.–Mexico border. Overall, support for building a border wall remained low among much of the U.S. public. In 2019, about 58% of the U.S. public opposed a border wall. For whites, it was a slim majority of 51% opposing expanding a wall along the southern border (since there is already fencing along some of the border). Republicans and conservatives, however, supported the expansion of a border wall at much higher rates than Democrats and liberals (Pew Research Center, 2019). About 80% of Republicans favored building a border wall (Public Religion Research Institute, 2019a). Hence, I expected that Republicans would have the highest levels of support for a border wall and Democrats the lowest. However, my expectations about moral traditionalism remain. Figure 3.7 shows the results for support for a border wall in 2016, when building a wall was not as favorable among Republicans as it became after Trump's election (Tesler, 2016a). In Table 3A.19, we see that both the interactions between party identification and moral traditionalism for independents and Republicans are positive and statistically significant from white Democrats. Figure 3.7 shows that higher levels of moral traditionalism increased support for building a wall for all party identifications. White Republicans start at a predicted probability of about 0.29 at the lowest level of moral traditionalism, and at the highest level of moral traditionalism most white Republicans support building a border wall. Hence, belief in moral traditionalism was an important aspect of pushing white Republicans to have more restrictive attitudes on immigration, which in this case does not confirm my expectation. This confirms the influence and significance of moral traditionalism even for Republicans. For white Democrats, however, moral traditionalism does increase restrictive immigration attitudes though not beyond Republicans'. Importantly, at the highest level of moral traditionalism, white Democrats surpass white independents in their support for a border wall. Hence my expectation for white Democrats is partially confirmed: Ideas about morality and social order play an important role in framing and dictating restrictive immigration attitudes. In fact, moral traditionalism is important for white Republicans as well, emphasizing the significance of morality and social order for white Americans.

Conclusion

Inherently, immigration is about whiteness; about U.S. ethos, values, and norms; and about belonging. The history of immigration to the United States (and possibly other countries) shows that it is a mechanism through which to preserve whiteness. However, white identity politics is complicated. It can be defined by measuring whites' perceptions of their white identity or their perceptions of discriminatory laws against them. White identity politics must also be defined, as I have argued, through socialized values and norms that come through predispositions.

To summarize, this chapter has shown that immigration is associated with maintaining the racial status for whites. In 2020, the association between decreasing legal levels of immigration, support for building a border wall, and increasing border security spending and opposing federal aid to Blacks were all positive and higher than 0.5. Additionally, whites who place higher importance on white identity and who have higher levels of white group consciousness are more likely to oppose aid to Blacks. Opposition to federal aid to Blacks is also positively and strongly associated with higher levels of racial resentment, moral traditionalism, anti-egalitarianism, and Republican identity. These findings join scholarship suggesting that whites are concerned not only with status threat but also with outgroups surpassing them in status and privilege (Yadon & Ostfeld, 2020). Aid to Blacks does not hurt the white ingroup materially, but as a policy whites find it threatening in that it might lead to an increase in social status for Blacks and give them the potential to exceed the societal status of whites.

This chapter also shows that, without controlling for predispositions, WRI influences support for policy checks and decreasing legal levels of immigration. Ethnocentrism, or higher levels of ingroup love, has the same effect and influences support for all restrictive immigration attitudes, including support for more punitive federal immigration policy. The most consistent measure of whiteness, a relational measure of group consciousness that blames minorities for whites' inability to find a job, also influences restrictive immigration attitudes. This measure of whiteness, in fact, remains consistent in its influence on restrictive immigration attitudes even after controlling for predispositions, which alone strongly influence immigration attitudes. White racial identity and ethnocentrism both lose significance in their influence on immigration attitudes once predispositions are considered except for influencing legal levels of immigration. However, in both cases the strength of each on legal levels of immigration diminishes.

Psychological predispositions matter, often above and beyond white identity and group consciousness. Once predispositions are considered, white racial identity is not a significant factor in white attitudes on immigration.

However, white group consciousness does remain important even after controlling for predispositions. In all cases, though, predispositions are often a stronger predictor of restrictive immigration attitudes. For whites, as psychologist Helms (1990) makes clear, racial identity is related to other cultural characteristics such as cultural value orientations, which are defined by "those dimensions that members of a particular group consider important and desirable—what it values, [what] guides the behavior of its individuals, forms the basis for group norms, and dictates lifestyles that are deemed appropriate for group members" (p. 106). Predispositions get to these value judgements. Without the consideration of these values, white racial identity politics is incomplete. Simply examining individuals who check "white" as their race and/ or who say being white is important to their identity is not enough to reveal the impact of whiteness. In fact, scholarship that rests on white racial identity based on these measures runs the risk of perpetuating notions of race that rest on ascription rather than power. Simply acknowledging that being white is important for one's identity does not acknowledge that "white" is but a socially constructed racial category. The workings of race are not embedded in categories without the meaning behind the categories and without an understanding of how those racial categories were formed—what type of racialization and socialization individuals in that category experience.

More specifically, moral traditionalism is one of the most consistent and strongest predictors of restrictive immigration attitudes. As previously theorized, I argue for the importance of all predispositions in understanding how whiteness operates, how it shows up in white attitudes in ways that are deeply embedded in whiteness. The values that undergird moral traditionalism have been connected to white nativist movements and continue to influence anti-immigration attitudes. New Right movements also base their message and rhetoric on moral traditionalist values, and importantly, these New Right movements understand that white supremacy is a fundamental part of U.S. society (Winant, 2004b). Hence moral traditionalist values ground the maintenance of this system such that to destroy it means destroying a fundamental part of what it means to be white in the United States. The findings of this chapter, that whiteness moderates the strength and importance of predispositions, confirms this understanding. The influence of moral traditionalism, in particular, is moderated by the saliency of WRI and ethnocentrism. High levels of moral traditionalism influence decreasing legal immigration levels among whites whose white identity is most salient and who express the most ingroup love but not among low white identifiers or whites who express outgroup love. White group consciousness also moderates the strength and importance of moral traditionalism.

Finally, party identification also moderates moral traditionalism, especially for white Democrats. This finding is novel and important given the current polarized nature of politics. From prior scholarship, we know that feelings about immigration have the capacity to move Democrats into the Republican Party (Abrajano & Hajnal, 2015) and that immigration beliefs are fundamental in understanding partisanship. However, we know less about what factors influence white Democrats in defecting or at least holding more conservative views relative to the norms of the Democratic Party. This work has found that moral traditionalism is a key factor that influences white Democratic partisanship. However, this is not the case for racial resentment. Party identification does not moderate the effect of high levels of racial resentment in influencing attitudes in favor of decreasing legal levels of immigration or building a border wall. The interaction between independents and racial resentment and Republicans and racial resentment is insignificant for both policies across racial resentment levels. Moral traditionalism's importance to and influence on white immigration attitudes is different. It has the capacity to supersede Democratic norms. White Democrats who express higher levels of moral traditionalism also express more conservative immigration attitudes.

These results matter deeply for U.S. politics and future immigration policy. Public opinion literature is interested in understanding the factors that play a role in the formulation of public opinion and political behavior. In political science, an emerging scholarship on white identity politics posits the importance of white racial identity for whites, often characterizing the Obama presidency and the 2016 elections as catalysts. However, this chapter has shown that white political behavior cannot be simplified to questions that ask just about whites' identity saliency. Given their status as the historical dominant group in U.S. society, these questions only get us so far. Preconceived ideas, norms, and values that they have learned influence whites' attitudes and behavior, and these predispositions are manifestations of how whiteness operates, how it shows up in daily life. Without an examination of these predispositions, white identity politics is not complete because the (im)moral choices whites make when visiting the voting polls or supporting policies did not start with Obama's presidency, but when whiteness became a strategy for power. In this sense, if white Americans are making decisions on immigration based on predispositions, what we should be focused on is not how much or how little whites recognize their whiteness or deem it important, but how they perform it through behavior. Importantly, whites' predispositions are inherently raced. Predispositions are learned through socialization and though they can change over time, they are still raced. Whites learn through the lens of whiteness; thus, this chapter has showcased that white identity, white group consciousness, and partisanship moderate when and how predispositions are important in whites' immigration attitudes. More specifically, this chapter has shown the importance of morally based values about the "right" social order.

4

White Racial Privilege and Progressive Immigration Attitudes

Why does white supremacy take hold of most whites but not all whites? Why do a minority of whites fight against the norms of white supremacy? A memoir by Mab Segrest (2019), *Memoir of a race traitor*, provides us with an example of what it might look like to go against the norms of white supremacy. From Segrest, we learn that white persons who choose to follow their moral compass do not betray themselves or their family but the ideology of white supremacy. In her memoir Segrest, a queer anti-racist activist, details her very troubled and haunting past growing up in Tuskegee, Alabama, and learning about the 1966 murder of Sammy Younge, a 21-year-old African American civil rights and voting rights activist, at the hands of her uncle Marvin Segrest. Throughout the memoir, we witness Segrest coming to terms with her own family's past. We learn that Segrest distances herself from her family as well as her family's attitudes about race. By the end of the memoir, though, Segrest is enveloped by her aging father's love, and she asks:

> When had my "racist daddy" contracted to himself—to one aging man— from the balloon into which I had inflated him: a caricature of everything in the culture that I hated, my archetypical white person, whom I could never convert because I could never accept, the him of me? (p. 184)

Segrest struggled to be at once both a member of her family and an avid anti-racist. Her memoir is illustrative of one kind of white socialization that happens under the system of white supremacy, the illusion that whites need to make a choice between belonging to a family unit and living life in isolation—as in Baldwin's representation of Jesse. Segrest comes to the realization and the choice that "It's not [her] people, it's the *idea* of race [she is] betraying" (p. 7). Key to Segrest's realization is her understanding of her white racial privilege, "the him of me."

Moral and Immoral Whiteness in Immigration Politics. Yalidy Matos, Oxford University Press.
© Oxford University Press 2023. DOI: 10.1093/oso/9780197656259.003.0005

Is Segrest's understanding of her own privilege generalizable to other whites, and might this realization answer the question at the start of this chapter? Do beliefs about whether whites have a racial advantage because of their skin color—a question that directly implicates whites' racial identity and privileges—push whites to be more progressive in their immigration policy attitudes? This chapter further examines white political behavior on immigration, focusing on what distinguishes whites who support progressive immigration policies. Furthermore, this chapter introduces a measure of whites' belief in white racial advantage to an examination of immigration attitudes. Using the 2016 American National Election Study (ANES) as well as the 2018 Cooperative Congressional Election Study (CCES), I focus on progressive immigration policy preferences to understand this political choice more fully using a series of logistic regression models. This examination furthers our understanding of how whiteness is implicated in macro-level outcomes, such as immigration policy, that have the capacity to alter immigrants' lives and equalize society.

B-Side: Progressive Immigration Attitudes

If Chapter 3 addresses the A-side, this chapter focuses on the B-side: whites who make the decision to do whiteness differently. Relevant to this book project is an examination of whites who have progressive immigration attitudes when progressive attitudes are not required by the group; on the contrary, they go against group norms. Many whites (and others) in the United States often express ambivalent attitudes toward certain aspects of immigration when given the chance. They say they neither favor nor oppose a policy and want to keep current levels of legal immigration the same without a clear understanding of, or in denial of, the restrictive nature of immigration policy. Very few whites express support for increasing levels of immigration or allowing undocumented immigrants to stay in the United States without penalty and with a pathway to citizenship. What are the underlying factors that influence these decisions for some white Americans? In this chapter, I argue that these individuals' socialization was either different or interrupted by external events or experiences. Hence these individuals have much lower levels of moral traditionalism, racial resentment, anti-egalitarianism, and authoritarianism. Additionally, I argue that what sets these white Americans apart from most whites who have more restrictive immigration attitudes is an awareness of their white racial advantages and privileges. This awareness leads whites to make different decisions. This awareness is a prerequisite for progressive immigration attitudes.

Although white supremacy affects everyone, white, Black, Latino, Asian, Indigenous, and everyone living under the regime of white supremacy (Metzl, 2019; Oliver & Shapiro, 1995), whites are the least likely to discuss their racial identities, the meaning of their race, and how race shapes their lives (Frankenberg, 1993; Yancy, 2004). Most whites hold a colorblind race ideology (Bonilla-Silva, 2014) that allows them to recognize past discrimination and racism (the pre-1965 kind) but claim that the Civil Rights Movement achieved its aims of equality. In other words, race no longer influences the lives, experiences, wealth, and success of non-whites. Based on this distorted view of U.S. history and contemporary society, whites who adhere to a colorblind ideology see the socioeconomic system as fair (Kinder & Sanders, 1996). They attribute differences in wealth to individual-level factors rather than structural ones (Hartmann, Gerteis, & Croll, 2009). In general, they deemphasize the structural nature of racism and discrimination.

As I argue throughout this book, whites' worldview, their ideological standpoint, and their choices are raced. However, for many whites their worldview is normative, natural: It just is. In what Barbara J. Flagg (1993) calls the "transparency phenomenon," whites tend "not to think about whiteness, or about norms, behaviors, experiences, or perspectives that are white-specific" (p. 957). This transparency or complete lack of white consciousness is undergirded by the pretense of colorblindness, what Ruth Frankenberg calls a move toward color and power evasiveness. This understanding, however, is not universal across all white Americans. A minority of white Americans are race conscious.

Race consciousness or race cognizance (Frankenberg, 1993) is the ability to recognize historical, cultural, political, and social difference. As Tehema Lopez Bunyasi (2015) argues, however, there are different kinds of race consciousness. Some have a type of consciousness that leads them to believe that whites are being victimized and discriminated against. Like those who adhere to colorblindness, they have either more ambivalent political attitudes or restrictive and punitive ones as they are most interested in maintaining the racial status quo and even strengthening their dominance. Others have a type of consciousness that prompts them to make more progressive political decisions than average white Americans. I argue that this explains progressive immigration attitudes among whites. The recognition that race makes a difference in people's lives and that racism shapes contemporary U.S. politics and society allows these white individuals to see the world differently, and thus whiteness does not distort their moral compass as much as it might, as whiteness is no longer evasive. Whites who recognize white racial advantages can understand how political policies harm non-whites.

Scholarship on whites who have an awareness of their white racial privilege finds that it is overall rare (Bonilla-Silva, Lewis, & Embrick, 2004). Expressions of white racial privilege might sound like white race-talk that articulates and acknowledges the benefits of being white, the difficulties of being non-white, and importantly, support for policies that help non-whites, such as affirmative action (Frankenberg, 1993). In this chapter, I examine awareness of white racial advantage in two ways. The first, using the 2016 ANES, combines three different questions that examine how aware whites are of their position in U.S. society vis-à-vis non-white individuals and their relationship to institutions, such as the police. These questions are necessarily relational, as whiteness cannot exist outside non-whiteness. They concern whites' perception of their influence in U.S. politics, whether the federal government treats them better than Black Americans, and whether the police treat them better than Black Americans. Whites who are aware of their advantages and privileges perceive whites as having too much influence in politics and that the federal government and the police treat them better than Black Americans. The second, using the 2018 CCES, examines a question that elicits the degree to which participants agree that white people in the United States have certain advantages because of their skin color. I expect that whites who are racially aware of their privileges will have more progressive immigration attitudes.

This chapter also continues to look at how white identity and white group consciousness influence whites' understanding of immigration attitudes. My expectation is that whites with higher saliency of white racial identity (WRI) will be more racially aware. It is only logical that people who are aware of advantages that accrue to them because of their whiteness see being white as a recognizable identity. However, this positive relationship does not indicate that the saliency of one's white identity influences progressive immigration attitudes. I would argue white racial identity can lead to both restrictive and progressive attitudes; however, the form of white identity matters. In most cases, as I have argued in the preceding chapters, WRI should be insignificant as a mere recognition of one's white identity is not enough to create progressive attitudes. However, WRI is different from whites' group consciousness. I expect that whites who want to work together because they perceive unfair laws toward their group and whites who blame minorities for their inability to find a job are by default conscious that they are white. Yet their belief in vic-timization is tied to an inability to be aware of white privilege or advantages and leads them to support restrictive immigration policies. This is because this group of whites see themselves as victims of discrimination and struc-tural bias. Hence, they blame minoritized groups, non-white people, and the federal government for what they see as white victimization.

Race cognizance is a moral choice for whites; colorblindness and white victimhood ideology, which are not necessarily different from one another (Lopez Bunyasi, 2015), are amoral. Colorblindness and white victimhood ideology often misunderstand unintentional race discrimination or racism precisely because the perpetrator, whether a person or an institution, is un-aware that race played a role in their action or the outcome. If they did not know, because of the transparency phenomenon, then they are not to blame and the outcome itself is not immoral. However, when a white person is clear about white racial privilege, they understand, I would argue, unintentional race discrimination is racist regardless of intent. Cognizant whites understand that discrimination on the basis of race is immoral regardless of intent. What distinguishes this group from whites who adhere to a colorblind ideology is that they understand that race neutrality only appears moral but it is in fact immoral in outcome. When it comes to actions, to behavior, colorblind whites refuse to go the extra step in supporting policies that would level the playing field, whereas cognizant whites' behavior will differ in both theory and praxis. The choice to be cognizant, to be aware of how race works in their own lives and how it affects the lives of others, is to make a moral choice that goes against the group's norms since most of the group is not racially conscious.

The following section details the data and empirical strategy employed in this chapter. The goal is to understand what factors influence more progres-sive immigration policy attitudes among white Americans and, in particular, the role of perceptions of white racial advantage, controlling for other alter-native hypotheses.

Information on Data

Immigration Policy Preferences

In the 2016 ANES, the main dependent variable is respondents' preferred federal policy toward unauthorized immigrants. For this chapter, I created a binary variable. Respondents who chose the first response became the first category (1; progressive attitudes), while respondents who chose the last response were relabeled into the zero category (punitive attitudes). However, I do run the models using the original four-item measure as well. The first two responses consist of allowing unauthorized immigrants to remain and eventually qualify for U.S. citizenship without penalties and allowing them to remain and qualify for U.S. citizenship if they meet certain requirements. The last two punitive responses include a policy for a guest worker program—such programs are exploitative and detrimental to workers—and making all unauthorized immigrants felons and sending them back to their home country.

In the 2018 CCES, I use two main dependent variables. The first one asks respondents whether they support or oppose withholding federal funds from any local police department that does not report to the federal government anyone they identify as an "illegal immigrant." The second asks whether they support or oppose sending to prison any person who has been deported from the United States and re-enters the United States. Higher values indicate the more progressive preference, which in these instances oppose both policies.

Measuring White Racial Advantage

Using the 2016 ANES, I use three proxy measures of white racial advantage that I have combined into an additive index scale. First, influence of whites in politics asks, "Would you say that whites have too much influence in American politics, just about the right amount of influence in American politics, or too little influence in American politics?" I recoded this question to binary, where one indicates respondents who answered too much influence, while all others were collapsed into the zero category. Second, perceptions of whether the federal government treats whites better asks, "In general, does the federal government treat whites better than [B]lacks, treat them both the same, or treat [B]lacks better than whites?" I recoded the answers as binary, with respondents who perceive the government as treating whites better in one category (1), and all others into the residual category (0). The final question asks, "In general, do the police treat whites better than [B]lacks, treat them both the same, or treat [B]lacks better than whites?" I recoded this variable in the same manner, where one is police treat whites better and zero is the collapsed categories of treat them both the same and treat Blacks better. These are prime questions to understand whether whites think they have advantages when it comes to how the government and the police treat their group as well as how much influence they believe they have in politics. Whites who answer in the affirmative (or 1) in all three questions are whites that have a high amount of white racial awareness of their advantages, while whites who answer zero to all questions have no awareness of their own privileges. Whites in the middle have some awareness.

The Cronbach's alpha for these three measures is 0.71. Based on this, I created an additive index scale and rescaled it to run from zero to one. Figure 4.1 depicts the distribution of the percentage of white respondents at each scale category. About 42% of whites in the sample have no recognition of white racial advantage. In all three questions, they answered that whites have the right amount of influence in politics or too little, that the federal government treats both Blacks and whites the same or Blacks better, and that the police treats both whites and Blacks the same or Blacks better. A little under 17% of whites answered that whites have too much influence and that the federal government and the police treat whites better. This percentage is in line with findings from other research for the percentage of racially cognizant whites. For example, in their research, Eduardo Bonilla-Silva and colleagues (2004) find a range of 12%–15%. In the intervening category 26% of whites answered one of the questions in the affirmative, while about 15% answered two of the three questions in the affirmative.

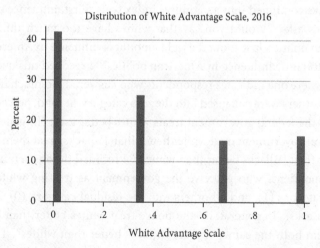

Figure 4.1 Distribution of White Advantage Scale, 2016 ANES, Weighted

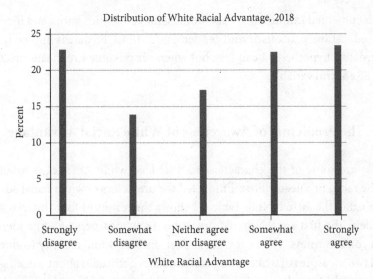

Figure 4.2 Distribution of White Racial Advantage, 2018 CCES, Weighted

In the 2018 CCES, one explicit question asks respondents to strongly agree, somewhat agree, neither agree nor disagree, somewhat disagree, or strongly disagree with the following statement: "White people in the U.S. have certain advantages because of the color of their skin." This question is used as a direct measurement for white racial advantage. Higher numbers indicate agreement with the statement. About 46% strongly or somewhat agreed with the statement, while about 37% strongly or somewhat disagreed. Figure 4.2 shows the complete distribution of white racial advantage in 2018.

Controlling for Relevant Factors

This chapter utilizes importance of white identity and white consciousness to examine differences between white identifiers using the same measures as in Chapter 3. Much as I did there, I control here for the main predispositions. Lower levels of racial resentment, moral traditionalism, anti-egalitarianism, and authoritarianism should result in whites being more likely to have progressive policy attitudes. The reverse for all is also true. In Appendix B, Tables 4A.1 and 4A.2 are descriptive statistics of relevant variables in the 2016 ANES data by white identification and white consciousness, respectively. The models include feeling thermometers for Asians, Hispanics, and undocumented immigrants. I also control for economic factors and income, age, education, patriotism, and gender. The 2018 CCES data is limited in the alternative hypotheses I can test, but wherever possible I replicate the 2016 ANES control variables.

The Predictors of Awareness of White Racial Advantage

What are some of the characteristics that lead white Americans to admit white racial privileges? First, I modeled the predictors of white racial advantage using the 2016 ANES. Table 4.1 shows the results of four ordered logit models. The first are the predictors without any measures of white identity and consciousness. The next three models include white identity (model 2) and two measures of white group consciousness: attitudes about working together to address the unfair laws toward whites (model 3) and beliefs about whites not finding a job due to employers hiring minorities (model 4). In the first model, I find that being a Democrat is positively associated with higher levels of awareness of white racial advantages compared to identification as a Republican. The same is the case for independents compared to Republicans. Higher levels of patriotism are negatively associated with white awareness of racial advantages. In other words, whites who are highly patriotic have a harder time grasping that they have racial advantages because they are white. Whites who say the national economy has gotten worse are less likely to be aware of their white advantages. The same negative relationship exists with older whites. White women are more likely than white men to be aware of their racial privilege. Finally, higher levels of education have a positive relationship with awareness of white racial advantages. Including the influence of white identity does not alter anything. In fact, white identity is insignificant to attitudes about white racial advantages. However, whites who believe that whites should work together to tackle the unfair laws toward whites (model 3) and whites who blame minorities for not finding a job (model 4) are less likely to be racially aware of their privilege.

One of the most important predictors of awareness of white racial advantage is levels of patriotism, which asks respondents how they feel when they see the American flag. Figure 4.3 shows the predicted probability of being fully racially aware (answering all three questions in the affirmative) based on levels of patriotism for white Democratic women with the modal education level of some college, all else equal. Most whites are fully racially aware at

Table 4.1 Predictors of White Racial Advantage, 2016

	(1) Base	(2) White ID	(3) Unfair Laws	(4) Blame Minorities
Democrat	1.419***	1.422***	1.362***	1.329***
	(0.119)	(0.119)	(0.120)	(0.120)
Independent	0.607***	0.612***	0.591***	0.567***
	(0.106)	(0.106)	(0.107)	(0.107)
Patriotism	−2.411***	−2.442***	−2.306***	−2.044***
	(0.248)	(0.250)	(0.249)	(0.251)
Natl economy	−1.049***	−1.045***	−1.006***	−0.897***
	(0.128)	(0.128)	(0.128)	(0.130)
Income	0.154	0.151	0.088	0.070
	(0.165)	(0.165)	(0.166)	(0.167)
Age	−0.358*	−0.356*	−0.318*	−0.366*
	(0.157)	(0.158)	(0.158)	(0.158)
Education				
1. HS diploma	0.276	0.280	0.242	0.195
	(0.250)	(0.251)	(0.251)	(0.252)
2. Some college	0.193	0.205	0.174	0.134
	(0.243)	(0.243)	(0.244)	(0.244)
3. BA degree	0.773**	0.783**	0.749**	0.605*
	(0.249)	(0.250)	(0.250)	(0.252)
4. Advanced degree	0.887***	0.892***	0.844**	0.689**
	(0.260)	(0.260)	(0.261)	(0.262)
Female	0.211*	0.205*	0.224*	0.261**
	(0.087)	(0.087)	(0.087)	(0.088)
White ID		0.060		
		(0.112)		
Unfair laws			−0.480***	
			(0.116)	
Blame Minorities				−0.368***
				(0.047)
Cut	−2.038***	−2.025***	−2.281***	−2.746***
	(0.346)	(0.348)	(0.350)	(0.359)
Cut	−0.629+	−0.618+	−0.862*	−1.306***
	(0.344)	(0.346)	(0.348)	(0.356)

(continued)

Table 4.1 Continued

	(1) Base	(2) White ID	(3) Unfair Laws	(4) Blame Minorities
Cut	0.483	0.496	0.258	−0.162
	(0.343)	(0.345)	(0.347)	(0.354)
N	2059	2056	2052	2056
Pseudo R2	0.130	0.129	0.133	0.142
Log Likelihood	−2328.843	−2326.266	−2313.208	−2293.875

Data: ANES 2016.

Note: *** p < .001 ** p < .01 * p < .05 + p < .10; standard error in parentheses; weighted.

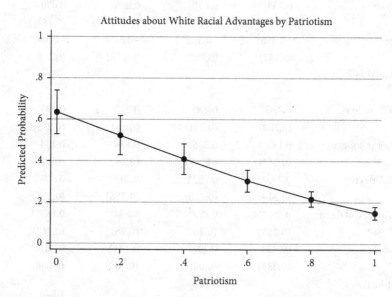

Attitudes about White Racial Advantages by Patriotism

Figure 4.3 Predicted Probability of White Racial Awareness by Levels of Patriotism; 2016 ANES; Table 4.1, Model 3

the lowest levels of patriotism, respondents who answered that they feel ex-tremely bad when they see the U.S. flag. At this level of patriotism, about 64% of white Democratic women with at least some college have racial awareness. At the next level, respondents who feel moderately bad when they see the American flag, about 52% of these women are racially aware. By the highest level of patriotism, the percentage of white Democratic women who are ra-cially aware decreases to about 15%. That is a 49-point difference between the lowest and highest levels of patriotism. Controlling for attitudes about white group consciousness does not change much substantively. At the lowest level of patriotism, the percentage of white Democratic women with at least some college and who feel that it is very or extremely important that whites work together to change the unfair laws that victimize them decreases to 59%, while at the highest level of patriotism it decreases to about 13%. Among white Democratic women with at least some college who believe it is not at all important that whites work together, about 70% with the lowest level of patriotism are racially aware while about 19% with the highest level of patriotism are racially aware. Hence, a lack of white group consciousness increases the percentages of white Democratic women with some college who are racially aware both at the lowest end of patriotism and at the highest, although at the highest end of patriotism, positive affect for the U.S. flag, is much more important than white group consciousness.

The following analysis examines the predictors of white racial advantages with the inclusion of predispositions (model 1) and with predispositions and white racial identity (model 2). I also ran two additional models, one with each white group consciousness measure (model 3, *Unfair laws*, and model 4, *Blame minorities*), neither of which were significant when included with the predispositions. There are five important findings. The first thing to note from all models in Table 4.2 is that all the predispositions are negatively associated with awareness of white racial advantage. In other words, as levels of racial resentment, moral traditionalism, anti-egalitarianism, and authoritarianism increase, awareness of white racial advantage decreases. The second important finding is that the coefficient for patriotism diminishes in size and strength. As a comparison, examining model 2, for a white Democratic woman with some college, there is only a 10-point difference between the lowest level of patriotism (0.18) and the highest level of patriotism (0.08) with respect to awareness of white racial advantage. About 18% of this population with the lowest level of patriotism is racially aware, far less than in Table 4.1, model 3, where the percentage was 69%. Patriotism is just not as important in Table 4.2. Third, although white racial identity was not significant in model 2 in Table 4.1, it is significant in model 2, Table 4.2. Higher saliency in white racial identity is positively associated with higher levels of awareness of white racial advantage. Fourth, the size and strength of Democratic identification also decreases, while independents are not significantly different from Republicans. Finally, education no longer significantly influences awareness of white racial advantage once predispositions are considered.

Table 4.2 Predictors of White Racial Advantage (Including Predispositions), 2016

	(1) Base	(2) White ID	(3) Unfair Laws	(4) Blame Minorities
Democrat	0.383**	0.377**	0.370**	0.388**
	(0.135)	(0.135)	(0.135)	(0.135)
Independent	0.089	0.101	0.082	0.095
	(0.115)	(0.115)	(0.115)	(0.115)
Patriotism	−0.842**	−0.905***	−0.832**	−0.806**
	(0.267)	(0.270)	(0.268)	(0.269)
Natl economy	−0.308*	−0.317*	−0.301*	−0.298*
	(0.139)	(0.139)	(0.139)	(0.139)
Income	−0.036	−0.016	−0.070	−0.040
	(0.172)	(0.173)	(0.173)	(0.173)
Age	−0.099	−0.138	−0.104	−0.105
	(0.169)	(0.170)	(0.169)	(0.169)
Education				
1. HS diploma	0.256	0.262	0.240	0.238
	(0.265)	(0.265)	(0.265)	(0.265)
2. Some college	0.145	0.161	0.132	0.137
	(0.257)	(0.258)	(0.258)	(0.258)
3. BA degree	0.330	0.356	0.326	0.310
	(0.267)	(0.268)	(0.268)	(0.268)
4. Advanced degree	0.364	0.378	0.359	0.338
	(0.280)	(0.281)	(0.281)	(0.281)
Female	0.071	0.065	0.075	0.079
	(0.091)	(0.091)	(0.092)	(0.092)
Racial resentment	−3.064***	−3.068***	−3.041***	−2.991***
	(0.235)	(0.235)	(0.235)	(0.240)
Moral traditionalism	−1.135***	−1.172***	−1.089***	−1.100***
	(0.243)	(0.243)	(0.244)	(0.244)
Anti-egalitarianism	−1.857***	−1.905***	−1.864***	−1.841***
	(0.269)	(0.271)	(0.270)	(0.270)
Authoritarianism	−0.594***	−0.609***	−0.589***	−0.581***
	(0.173)	(0.173)	(0.173)	(0.174)
White ID		0.316**		
		(0.119)		
Unfair Laws			−0.149	
			(0.123)	

(continued)

Table 4.2 Continued

	(1) Base	(2) White ID	(3) Unfair Laws	(4) Blame Minorities
Blame Minorities				−0.204
				(0.155)
Cut	−4.535***	−4.474***	−4.611***	−4.539***
	(0.391)	(0.392)	(0.393)	(0.391)
Cut	−2.858***	−2.794***	−2.931***	−2.862***
	(0.384)	(0.385)	(0.387)	(0.384)
Cut	−1.470***	−1.403***	−1.545***	−1.474***
	(0.378)	(0.379)	(0.380)	(0.378)
N	2039	2036	2034	203
Pseudo R2	0.218	0.219	0.218	0.219
Log Likelihood	−2072.311	−2066.914	−2066.857	−2068.074

Data: ANES 2016.

Note: *** p < .001 ** p < .01 * p < .05 + p < .10; standard error in parentheses; weighted.

Figure 4.4 depicts the predicted probability of each of the categories of white racial advantage by racial resentment and moral traditionalism. At the lowest level of racial resentment, the predicted probability of white Democratic women with some college expressing no racial awareness is 7%, while at the highest level, 63% express no racial awareness. White Democratic women's (with some college) expression of full racial awareness decreases from 38% to 3% as racial resentment levels go from zero to one. The same pattern can be found with levels of moral traditionalism; from the lowest to the highest level of moral traditionalism expressions of full racial awareness go from 16% to 5% and expressions of no racial awareness go from 20% to 44%. In summary, levels of predispositions influence the ability of whites to be racially aware.

In 2018, 22.5% and 23.4% of whites somewhat agree and strongly agree, respectively, that they have racial advantages due to their skin color. This model can be found in Table 4A.3 in Appendix B. An examination of the 2018 CCES indicates that white women who are younger, more educated, and have higher incomes are slightly more likely to agree that whites have racial advantages. Democrats and independents are more likely to agree that whites have racial privileges than Republicans, who are less likely to agree.

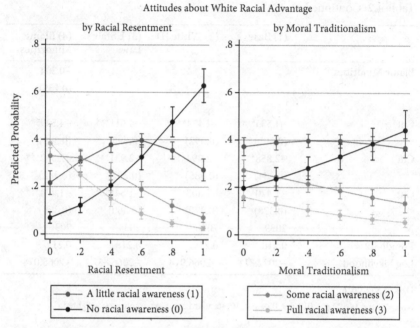

Figure 4.4 Predicted Probability of Attitudes about White Racial Privilege by Racial Resentment and Moral Traditionalism; 2016 ANES; Table 4.2, Model 2

Finally, in 2018, racial resentment is negatively associated with awareness of white racial advantage.

The following section examines the role of awareness of white racial advantage on progressive immigration attitudes. The section is also concerned with the influence of WRI and white group consciousness on progressive immigration attitudes.

The Influence of White Racial Advantage on Progressive Immigration Attitudes

Does awareness of white racial advantage or privilege move white Americans to have more progressive immigration attitudes? Table 4.3 shows whether admitting to white racial privileges is positively associated with progressive immigration policies. The immigration policy outcome is a binary outcome where zero (0) is the most punitive policy attitude (making immigrants felons and deporting them) while one (1) is the most progressive

Table 4.3 Influence of White Racial Advantage on Immigration Policy, 2016

	(1) Base	(2) White ID	(3) Unfair Laws	(4) Blame Minorities
White Racial Advantage	1.868**	1.886**	1.728**	1.611**
	(0.598)	(0.601)	(0.611)	(0.613)
White ID		0.233		
		(0.499)		
Unfair Laws			−1.022*	
			(0.513)	
Blame Minorities				−1.198+
				(0.614)
N	562	560	562	561
Pseudo R2	0.701	0.700	0.707	0.707
Log Likelihood	−103.356	−103.234	−101.393	−101.429

Data: 2016 ANES; weighted results.

Note: *** p < .001 ** p < .01 * p < .05 + p < .10; standard error in parentheses.

policy attitude (allowing immigrants to remain and qualify for citizenship without penalties). Table 4.3 includes all control variables except for all predispositions. Models 2–4 include a measure of white identity or white group consciousness. The full table can be found in Appendix B (Table 4A.4). Table 4A.5 shows these models with the full immigration policy outcome variable. The main findings remain the same.[1]

Awareness of white racial advantage consistently influences progressive immigration policy attitudes. In essence, admitting to white racial privilege influences whites to be more progressive on immigration even after controlling for partisanship, affect toward undocumented immigrants, and patriotism. White racial advantage also remains significant after controlling for measures of white identity saliency and white group consciousness. The saliency of white identity is insignificant in model 2, while the group consciousness measures are significant. Whites with higher levels of white group consciousness, those who want to work together to change unfair laws toward them and those who blame minorities for the perception of lack of jobs available to whites (only slightly significant), are less likely to prefer the most progressive immigration policy.

Figure 4.5 depicts the predicted probability of the most progressive immigration policy attitude by level of awareness of white racial advantage

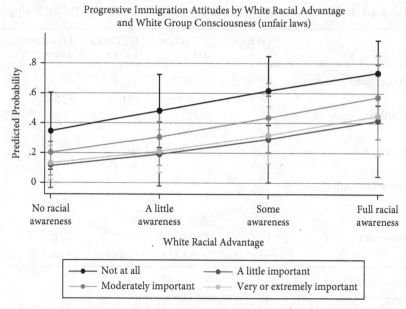

Figure 4.5 Predicted Probability of Progressive Immigration Policy Attitude by Levels of White Racial Advantage and White Group Consciousness (Unfair Laws); 2016 ANES; Table 4.3, Model 3

and white group consciousness (*Unfair laws*) among Democratic women. Awareness of white racial advantage influences all levels of group consciousness in the positive direction. However, it influences some more than others. For white Democratic women who express that it is not at all important to work together to change the unfair laws, going from no racial awareness to full racial awareness increases the likelihood of progressive immigration attitudes from 35% to 74%. In other words, among these women, full awareness of their privilege (even some awareness) influences their progressive immigration attitudes if they also express a lack of white group consciousness. If they do have white group consciousness and believe it is very or extremely important to work together, then the predicted probability of supporting a progressive immigration policy goes from 13% with no racial awareness to 45% with full racial awareness. In other words, even among these women, white racial awareness increases the possibility of more progressive attitudes. Substantively, 45% is below the midpoint, but the jump is large and significant. There is also a large jump among those who believe it is moderately important to work together (from 20% to 57%). Among those who say it is only a little important, levels of white racial advantage are insignificant except for full racial awareness.

Awareness of white racial advantage is important for understanding whites' progressive immigration attitudes. Table 4A.6 (in Appendix B) replicates Table 4.3 but with the inclusion of predispositions, which are highly significant and important factors influencing immigration attitudes. In these models, where policy attitudes are binary, the significance of awareness of white racial advantage disappears completely, as do all measures of white identity and group consciousness. Two out of the four predispositions are significant: racial resentment and moral traditionalism. Higher levels of both have a negative relationship with the progressive attitude of allowing immigrants to stay in the United States with a pathway to citizenship without penalties. Figure 4.6 is a depiction of the predicted probability of having the most progressive immigration policy attitude by levels of moral traditionalism and by party identification (Figure 4A.1 in Appendix B shows the results for racial resentment). The influence of moral traditionalism is strongest for Democrats, decreasing progressive attitudes from about 60% to 19% from the lowest level of moral traditionalism to a level of 0.6, after which levels are insignificant. For Republicans, levels of moral traditionalism also decrease progressive attitudes, although the a priori assumption is that not many Republicans believe in progressive immigration policy. The threshold for Republicans is also 0.6. At the lowest level of moral traditionalism, white female Republicans have a 40% likelihood of choosing the progressive immigration policy attitude, all else equal, while at a moral traditionalism level of 0.6 that number decreases to 9%. Independents are no different from Republicans and are even subsumed by Republicans in the figure.

An examination of the same model but with the full range of policy options, Table 4A.7 in Appendix B, however, does show that higher levels of awareness of white racial advantage influences more progressive immigration policy attitudes, controlling for all predispositions, which diminish in strength and size but remain mostly significant. The variation allows for these differences in results; however, this chapter is interested in whites with progressive immigration attitudes rather than something in between. Hence, when whites who are aware of their racial advantage are presented with more options the fact that they are more aware matters, but it matters less once predispositions are considered.

An examination of the 2018 CCES (Table 4.4) reveals that among whites who believe that whites have white racial advantages those who also believe

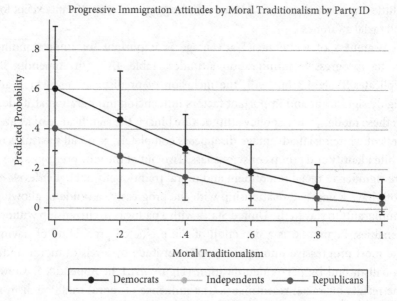

Figure 4.6 Predicted Probability of Progressive Immigration Policy Attitude by Levels of Moral Traditionalism and Party ID; 2016 ANES; Table 4A.6, Model 1

that racial problems in the United States are not rare and isolated situations are more likely to choose the progressive immigration policy option. Whites who are more aware of their racial advantage because of the color of their skin are more likely to oppose withholding federal funds from any local police department that does not report to the federal government anyone they identify as an "illegal immigrant" and sending to prison immigrants who have re-entered the United States after being returned once. Controlling for racial resentment, which also has a significant and negative relationship with progressive immigration attitudes in both models, and demographics, these results remain the same. The common content of the CCES is limiting in that not all alternative hypotheses can be controlled for. However, a replication of the same models on a subset of whites using a smaller module reveals very similar results (shown in Table 4A.8, Appendix B). Whites who admit to having white racial advantages are more likely to oppose anti-sanctuary measures (slightly significant p-value 0.06) and making it a crime for immigrants to attempt to re-enter the United States after being deported once before.[2]

Table 4.4 Influence of White Racial Advantage on Immigration Policy Attitudes, 2018 CCES

	Funds	Re-entry
White Racial Advantage	0.955***	0.584***
	(0.075)	(0.069)
Racial Resentment	−3.012***	−2.588***
	(0.099)	(0.088)
Racism Rare	0.975***	0.445***
	(0.078)	(0.070)
National Economy	1.981***	1.060***
	(0.088)	(0.077)
Lost Job	−0.199*	−0.028
	(0.088)	(0.077)
Age	−0.013***	−0.014***
	(0.001)	(0.001)
Female	0.228***	0.061+
	(0.041)	(0.036)
Education	0.414***	0.239***
	(0.075)	(0.065)
Married	−0.025	−0.051
	(0.043)	(0.038)
Registered Voter	0.195**	0.166**
	(0.065)	(0.060)
Republican	−1.149***	−0.733***
	(0.045)	(0.043)
Income	0.233**	0.142*
	(0.080)	(0.069)
Constant	0.274+	0.798***
	(0.146)	(0.131)
Pseudo R2	0.462	0.311
N	22250	22242
Log Likelihood	−8292.571	−10526.588

Data: 2018 CCES; weighted results.

Sample: Non-Hispanic whites, third generation only.

Note: *** p < .001 ** p < .01 * p < .05 + p < .10; standard error in parentheses.

These results also point to the fact that whites make decisions as white people, not as individuals who are race-less, and these decisions are made as part of a larger group. Whites make group-centered political decisions, and a part of that calculation involves recognizing one's own racial positioning.

The Importance of Awareness of White Racial Advantage on Immigration Attitudes

The results for whites who admit white privilege exists are in line with the scholarship that suggests this admission leads to more progressive policies (Branscombe et al., 2002; Lopez Bunyasi, 2015; Powell et al., 2005). Even though only a minority of whites admit to white racial advantage, about 17% in 2016 and 23% in 2018, this admission to themselves and about themselves has political consequences. In 2016, beyond shifting attitudes toward a more progressive orientation, whites who are aware of their racial privileges tended to feel angrier about Donald Trump and to report feeling proud because of Barack Obama's election. Predispositions, especially racial resentment and moral traditionalism, strongly influence whites who have no racial awareness of whiteness and how it operates. Higher levels of racial resentment and moral traditionalism push whites to be less racially aware. Other factors that influence awareness of white racial advantage include Democratic identification, higher levels of education, being female (although in many instances gender is insignificant once other factors are considered). Higher levels of education make sense given the literature in critical whiteness studies and political socialization suggest that, because young adults are impressionable, higher education can counteract previous socialization for whites (Kinder & Sears, 1985; Neundorf & Smets, 2017). Without the consideration of predispositions, white identification is insignificant, though once predispositions are accounted for it does become significant, and whites with higher white identity saliency are more likely to be racially aware. The reverse is true for white group consciousness; without considering predispositions, white group consciousness is negatively associated with white racial awareness but insignificant once predispositions are accounted for. All predispositions are important in influencing awareness of white racial advantage. Higher levels of racial resentment, moral traditionalism, anti-egalitarianism, and authoritarianism all decrease the likelihood of racial awareness for whites.

In addition to the importance of the impact of whites' white racial privilege on immigration attitudes, an important finding is patriotism's influence on awareness of white racial advantage. Higher levels of American patriotism decrease whites' ability to be racially aware of how their whiteness advantages them. American patriotism and whiteness are woven together in the same fabric. A pro-nationalist discourse of American patriotism results in commitments to freedom, equality, democracy, and bootstrap ideology (that if you just pull yourself up by your bootstraps and work hard you would have just as much as white people). This commitment is to a patriotism that is raced as white, to a democracy that really is a *Herrenvolk* white democracy, one that reconciles equality and subordination, one that is committed to both liberal ideals and racial hierarchy. American patriotism was taught in the same sentence as slavery was extolled, as Lillian Smith (1949) detailed in her autobiography, when she wrote, "I learned to believe in freedom, to glow when the word *democracy* was used, and to practice slavery from morning to night" (p. 19). The construction of whiteness and of a patriotic identity happens simultaneously (Miller, 2020). This kind of patriotism does not engage in critical thinking about whiteness. Quite the opposite; it suppresses any critical thinking of one's own race, positioning, and culpability in the kind of patriotism and democracy that privileges whites and oppresses non-whites (Beltrán, 2020). In the 2008 presidential election, racial resentment and patriotism were important factors in opposition to candidate Barack Obama. Appeals to working-class whites, for example, focused on Obama's supposed lack of patriotism (Parker, Sawyer, & Towler, 2009). Christopher Parker and colleagues find that higher levels of patriotism dampened Obama's support among whites, especially working-class whites. National pride is connected to racial antipathy because an "insistence upon universal freedom and equality, for which democracy is known, is restricted to conationals" (Parker et al., 2009, p. 197; also see Viroli, 1997), and those who are perceived to be prototypical Americans are white (Devos & Banaji, 2005). Whites, then, weaponize U.S. symbols, like the U.S. flag, to dominate other groups (both internationally and domestically). Per social dominance theory, patriotism and symbols connected to it are associated with negative feelings toward subordinates and thus an endorsement of the country's hierarchical structure (Sidanius & Pratto, 1999). A commitment to this type of American white hierarchy, this type of patriotism, which is very much akin to racism, is a commitment to the status quo, to the maintenance of whites' position, a position that requires colorblindness and power and color evasiveness, not awareness.

Another important finding is that higher expressions of racial resentment and moral traditionalism can suppress white racial awareness. Higher levels of racial resentment indicate a lack of understanding or recognition of structural racism, or a belief that structural racism is no longer a problem and that the problem is really the individual's lack of Protestant work ethic (Kam & Burge, 2018). This belief is antithetical to white racial awareness, which necessitates an awareness of structural racism and how structural racism continues to affect the lives of non-whites. In fact, a look back at Chapter 2 indicates that whites who disagree that whites have certain advantages have higher levels of racial resentment and are stronger Republicans. Racial resentment has also been conceptualized as a measure of colorblindness, a belief that we are all equal and that any effort the federal government makes to remediate the disadvantage of Black Americans is unfair. Hence, this preadult socialization—both abstract and moralistic (Kinder & Sears, 1981)—toward a colorblind ideology actually prevents whites from being racially aware. It keeps whites from being aware of how their whiteness privileges them and thus how it deprivileges non-whites. The moral values attached to racial resentment are misaligned with what most white people believe about themselves, that they are where they are due to hard work and individual effort (and in many cases because of God). They adhere to a meritocratic myth quite intimately tied to a U.S. patriotic understanding. Recognizing that the mere coincidence of their whiteness is what allows for their dominant position would result in a moral crisis. At the end of that crisis lies either an awareness of white racial advantages, and thus more progressive attitudes, or a denial of how race and whiteness operate, which results in a disbelief in structural racism.

Higher levels of moral traditionalism also indicate a violation of traditional values. Right-wing organizations see themselves as the protectors of Protestantism. These moral values, this "right" way of living is indicative of "real" and "true" Americans (Boissoneault, 2017; Parker & Barreto, 2013). The moral social order is what is at stake for moral traditionalists; these individuals are not interested in change and are more interested in maintaining a social order that works and benefits their group, that maintains their dominance (Barreto et al., 2011; Conover, 1988). An awareness of white racial privilege is a major change because it can then dictate how one thinks of oneself and how one operates in the world with others and one's political behavior, which can shift the social order. Thus, the two are also antithetical. There is a moral superiority and propriety attached to expressions of moral traditionalism; hence, to express higher levels of moral traditionalism is to believe that one's ingroup is morally superior and does not need to change to become aware of anything, especially anything that points the finger back at themselves for wrongdoings. It seems, however, that higher levels of racial resentment and moral traditionalism counteract Democratic norms among Democrats while reiterating Republican norms.

Republican identification alongside its norms go hand in hand with restrictive immigration attitudes, with higher levels of racial resentment, and with a deep connection to moral traditionalism. In fact, the Republican strategy has been to graft moral traditionalist norms onto what it means to be patriotic and thus what it means to be loyal to one's country and hold high traditional Republican values (Gregory, 2005). Hence, higher levels of racial resentment and moral traditionalism are in alignment with what it means to identify as Republican, whereas the gap between racial resentment and moral traditionalism is wider for Democrats and thus high levels of these predispositions should have more of an influence on Democrats than Republicans. This is exactly what this chapter finds. Even though Democrats have higher propensities to admit to white racial advantages, higher levels of racial resentment and moral traditionalism have the capacity to counteract this awareness. A distorted understanding that denies structural racism exists, purports equality in theory, and perceives itself as morally superior is too strong to counteract Democrats' racial awareness. White Democrats' support for the most progressive immigration policy preference goes from 60% to 19% as moral traditionalism moves from 0 to 0.6. Their support for allowing undocumented immigrants to stay in the United States with a pathway to citizenship without penalty goes from almost 70% to about 22% when levels of racial resentment go from 0 to 0.6. A belief in moral traditionalism, in moral superiority and a particular moral social order, is enough to push Democrats to behave more like Republicans and to adhere more to colorblindness than to racial awareness.

Conclusion

In summary, awareness of white racial advantages among whites is politically important and pushes whites toward more progressive attitudes. Predispositions, byproducts of socialization, inform whether whites are pushed toward awareness or away from it. Patriotism is an important factor in determining white racial awareness. Finally, the influence of white racial awareness and predispositions are particularly telling for white Democrats.

This chapter showed that when whites admit to having unearned and undeserved racial privileges due to the color of their skin (de-normalizing whiteness), they tend to be more progressive with respect to immigration policies. This aligns with previous works on whites who perceive racial privileges (Lopez Bunyasi, 2015). Whites who admit to white privilege are more progressive, even after controlling for education, psychological predispositions and personality traits. In essence, the findings of this chapter indicate that a way forward to a more equitable society rests on whites' moral compulsion to admit that they have unearned racial privileges that do not spring from mere hard work.

Whites make ingroup-centered political decisions as white people in relationship to their group position and standing vis-à-vis outgroups. Whites' decisions are utility-based. Whites are often invested in their group's social and racial position and interested in maintaining material or psychological benefits, while others are less invested in this maintenance. Social group racial identity influences whites' political behavior. Predispositions that are grounded in whites' socialization and whites' perceptions of their white racial advantages due to their skin color influence both whites' public opinion and political behavior. Whites' policy preferences are a way for whites to choose their ingroup and for some whites to repudiate the system of whiteness that is detrimental to many. Another way is through the election of particular political candidates as presidents or as their representatives. Chapter 5 examines the consequences of whites' decision-making in electing state-level representatives who make decisions about how immigration is enforced in their state.

5

Enacting Whiteness through State-Level Immigration Laws

Federal and state governments have a long history of disagreement over matters of state sovereignty and the supremacy of federal law (Tichenor & Filindra, 2012). In 1850, William Lloyd Garrison, a white abolitionist, referenced one of the more famous instances when he alerted readers in his Boston anti-slavery newspaper *The Liberator* of the presence of slave hunters in the city. He warned of "two prowling villains" from Macon, Georgia, "for the purpose of seizing William and Ellen Craft, under the infernal Fugitive Slave Bill" (Garrison, 1850). The Fugitive Slave Law of 1850, passed on September 18, required that fugitive slaves be returned to their "owner" and made it a crime, punishable by a fine of up to $1,000 and six months of prison, to "harbor or conceal fugitives" (Fugitive Slave Law of 1850, Sec. 7). The Fugitive Slave Law of 1850 was part of U.S. Senator Henry Clay's Compromise of 1850—a group of bills that helped dampen calls for Southern secession. Clay had conflicting stances on slavery but he is famous for, in part, balancing western expansion of mostly free states and assuaging Southern slaveholders' desire to maintain and expand slavery. The Fugitive Slave Act of 1850 granted everyday citizens the power (and role) to assist in the capture of runaways; indeed, it compelled them to do so. Garrison and some others, including Black abolitionists such as Harriet Tubman and Frederick Douglass, flouted the law, regarding the Fugitive Slave Law itself as a violation of an individual state's rights to prohibit slavery within its borders. In fact, federalism makes states relevant to this legislation because the U.S. Constitution allows states and localities to pass their own policies and legislation (Gimpel & Schuknecht, 2009). Consequently, some Northern states passed their own sanctuary or personal liberty laws to protect runaway slaves and free Blacks in violation of the law.

The turn of the 21st century saw another conflict between federal and state law with respect to the freedom of persons, in this case immigrants. The

Moral and Immoral Whiteness in Immigration Politics. Yalidy Matos, Oxford University Press.
© Oxford University Press 2023. DOI: 10.1093/oso/9780197656259.003.0006

leaders of several U.S. states, frustrated with the federal government's inaction on imigration reform, started to pass anti-immigration and restrictive immigration laws. Legal scholars suggest some states crossed the line that separates states' rights and federal plenary power. State-level immigration omnibus legislation—consisting of a law with multiple provisions—were passed in Alabama, Arizona, Nebraska, Oklahoma, and South Carolina, among others. Many of these laws use the words "harbor" or "harboring," much as the Fugitive Slave Law did, to criminalize transporting, shielding, or concealing unauthorized immigrants. Among the states that passed omnibus immigration legislation, only Indiana was a non-slaveholding state in 1860 but the non-slaveholding state with the most restrictive provisions regarding the free movement of Blacks, free or otherwise, in 1850 (Colbern, 2017; Middleton, 1993).

Much as citizens and police could have demanded documentation from free Blacks in any part of the country in 1850—although such documentation was no guarantee of safety—state-level immigration laws passed a century and a half later have "show me your papers" provisions.[1] This allows local police to essentially serve as U.S. Customs and Immigrant Enforcement (ICE) agents and stop anyone they deem suspect of being in the country illegally and has led to rampant racial profiling predicated on stereotypes that target individuals based on how they look and sound (Olivas, 2007; Wishnie, 2001).

"Show me your papers" is a surveillance tactic using documentation, such as a driver's license or another valid ID, to "prove" citizenship and, therefore, belonging and humanity in the eyes of the law. To be unauthorized is to be an "alien," an *other*, a foreigner, someone who does not belong. Unauthorized status is not a physical marker, but the racial profiling of non-white Latinos and non-white people in general indicates that non-whiteness is attached to an inability to belong. In the same way, slave patrols and bounty hunters tracked blackness as property, outside of the categories of human and free (Browne, 2015). The genealogy of the passport—the ultimate piece of paper that defines Americanism—is linked to "the tracking, accounting, and identification of the racial body, and in particular the black body and black social life" (p. 70). "Show me your papers" provisions track non-whiteness and illegality through immigration law, through the surveillance of mobility.

Like states that passed personal liberty laws in the 19th century, states and municipalities in the contemporary United States have also passed sanctuary legislation. Northern liberty laws were designed to provide protection to free Blacks and runaways and to constrain enforcement of the

Fugitive Slave Law. Massachusetts, New York, and Pennsylvania led in providing sanctuary protection for runaway and free Blacks. In similar fashion now, states, cities, counties, and other municipalities have also passed executive actions, resolutions, and legislation deeming their jurisdictions sanctuary spaces. Legally, there is no one definition of sanctuary policies; municipalities use many tactics and different policies. For example, some cities have explicitly forbidden city or law enforcement officials from inquiring about immigration status, while others forbid cooperation with ICE (Collingwood & Gonzalez O'Brien, 2019). Sanctuary policies can also forbid holding people beyond their release date based on an immigration detainer placed by ICE (Wong, 2017). The bottom line of contemporary sanctuary policies is that they mandate non-cooperation with ICE or federal government programs like 287(g) and Secure Communities. In the last decade, California, Connecticut, Illinois, Massachusetts, New York, Vermont, and other states have passed legislation that deem them sanctuary states (Griffith & Vaughan, 2020).[2]

The passage of Fugitive Slave Laws and personal liberty laws as well as contemporary restrictive immigration laws (federal and state) and sanctuary policies are all exemplary of whiteness enacted. Whiteness structures immigration attitudes. On the one hand, whiteness is enacted to maintain white supremacy by legislating human movement and by defining some people as sub-human and/or perpetually foreign and un-American. On the other hand, whiteness is enacted to resist or at least attempt to resist a system that uses immigration laws as a tool of white supremacy. Whites who are aware of their own racial advantage are less likely to support collaboration between local police and federal authorities and are more supportive of sanctuary policies (Casellas & Wallace, 2020). A direct link exists between individual whites' moral choices and the kinds of policies that get enacted. These laws are to at least some degree manifestations of the individual opinions of constituents. This chapter connects individual-level immigration public opinion, on which the previous chapters have focused, to the collective and dynamic policy consequences based on whites' candidate selection.

Individual people elect legislators and self-select into neighborhoods. The argument of this chapter rests on the fact that white individuals *choose* to elect legislators that are "like them," and most of the time share their immigration views. This decision does not exist outside of their identity as white people and their motivation to maintain their status (Petrow, Transue, & Vercellotti, 2018). Petrow et al. (2018) argue and find that the mere presence of a Black candidate on a ballot cues white identity, reducing support for Black candidates among whites. Furthermore, I link whiteness and vote choice by mapping the districts where these elected legislators voted for punitive immigration policies and the white population of the district. Ultimately, I find that whiteness structures the geography of exclusionary immigration legislation.

I argue that contemporary immigration politics at subnational levels should be understood not only as a story about demographic changes and strictly partisan politics but also as a story about the sociohistorical racialized legacies of places, in particular the legislating of mobility. I am not arguing that undocumented immigrants are the same as people escaping chattel slavery. However, the evidence suggests that the historical racialized legacy of this country and of particular localities is linked with the current immigration enforcement regime, as it is also founded on racialized power (white supremacy) through social control. The historical legacies of both sanctuary jurisdictions and those with "show me your papers" laws play a role in their policies and the factors that have led to the successful passage of restrictive immigration laws. In conjunction with affective partisanship, the historical processes of race and the differing ways in which places get racialized influence whether representatives support restrictive immigration policies. Immigration policy continues to be a vehicle for contesting the politics of whiteness and, by association, power, by way of legislating mobility.

In this chapter, I examine roll call votes of elected representatives on restrictive (anti-sanctuary) and non-restrictive (sanctuary) immigration legislation.[3] The intervening mechanism between individual opinion and collective action on an issue is electoral, the election and re-election of the state legislature. I home in on district-level factors that might be associated with those decisions. I first provide information about all states' ideologies and the tone of their immigration policies and then select several states as case studies that have passed anti-sanctuary and pro-sanctuary policies.

For the states selected, I examine the roll call votes and link representatives back to the constituencies they serve. Focusing on roll call votes allows me to emphasize the link between how whiteness operates at the individual level, by means of vote choice for representatives, and how it operates at the institutional state level, by way of elected representatives. Political actors create meaning and frame debates. Their meaning-making power comes into play when new legislation is introduced. The sponsors and co-sponsors of the legislation and the debates and meetings about legislative language all produce meaning. The legislation itself is ultimately a meaning-making document, in which those who are advantaged and those who are disadvantaged are given a frame, a body, characteristics, and visible and invisible markers (i.e., meaning). Policing, in this case policing movement, performs a foundational role in assigning racial meaning, which produces whiteness as the subject of protection, of maintenance, and blackness (or non-whiteness) as an object of regulation (Burton, 2015).

This chapter's focus on the relationship between the passage of state-level immigration legislation and whiteness illustrates the moral and political project of whiteness. This project is enacted at the individual level, where whites make (im)moral choices to support or oppose immigration policy and whites' equally (im)moral choices of elected officials (elites) that serve a major role in the continuation of the racial status quo. The focus on how elites are voting at the state level links individual whites with how the status quo gets maintained through elected officials whose role is to represent the people that elected them. As with the Fugitive Slave Law of 1850, the state has a role in the maintenance of whiteness. This chapter focuses on this maintenance as it occurs at the state level and in relationship to the connection between partisanship and whiteness.

The "New" Immigration Federalism

In 1994, California, a state generally perceived as open-minded and racially progressive, led the way in state-level restrictive immigration legislation when it passed Proposition 187. Had it gone into effect instead of being the subject of a court injunction three days after its passage and declared unconstitutional the following month, Proposition 187 would have denied all undocumented immigrants access to public benefits, education, and health services; required public employees to report anyone applying for benefits (including students enrolling in school or patients seeking care at a hospital) they suspected of being an undocumented immigrant to law enforcement; and required law enforcement officials to report such individuals to the federal Immigration and Naturalization Services (INS)[4] (Hosang, 2010, chap. 6). While the law never went into effect, it paved the way for the federal 1996 Illegal Immigration Reform and Immigrant Responsibility Act (IIRIRA), which included many of Proposition 187's provisions including limiting or cutting social services to undocumented individuals, and the Personal

Responsibility and Work Opportunity Reconciliation Act (PRWORA), which further restricted social benefits for non-citizen immigrant women.

Between 2005 and 2009 six states enacted omnibus bills on immigration, including Georgia's Senate Bill (SB) 529 and House Bill (HB) 2, Nebraska's Legislative Bill (LB) 403, Oklahoma's HB 1804, Missouri's HB 1549 and HB 390, South Carolina's HB 4400, and Utah's SB 81. Many of the bills had similar provisions. In Missouri, for example, the law requires state highway patrol to be trained to enforce immigration law and the reporting of individuals arrested for being unlawfully present in the United States. South Carolina's HB 4400 includes providing civil cause of action for a terminated authorized employee if replaced by an unauthorized employee, requiring a Memorandum of Agreement (MOA) with the Department of Homeland Security (DHS), and making it a felony to "harbor, transport, or conceal" unauthorized immigrants. Utah's SB 81 states that local governments may not prohibit law enforcement officers from cooperating and communicating with federal immigration officials. Finally, Nebraska's LB 403 focuses primarily on employment and verification of work eligibility.

Arizona's SB 1070 (and the later amended policy HB 2162) gained more national attention than legislation prior to it, including Proposition 187. Enacted in 2010, SB 1070 criminalizes being in the country illegally; grants police power to stop and verify the immigration status of anyone they *suspect* of being an undocumented immigrant; and makes sheltering, hiring, and/or transporting undocumented immigrants illegal. The legal battle that ensued after the passage of SB 1070 maintained the "show your papers" provision, enshrining racial profiling of Latinos in law, but struck down the other provisions, maintaining violations of criminal law as strictly civil violations and eliminating the provisions criminalizing interactions with undocumented immigrants by citizens and documented individuals.[5] By March 2011, at least 16 states were trying to pass copycat bills. These measures failed in California, Florida, Illinois, Maine, Michigan, Mississippi, North Carolina, and Ohio, among others (see the National Conference on State Legislature; Wessler, 2011), but Alabama (HB 56), Georgia (HB 87), South Carolina (SB 20), Indiana (SB 590), and Utah (HB 497) all have "show me your papers" provisions.

Many of these omnibus laws also included anti-sanctuary measures that required localities to enforce immigration law and work with federal authorities to do so. Table 5.1 lists the states that were able to pass state-level anti-sanctuary legislation (not cities or localities) as well as states that passed

Table 5.1 Sanctuary and Anti-Sanctuary State Policies

Sanctuary			Anti-Sanctuary		
State	Year	Bill	State	Year	Bill
California	2017	S 54	Alabama	2011	H 56[a]
Colorado	2019	H 1124	Arkansas	2019	S 411
Connecticut	2019	S 992	Florida	2019	S 168
Illinois	2017	S 31	Georgia	2006	S 529
				2011	H 87
Massachusetts	2017	*Lunn vs. Commonwealth*, 477 Mass. 517[c]	Indiana	2011	S 590[b]
New Jersey	2018	Immigrant Trust Directive NO. 2018-6 v2.0	Iowa	2018	SF 481
New York	2019	Green Light Law[d]	Mississippi	2017	S 2710[e]
Oregon	1987	1987 c.467 §1; 2003 c.571 §1[f]	Missouri	2008	H 1549
				2009	H 390
Vermont	2017	S 79	North Carolina	2018	N.C. Gen. Stat. §§ 153A-145.5, 160A-205.2
Washington	2019	S 5497	Oklahoma	2007	H 1804
			South Carolina	2011	S 20
			Tennessee	2009	H 1354
				2018	H 2315
			Texas	2017	S 4
			Utah	2008	S 81
				2011	H 497

[a] See AL Code § 31-13-22 (2018).

[b] See IN Code § 5-2-18.2-7 (2018).

[c] In 1986, Massachusetts' governor issued an executive order.

[d] In 1986, the New York State Assembly passed a resolution declaring the state a sanctuary for refugees from El Salvador and Guatemala.

[e] See MS Code § 25-1-119 (2018).

[f] ORS 181.850.

pro-sanctuary legislation between 1980 and 2019. These are either House or Senate bills or court-ordered legislation, excluding proclamations or executive orders. In the broadest definition, pro-sanctuary policies require non-cooperation with federal authorities on several immigration-related enforcement issues. For example, New York allows undocumented immigrants to get driver's licenses and stops the sharing of data with federal agencies. This is narrower than California's SB 54 which prevents state and local law enforcement agencies from using their resources on behalf of federal immigration enforcement agencies. Oregon's sanctuary policy has been on the books since 1987, while other states have passed theirs more recently. This chapter focuses directly on contemporary immigration sanctuary and anti-sanctuary policies as examples of two different responses to the surveillance and control of non-white bodies through policy.[6]

What factors contribute to some states passing pro-sanctuary policies while others pass anti-sanctuary and restrictive omnibus immigration legislation? A myriad of explanations around this "new" immigration federalism exists, namely demographic changes, partisanship, or a combination of the two. What follows is a brief overview of these top two narratives as well as a previously overlooked concept, sociohistorical racial legacies as part and parcel of affective partisan alignments.

Narratives Explaining the "New" Immigration Federalism

Demographic Changes

Starting in 2005, scholars as well as journalists tried to make sense of the proliferation of state-level restrictive immigration laws across the country. One narrative that began to appear in the headlines as well as scholarly work was based on the demographic changes happening across the country in places labeled "new immigrant destinations" (Hopkins, 2010; Newman, 2012; Newman, Johnson, Strickland, & Citrin, 2012; Ramakrishnan, 2005; Ramakrishnan & Baldassare, 2004; Sabia, 2010). The U.S. South, in particular, has seen a dramatic growth in new immigrants—most prominently Latino immigrants—and a reshaping of the demographics, such that people have been referencing "the *nuevo* New South" (Mohl, 2002; Winders, 2007). Immigrants are not migrating to well-known immigrant hubs like New York City, Los Angeles, and Chicago, but have begun to spread across the United States and into new destinations like Alabama and South Carolina. Of the top 10 immigrant-receiving states with the highest immigrant population growth between 2000 and 2010, seven are Southern states (Camarota, 2012). A myriad of scholarship has focused on the effect of changes vis-à-vis immigrant population since 2000, and especially post Arizona's SB 1070 (Marquez

& Schraufnagel, 2013; Monogan, 2013; Wallace, 2014). Between 2010 and 2019, top immigrant-receiving states included South and North Dakota, Kentucky, Delaware, and South Carolina.

Contact and threat theories serve as competing alternatives hypothesizing the effects of demographic changes, especially the influence of increasing immigrant and foreign-born populations in a particular locality, on immigration policy preferences (Allport, 1954; Key, 1949). The racial threat hypothesis indicates that higher levels of an outgroup will increase restrictive policy preferences, while the contact theory suggests the opposite—that increased contact between ingroup and outgroup members will increase sanctuary policy preferences. The evidence, however, has been mixed. Some scholars find no relationship between immigration populations and attitudes toward that group (Citrin et al., 1997; Scheve & Slaughter, 2001). The results are mixed even among those who do find significant findings; in some cases proximity to Asian Americans or Latinas/os has a positive influence on progressive immigration policy (Hood & Morris, 1997), and in others it leads to hostility (Ha, 2010). However, several theories have helped explain the mixed results. For instance, the scholarship on proximal contact differentiates the type of contact one has with outgroups, whether a loved one or an acquaintance (Ellison, Shin, & Leal, 2011; Walker, 2020). Other scholarship also focuses on the nature of prejudice (Dixon, 2006), the geographical unit (Enos, 2017), population size versus growth (Hopkins, 2010), and levels of segregation (Arora, 2020; Oliver & Wong, 2003; Rocha & Espino, 2009).

The full story, I argue, is not found in demographic changes, especially since we observe the full range of outcomes: Some states decided not to pass restrictive legislation, plenty of states tried to pass it but were not able to, and still others enacted integrationist immigration legislation.[7] These differences do not align with demographic changes. In fact, research shows that outgroup size measures positively influence both restrictive and progressive immigration policy preferences, while population growth yields no results (Filindra, 2019).

Partisanship

According to Pratheepan Gulasekaram and Karthick Ramakrishnan (2015), state-level immigration restriction did not arise due to immigrants moving to *new* destinations (i.e., demographic changes) but rather from immigrants moving into Republican-heavy destinations. The authors argue that partisanship is at the center of subnational immigration law. In their work, the authors find that partisanship has strong and consistent effects on restrictive immigration laws. More specifically, Republican-heavy states and localities are more likely to propose restrictive ordinances and more likely to pass such ordinances than Democratic-heavy places. Marisa Abrajano and Zoltan Hajnal (2015) argue that the public's views on immigration predicts individual defections from the Democratic Party to the Republican Party. However, Abrajano and Hajnal also argue that both immigrant population size and growth are part of the larger conversation about how immigration has led to "white backlash," a deviation from Gulasekaram and Ramakrishnan, who argue for partisanship's exclusive role. Overall, partisanship plays a role in the proliferation of state-level immigration laws (Ramakrishnan & Wong, 2010).

The role of history, and more specifically, of historical legacies of particular places at particular times vis-à-vis the proliferation of state- and local-level immigration laws, however, has not been sufficiently examined. Furthermore, partisanship's racialized and affective nature has not been properly incorporated into understandings of its effect on immigration restrictive attitudes (García Bedolla & Haynie, 2013; Mason, 2018; Weller & Junn, 2018).

Historical Racial Legacy

How do historical legacies of race relations play a role in contemporary immigration politics and policy? An increasing number of scholarly works focus on the significance of racial legacy on contemporary political behavior. For example, the political legacy of slavery continues to affect contemporary attitudes. White Americans who currently live in Southern counties that had high shares of slaves in 1860 are less likely to identify as Democrat, more likely to oppose affirmative action policies, and more likely to express racial resentment toward Blacks than their counterparts in Southern counties that had lower shares of slaves (Acharya et al., 2016). Avidit Acharya and colleagues' (2016) work exemplifies how the historical legacy of slavery and racism influences contemporary political outcomes. Racism has played and continues to play a significant role in shaping attitudes toward foreigners (Higham, 1958) and immigration policies (Tichenor, 2002).

Debra Sabia (2010) highlights that a Republican from the predominately white suburban county of Cherokee introduced Georgia's restrictive immigration law SB 529.[8] I concur with her that this is no accident. Contemporary homogenous white spaces are not void of history. Race and space have combined over time to create the contemporary geography of U.S. cities and suburbs (Jackson, 1985; Katz, 1993; Massey & Denton, 1993; Sugrue, 1996), and that history continues to play a significant role in race relations today. Predominately homogenous white spaces tend to be less tolerant (Cain, Citrin, & Wong, 2000), which indicates a convergence of whiteness, partisanship, racism, and place rather than simply demographic changes or partisanship. The history of racial segregation, redlining, racial covenants, and white flight foreground the existence of predominately white spaces. Hence, the historical racialized legacy of places may drive the proliferation of sanctuary and anti-sanctuary and restrictive immigration laws in certain states, as I hypothesize here.

Information on Data

This chapter uses case studies to delve more deeply into the passage of state-level immigration law. The first step was to obtain data from all 50 states on restrictive and progressive immigration laws, as well as state-level ideology.[9] The data came from James Monogan's (2011) replication data for his 2013 article covering immigration-related enacted legislation from 2005 through 2011. The dataset includes 1,637 pieces of legislation drawn from the National Conference of State Legislatures immigration database.[10] I used a modified version of Monogan's weighted count measure, which takes into consideration the impact of immigration legislation, and created a histogram of independent variables based on the immigration tone of each state, which considers both restrictive and progressive immigration legislation. I modified the weighted count measure by eliminating all symbolic legislation to gauge immigration bills that had an enforcement mechanism and went beyond being performative by creating committees and similar provisions and legislation. The key alternative independent variable is state-level ideology obtained by averaging the 2000–2009 estimates of the ideal points of lower and upper chamber medians reported by Shor and McCarty (2011). I compared states that passed anti-sanctuary policies (often included in their omnibus immigration law) and states that passed state-level sanctuary based on states listed in Table 5.1. For the purposes of the analysis, I selected states that passed their anti-sanctuary and sanctuary legislation through their state legislature rather than via court cases or directives. Figure 5.1 presents the distribution of ideology.

My selection mechanism included selecting states on both sides (sanctuary and anti-sanctuary) that varied in ideology as much as possible. The universe of available states is constrained to the states that have been able to pass state-level immigration legislation—excluding cities, counties, or localities that have passed similar legislation. There is greater ideological diversity among states that have been able to pass sanctuary policies than among states that have passed restrictive or anti-sanctuary policies. I also tried to choose states that varied in the proportion of the immigrant population. For example, both California and Texas have a large immigrant population while Vermont and Alabama have very small immigrant populations. Overall, the states selected represent a varied sample that can reveal different patterns.

This chapter draws on data from various sources to obtain lower chamber district roll call votes for selected states that passed anti-sanctuary and sanctuary immigration laws after 2010. First, I obtained the roll call votes from each of the official state legislature websites. I then created an Excel sheet with the roll call vote, the name of the representative during the appropriate

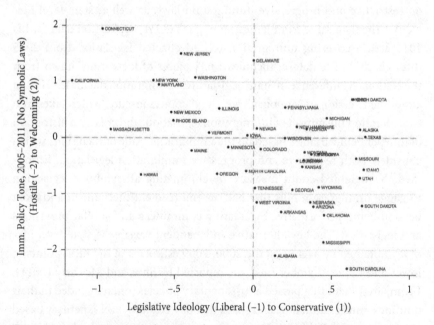

Figure 5.1 Immigration Policy Tone by State and Legislative Ideology

congressional session, the party of the legislator, and the district represented at the time of the vote. It is important to note that I used the roll call vote for the first official passage of the bill in the lower House, often after the third reading, rather than votes on individual amendments between the lower and upper chambers. I then merged this data with data from the American Community Surveys (5-Year Estimates) from Social Explorer.[11] I used the appropriate year to align with the passage of the laws. From the Census website, I downloaded TIGER/Line Lower Chamber shapefiles[12] for each state and merged the community and legislative data with the shapefile[13] using R statistical software to create the map visualizations. The maps were created using GeoDa.[14]

By examining the roll call votes we can extend our understanding of immigration politics. Specifically, we can trace the link between demographics, partisanship, and race at the legislative level by examining the racial and ethnic population that legislators represent and how these legislators vote on immigration-related laws. Examining the racial and ethnic makeup of the districts is useful in that it says something about the convergence of demography and geography; what a place looks like is connected to the history of that place. U.S. geography cannot be understood without also understanding U.S. imperialism and racism. Localities carry with them distinct and sometimes similar historical legacies that can explain, in part, the geography of subnational immigration laws.

Anti-Sanctuary Policies

Table 5.2 shows the legislative roll call votes of the selected states that have enacted anti-sanctuary legislation. The table includes the votes in support

Table 5.2 Selected Anti-Sanctuary Legislative Roll Call Votes

Year	State	Bill	Yea	Nay	Absent	Abstain
2011	Alabama	H 56	73	28	2	1
2011	Indiana	S 590	64	32	4	0
2011	South Carolina	S 20	65	39	3	17
2017	Texas	S 4	94	53	2	1
2011	Utah	H 497	59	15	1	0

for (yea) and in opposition to (nay) the respective legislation in addition to the votes counted as absent or excused and those who chose to abstain from voting. What follows is an examination of district-level roll call votes, demographics, and partisanship.

District-Level Demographics and Vote Choice

In South Carolina, House members representing districts with higher percentages of the foreign-born ($t = -3.49$ [102], $p = 0.001$) and the Latino population ($t = -2.32$ [102], $p = 0.02$) were more likely to vote for the restrictive immigration bill. In Alabama, the results are similar for the foreign-born ($t = -2.36$ [99], $p = 0.02$) and the Latino population ($t = -2.34$ [99], $p = 0.000$). In addition, in both states, members representing districts with higher percentages of naturalized foreign-born individuals were more likely to vote in the affirmative. However, only a weak to moderate correlation exists between voting to support the restrictive legislation and the percentage of the foreign-born and Latino population. In Alabama, the correlation between vote choice (yea vote) and foreign-born population is 0.23, $p = 0.02$. The same is the case for the Latino population in both Alabama (0.23, $p = 0.02$) and South Carolina (0.22, $p = 0.02$). In South Carolina, the correlation between vote choice (yea vote) and the foreign-born population is moderate at 0.33, $p = 0.001$. Although significant, these numbers indicate a weak to moderate association.

In Indiana, Utah, and Texas, in districts with higher percentages of foreign-born and Latino populations, representatives were more likely to vote against the respective immigration state bills. In Indiana, the results indicate a statistically significant difference between the mean percentage of Latinos in the legislative districts whose representatives voted yes on SB 590 and legislative districts whose representatives voted no on SB 590 ($t = 5.51$ [94], $p = 0.000$). In other words, those who voted no had a statistically significantly higher percentage of Latinos in their legislative district (9.96%) than those who voted yes (4.11%). The same is the case for the percentage of foreign-born by lower chamber district ($t = 3.88$ [94], $p = 0.000$). In Texas, the same pattern is present for both the foreign-born ($t = 8.13$ [145], $p = 0.000$) and the Latino population ($t = 12.94$ [145], $p = 0.000$). In Utah, the results indicate a statistically significant difference between the mean percentage of foreign-born in the legislative districts whose representatives voted yes on HB 497 and legislative districts whose representatives voted no on HB 497 ($t = 4.04$ [94], $p = 0.000$). However, the results for the percentage of the Latino population did not reach significance at the .05 level ($t = 1.84$ [72], $p = 0.07$). In all these states, except for Utah, the correlation between the Latino population and vote choice is moderate (Indiana) to strong (Texas).

These results indicate that demographic changes and diversity may account for some aspects of restrictive state-level immigration legislation in some states, but not others. In Indiana and Utah, lower percentages of foreign-born and the Latino population worked in the opposite direction. For some representatives, foreign-born and Latino populations decreased the likelihood that they voted for the state omnibus legislation. The political effects of demographic differences, then, are not uniform across states.

District-Level Party Affiliation and Vote Choice

Ample evidence shows the significance of partisanship on state-level politics and in particular immigration-related state- and local-level politics. Generally, Republican-led states jumped on the Arizona SB 1070 bandwagon more often than Democratic-led states. These results concur with the literature on partisanship; it matters. Importantly, not all conservative states during this time were able to enact state-level anti-sanctuary immigration legislation. In fact, many conservative states introduced bills but were unable to pass them (see Wallace, 2014), including Colorado, Florida, Michigan, Mississippi, and Pennsylvania. States that introduced an SB 1070–like bill with anti-sanctuary measures were predominately Republican, but Democratic or split-controlled states also introduced such bills, and some Republican-controlled states did not introduce such bills at all. Partisanship is important and not the only part of the story.

The first thing I ran was a Fisher's exact test, which indicates that partisanship is significant in the assumed ideological direction. That is, in all states, Republicans are more likely to vote for the restrictive immigration legislation, while Democrats are less likely to vote in the affirmative.[15] In all states, the correlation between vote choice and party is statistically significant; the extent to which legislator party identification accounts for the variation varies slightly by state.

In South Carolina, the correlation coefficient describing the relationship between vote choice and party identification is high, at 0.98. South Carolina had 17 members not voting and three absences. The Pearson correlation does not account for the 20 members who did not cast a vote. Seven of those not voting were Democrats and 10 were Republicans; one excused absence was Democrat and two were Republicans. The high number of House members who did not vote makes South Carolina different from other states, especially because the non-voting members include both Democrats and Republicans. The explanation for this lack of voting is not clear.

An examination of employment and industry occupation in South Carolina does not provide an explanation for the abstentions. Compared to members who voted for SB 20, those who did not vote have a statistically significant higher percentage of employed civilian population 16 years and over in the "farming, fishing and forestry" ($t = -2.23$ [80], $p = 0.03$) and "building and grounds cleaning and maintenance" ($t = -2.36$ [80], $p = 0.02$) occupations. While more of the abstainers are Republicans, Democrats drive these results because their districts are particularly high in these professions. This makes little intuitive sense, since these Democratic members could have voted to oppose a bill that does not align with their national party platform and that would make it harder for farmers to obtain labor; it seems odd that they would choose not to cast a vote at all. South Carolina shows a slightly significant difference of means between the seven Democrats who did not cast a vote and those who did in relation to the percentage of non-Hispanic whites in their district. The seven non-voting districts controlled by Democrats had a slightly higher percentage of whites than districts controlled by Democrats who did cast a ballot ($t = 1.95$ [43], $p = 0.058$). Considering what we have learned about white Democrats in previous chapters, the presence of more white constituents might have pushed these elected Democrats to abstain from voting. In South Carolina, although party identification was associated with support for or opposition to the restrictive immigration law, it is not perfectly associated. South Carolina is depicted in Figure 5.2.

The same pattern holds in Utah where party is a strong and significant predictor of support or opposition to immigration bills ($r = 0.92$), and there was only one absent vote. The pattern is stronger in Texas. For example, the Pearson correlation coefficient is 1.00 in Texas, describing the relationship between vote choice and party identification perfectly. Texas had only one non-voter, a Republican, and two absent votes, both Democrats.

Finally, the Pearson correlation coefficient between partisanship and vote choice in Alabama is 0.75 and in Indiana is 0.60, which indicates that partisanship does not perfectly explain vote choice on HB 56 and SB 590,

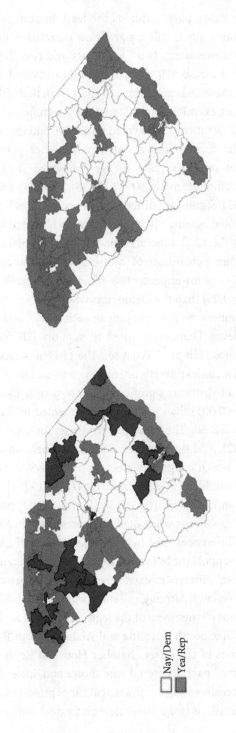

Party

Vote

☐ Nay/Dem
■ Yea/Rep

Figure 5.2 South Carolina Vote Choice and Party Identification of House Members

Note: Dark gray districts indicate absent or abstentions.

respectively. Of all the states, party explains the least amount of variation on vote choice in Indiana, albeit still a significant correlation (see Figure 5.3). Indiana saw four abstentions, two Democrats and two Republicans. Twelve Democrats voted for SB 590 and six Republicans voted against SB 590. Does anything set these 18 representatives apart from their fellow party identifiers? After further examination, a statistically significant difference emerges between the 12 Democrats who voted for SB 590 and the Democrats who voted against: The former had a statistically higher percentage of the civilian population over 16 years of age employed in agriculture ($t = -2.43$ [38], $p = 0.02$), manufacturing ($t = 2.13$ [38], $p = 0.04$), and farming ($t = -1.98$ [38], $p = 0.055$). Significant differences in occupations between the six Republicans who voted against SB 590 and those who voted for SB 590 also exist. Importantly, the 12 Democrats who voted for SB 590 in Indiana had a statistically higher percentage of non-Hispanic white population ($t = -2.36$ [38], $p = 0.02$) and lower percentage of non-Hispanic Black population ($t = 2.01$ [38], $p = 0.05$) than the Democrats who voted against SB 590.

In Alabama, two members did not vote (one in each party), and one voted absent (Democrat). Eleven Democrats voted to support HB 56 and one Republican voted to oppose HB 56.[16] What sets the 11 Democratic districts supporting HB 56 apart includes poverty, unemployment, and manufacturing and farming. In these 11 districts, significantly more people lived in poverty ($t = -3.65$ [71], $p = 0.001$) than in districts represented by Republicans who also voted yes on HB 56. The same pattern exists for unemployment ($t = -3.25$ [71], $p = 0.002$). Additionally, Democratic members who voted yes represented districts in which a higher percentage of the civilian population over 16 years of age was employed in manufacturing ($t = -3.13$ [71], $p = 0.003$) and "farming, fishing, and forestry" ($t = -2.38$ [71], $p = 0.02$) occupations than the districts that Republicans who voted yes represented. In all cases, no statistically significant differences exist between the districts of Democratic members who voted to support the bill versus those who voted against it.

At the subnational level differences exist across states that passed restrictive omnibus immigration laws. Although all states leaned Republican during the time of the voting, not all members of the legislature voted as their party would expect. In states like South Carolina and Alabama, both Republican and Democratic members of the lower chamber House of Representatives defected from the assumed party-centered vote choice and, instead, decided not to vote or to abstain from voting, tactics that at times prove to be political and not just personal decisions (for an overview on tactical voting see Riera,

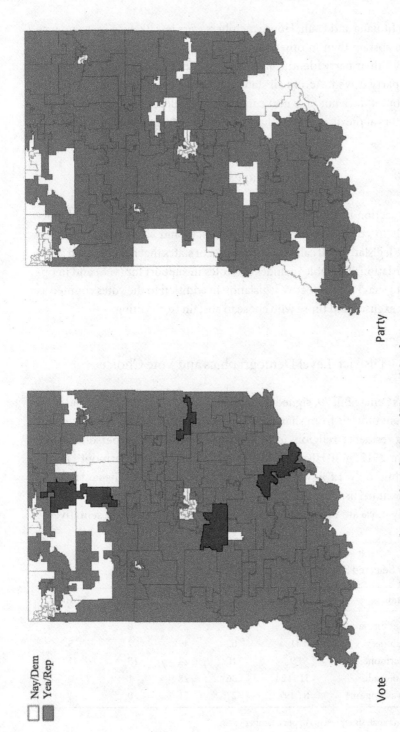

Party

Vote

Figure 5.3 Indiana Vote Choice and Party Identification of House Members

Note: Dark gray districts indicate absent or abstentions.

Nay/Dem

Yea/Rep

2016). In Indiana and Utah, House members were less likely to cast a no vote and/or to abstain than in other states. Finally, in Texas, all members voted in line with their party identification, making Texas politics stand out as ultimately party driven. Across all states, party identification of the legislator matters, but it does not take into consideration defections, abstentions, and other factors at the district level, namely the constituencies represented.

Sanctuary Policies

The next section uses the same methods to analyze states that passed sanctuary bills to compare district-level differences and similarities. Table 5.3 shows the legislative roll call votes of a subset of states that have enacted sanctuary legislation. The table includes the votes in support for (yea) and in opposition to (nay) the respective legislation in addition to the votes counted as absent or excused and those who chose to abstain from voting.

District-Level Demographics and Vote Choice

Vermont's Senate Bill 79, signed on March 28, 2017, prohibits state and local government officials from sharing information with the federal government regarding residents' religion, immigration status, and other personal information. In 2017, non-Hispanic whites made up 93.2% of Vermont's population, while only 1.8% were Hispanic/Latino, 1.2% non-Hispanic Black, and 1.5% non-Hispanic Asian. Most of the state is native-born (95.5%), while only 4.5% are foreign-born. The Vermont House of Representatives is

Table 5.3 Selected Sanctuary Legislative Roll Call Votes

Year	State	Bill	Yea	Nay	Absent	Abstain
2017	California	S 54	51	26	0	2
2017	Illinois	S 31	62	49	2	5
2017	Vermont	S 79	110	24	15	1
2019	Colorado	H 1124	36	28	1	0
2019	Washington[a]	S 5497	27	21	0	1

[a] Washington's analysis represents upper chamber votes.

unusual in that the districts are represented by one or two members. I provide results here only for the lower chamber given that the Vermont Senate voted 30-0 for the bill. The Senate then comprised seven Republicans, all of whom voted in the affirmative. The lower chamber voted on and passed SB 79 on March 14, 2017. An examination of all districts in the House reveals that those who voted for the sanctuary bill represented districts with slightly fewer non-Hispanic whites ($t = 2.53$ [132], $p = 0.013$), slightly more Latinos of any race ($t = -1.92$ [132], $p = 0.06$) and Black Americans ($t = -1.85$ [132], $p = 0.07$), more Asians ($t = -2.51$ [132], $p = 0.013$), and a higher foreign-born population ($t = -2.29$ [132], $p = 0.02$). An examination of only the 60 districts with one member (37 of which were represented by Democrats/Progressives, four by independents, and 19 by Republicans) does not yield significant differences across personal or district demographics and vote choice.

The Illinois TRUST Act, or SB 31, among many provisions, makes it illegal for a law enforcement agency or official to detain an individual solely based on an immigration detainer or warrant. In addition, it limits the sharing of information on individuals with immigration agents. In 2017, non-Hispanic whites made up 61.9% of the population, while non-Hispanic Black Americans made up 14.1%, Asians 5.2%, and Latinos 16.8%. About 14% of the population is foreign-born. Representatives who voted for the bill represented districts with lower percentages of non-Hispanic whites ($t = 13.88$ [109], $p = 0.000$) and higher percentages of Black Americans ($t = -5.88$ [109], $p = 0.000$), Latinos ($t = -6.03$ [109], $p = 0.000$), Asians ($t = -2.70$ [109], $p = 0.01$), and foreign-born populations ($t = -6.78$ [109], $p = 0.000$). House members who voted to pass a sanctuary bill represented much more diverse districts than those who voted to oppose the bill.

Colorado passed HB 1124 on April 23, 2019, with a 36-28 House vote. The law prohibits law enforcement from arresting or detaining individuals solely based on an immigration detainer and prohibits a probation officer or department employee from providing personal information to federal immigration authorities. However, it does allow for the execution of a warrant issued by a federal judge or magistrate. Contextually, in 2018, Colorado was 68.3% non-Hispanic white, 3.9% Black American, 3.1% Asian, and 21.4% Latino. An overwhelming majority of Colorado is native-born (90.2%). House representatives who voted for the bill served districts with lower percentages of non-Hispanic whites ($t = 4.82$ [62], $p = 0.000$) and higher percentages of Black Americans ($t = -2.50$ [62], $p = 0.02$), Asians ($t = -2.25$ [62], $p = 0.03$), Latinos ($t = -4.21$ [62], $p = 0.000$), and foreign-born populations ($t = -4.06$

[62], $p = 0.000$). The pattern found in Illinois is the same in Colorado. House members with more diverse districts and lower percentages of non-Hispanic whites vote for the sanctuary bill.

On April 12, 2019, Washington's upper chamber voted to pass SB 5497 (27-21). Washington's lower chamber has multiple representatives per district, so to examine votes by district, I focused on upper chamber votes.[17] The policy, among other provisions, authorized the state attorney general to publish model policies for limiting immigration enforcement to the fullest extent possible under federal law at public schools, health facilities, courthouses, and shelters. Additionally, it prohibits state agencies, including law enforcement, from using state funds, facilities, property, equipment, or personnel to investigate, enforce, cooperate with, or assist in the investigation of enforcement of federal registration or surveillance programs that target residents on the basis of race, religion, immigration, or citizenship status. In 2018, the state of Washington was 69.1% non-Hispanic white, 3.6% Black American, 8.3% Asian, and 12.5% Latino. Washington's population in 2018 was 86% native-born and 14% foreign-born. In 2019, senators who voted for the bill had lower percentages of non-Hispanic whites ($t = 2.07$ [46], $p = 0.04$) and Latinos ($t = 2.36$ [46], $p = 0.02$) and higher percentages of Black Americans ($t = -2.90$ [46], $p = 0.01$), Asians ($t = -5.28$ [46], $p = 0.000$), and foreign-born populations ($t = -3.79$ [46], $p = 0.000$), compared to senators who voted in opposition. Again, the pattern remains except for Latinos. Given that the upper-level districts are larger, the results for Latinos might be due to district size.

On September 15, 2017, the California lower chamber voted to pass SB 54 (51-26). The law repeals existing law that allows an arresting agency to notify DHS when there is reason to believe that the arrestee is undocumented. The law, among other provisions, also prohibits state and local law enforcement agencies, including school police and security departments, from using resources to investigate, interrogate, detain, or arrest persons for immigration enforcement purposes. In 2017, California was a majority-minority state consisting of 37.9% non-Hispanic white, 5.5% Black American, 8.8% Asian, and 38.8% Latino of any race. Representatives who voted for the bill represented districts with lower percentages of whites ($t = 4.54$ [75], $p = 0.000$), slightly more Black Americans ($t = -1.95$ [75], $p = 0.06$), slightly more Asians ($t = -1.68$ [75], $p = 0.10$), more Latinos ($t = -2.55$ [75], $p = 0.01$), and higher percentages of foreign-born populations ($t = -5.76$ [75], $p = 0.000$).

Generally, representatives who voted for the sanctuary bills served constituencies that were less white and more diverse, while those who voted against the bills served more non-Hispanic whites. In Vermont, however, because the state itself is predominately white, the results are not significant when examining only single-member districts.

District-Level Party Affiliation and Vote Choice

In Vermont, 25 self-identified Republicans, six independents, and all Democrats and Progressives voted for the sanctuary bill. Twenty-four Republicans voted against the bill. Republicans who voted for the bill had slightly more Asians in their district ($t = -2.21$ [47], $p = 0.03$), while no other demographic group reaches statistical significance in Republican-led districts. To better understand the split in Republican voting, I examined the difference in means by industry. I found that Republicans who voted against SB 79 had higher numbers of employed civilian population in the agriculture ($t = 3.38$ [47], $p = 0.001$) and manufacturing ($t = 2.24$ [47], $p = 0.03$) industries. This makes sense for Republican representatives who believe that immigrants threaten American jobs in their district in these immigrant-heavy industries. Finally, Republicans who voted yes represented districts with higher levels of poverty ($t = -2.12$ [47], $p = 0.04$). An examination of only the single-member districts reveals non-significant findings other than the 19 Republicans representing slightly more non-Hispanic whites ($t = -1.74$ [57], $p = 0.09$).

The Illinois lower chamber voted and passed SB 31 on May 29, 2017, with a 62-49 vote. Figure 5.4 depicts two maps of Illinois by lower chamber districts. The left-hand map illustrates vote choice, while the right-hand map shows party affiliation of the representative. Most Democratic representatives voted for the sanctuary state law, while most Republican representatives voted against it. The correlation between vote choice and party affiliation is high and significant ($\chi^2 = (1, N = 111) = 91.81$, $p = 0.000$). It does not account for five non-voting members, including four Republicans and one Democrat, two of whom were excused absences. Four Democrats voted against the bill and one Republican voted for SB 31. According to the data, the four Democrats who voted against the bill represented a larger percentage of non-Hispanic whites ($t = 3.52$ [63], $p = 0.001$), a lower percentage of Latinos ($t = -1.85$ [63], $p = 0.07$), and a lower percentage of foreign-born ($t = -2.72$ [63], $p = 0.01$)

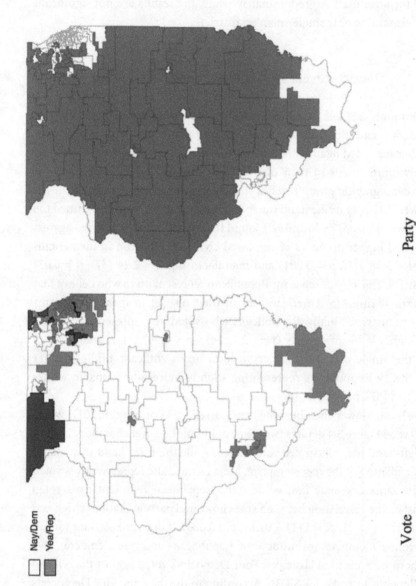

Vote   Party

Figure 5.4 Illinois Vote Choice and Party Identification of House Members

Note: Dark gray districts indicate absent votes and abstentions.

than Democrats who voted in the affirmative. Republicans who did not cast a ballot represented districts with lower percentages of non-Hispanic whites (t = 3.45 [47], p = 0.001) and higher percentages of Latinos (t = -1.98 [47], p = 0.05), Asians (t = -2.71 [47], p = 0.01), and foreign-born population (t = -2.32 [47], p = 0.025) compared to Republicans who voted against the bill.

Colorado displays a strong and significant correlation between party affiliation and vote choice (χ^2 = (1, N = 64) = 49.37, p = 0.000). Republican members represented higher percentages of non-Hispanic whites (t = -4.00 [63], p = 0.000) and lower percentages of Black Americans (t = 2.11 [63], p = 0.04), Asians (t = 2.68 [63], p = 0.01), Latinos (t = 3.28 [63], p = 0.001), and foreign-born populations (t = 4.44 [63], p = 0.000) compared to Democratic members. Four Democratic members voted against the bill, while no Republicans voted for the bill. The four Democrats who voted against the bill represented districts with higher percentages of non-Hispanic whites (t = 2.08 [38], p = 0.044) and lower percentages of Latinos (t = -2.07 [38], p = 0.05) than Democrats who voted in the affirmative. While partisanship remains important, the intersection of partisanship and constituent demographics are telling. Republicans represented more non-Hispanic whites and fewer diverse communities, while Democrats who voted with their Republican colleagues also represented larger percentages of non-Hispanic white Americans.

In Washington, one Democrat voted against the bill, while another Democrat did not cast a ballot. No Republicans voted for the bill. Vote choice and party correlate significantly (χ^2 = (1, N = 48) = 44.08, p = 0.000). Republicans represented slightly more non-Hispanic whites but the difference was not statistically significant at the 95% percent confidence interval (t = -1.63 [47], p = 0.11), more Latinos (t = -2.59 [47], p = 0.01), and fewer Black Americans (t = 2.62 [47], p = 0.01), Asians (t = 4.68 [47], p = 0.000), and foreign-born populations (t = 3.14 [57], p = 0.003).

California also exhibits a strong correlation between vote choice and party affiliation (χ^2 = (1, N = 77) = 68.39, p = 0.000). Two Democrats voted against the bill, while no Republicans voted for the bill. Republicans in California represented districts with higher percentages of non-Hispanic whites (t = -4.87 [77], p = 0.000), fewer Black Americans (t = 2.26 [77], p = 0.03), slightly fewer Asians (t = 1.66 [77], p = 0.10), and fewer Latinos (t = 2.71 [77], p = 0.01) and foreign-born populations (t = 5.65 [77], p = 0.000) compared to Democrats. In California, the association between party and all demographic groups is moderate and significant in the direction theorized in this chapter. In California, like Colorado and Illinois, the factors that significantly influence voting against the sanctuary bill are partisanship and representing non-Hispanic white constituents.

In all state legislatures, party affiliation matters. In addition, in California, Illinois, and Colorado, Republicans who voted against the sanctuary bill usually represented more non-Hispanic whites in their district, as did Democrats who voted against the bill. Generally, Republicans represent more non-Hispanic whites than do Democrats. Partisanship cannot be examined outside the realm of historical and contemporary race relations. The data make clear that partisanship implicates whiteness and power. In certain instances, namely in Vermont, the race of the constituents is not significant given that Vermont is over 90% white, leaving very little variation to examine. In Vermont, however, occupational industries are important factors to consider.

Individual to Collective Whiteness through Representation

Whiteness, and race more broadly, has influenced and continues to influence ideology. Conservatism and liberalism and their relationship to the Republican and Democratic Parties, respectively, are rooted in race relations in the United States. Any conversation about conservatism as it relates to the Republican Party inherently introduces a conversation about whiteness and race (Courtwright, 2013; García Bedolla & Haynie, 2013; Heersink & Jenkins, 2020a, 2020b, 2020c; Maxwell & Shields, 2019). A prime example is the Southern strategy. In the 1960s and 1970s, the Republican Party used the Southern strategy to increase the number of white voters in the South by appealing to racism against African Americans (Maxwell & Shields, 2019). The confluence of race and party is an association that continues to influence public opinion and political behavior. The partisan composition of the state legislature matters, but so does the history of how the Republican Party became known as the party of whites and the Democratic Party as the party of people of color. This history is integral in how we think about partisanship today.

For the selected states that passed anti-sanctuary bills, there is a significant association between the percentage of non-Hispanic whites in a district and the party identification of the legislator representing that district. In Alabama ($r = 0.73$, $p = 0.000$), Indiana ($r = 0.62$, $p = 0.000$), South Carolina ($r = 0.82$, $p = 0.000$), and Texas ($r = 0.85$, $p = 0.000$) the relationship is strong, whereas Utah ($r = 0.40$, $p = 0.000$) exhibits a more moderate relationship. Additionally, the difference of means is statistically significant between Republican-led districts and districts represented by Democrats in all states in the percentages of non-Hispanic white constituents (Utah, again, being the exception). Republicans controlled the Alabama, Indiana, South Carolina, Texas, and Utah state legislatures when the bills were signed into law.

In states that passed sanctuary legislation, the correlation between the percentage of non-Hispanic whites and vote choice is strong to moderate and significant: Illinois ($r = 0.76$, $p = 0.000$), Colorado ($r = 0.45$, $p = 0.000$), California ($r = 0.49$, $p = 0.000$).[18] The right-hand side map in Figure 5.5 illustrates the percentage of non-Hispanic whites in Illinois and makes visually clear the political power of whiteness, even in a state that passed a sanctuary bill. To the left is a map of Illinois by party affiliation of the representative and to the right is a map of Illinois's white population. Compared to the map on the left-hand side of Figure 5.5, predominately white districts are represented by Republicans. Further, most of these Republican representatives voted against a sanctuary bill.

The reverse in demographics and the elected representatives' partisan affiliation is also true. In these states higher levels of non-whites are negatively associated with Republican representation. In Illinois, for example, the association is negative between Republican representation and higher percentages of Black Americans ($r = -0.50$, $p = 0.000$), Latinos ($r = 0.46$, $p = 0.000$), Asians ($r = -0.18$, $p = 0.05$), and foreign-born populations ($r = -0.46$, $p = 0.000$). In Colorado, the associations between Republican representatives and all other groups are all negative, with the strongest association being between foreign-born and Republican members of the House ($r = -0.49$, $p = 0.000$). In California, the association between Republican representatives and all other groups, except Asians, are negative, with the strongest association again between foreign-born and Republican members of the House ($r = -0.54$, $p = 0.000$). Democrats controlled the California, Colorado, Illinois, Vermont, and Washington state legislatures. At the time of the signing of the sanctuary bills, Vermont and Illinois had Republican governors.

Individuals vote for their state senators and representatives; in doing so, their voting choices embody their own self-interests and thus their group interest (Brewer & Gardner, 1996; Tajfel & Turner, 1986; Turner, Oakes, Haslam, & McGarty, 1994). Voting for representatives is a utility-based political decision intricately attached to identity (Knuckey & Kim, 2020; Mason, 2018; Petrow et al., 2018; Weller & Junn, 2018). Figure 5.5 is indicative of

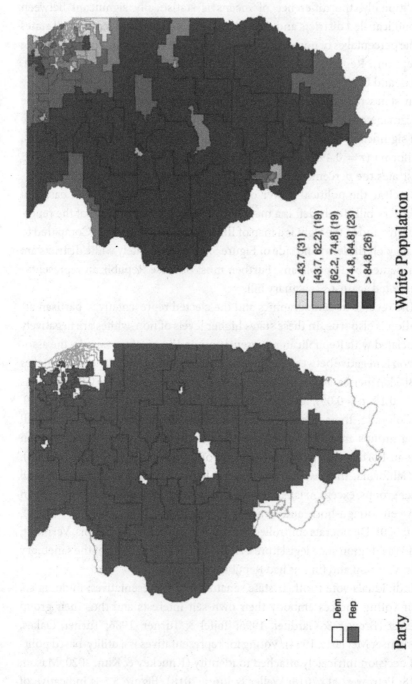

Figure 5.5 Illinois Party Affiliation and White Population

White Population

- < 43.7 (31)
- [43.7, 62.2) (19)
- [62.2, 74.8) (19)
- (74.8, 84.8) (23)
- > 84.8 (26)

Party

- Dem
- Rep

this conclusion. Elections reflect voters. Identity politics affect the behavior of white people as well as other groups (Eckhouse, 2018). Scholarship on racially polarized voting shows that whites are reluctant to vote for minority candidates (Ebonya, 2006; Keith, 1997; McDermott, 2016; Terkildsen, 1993), although the research produces mixed results (Sigelman, Sigelman, Walkosz, & Nitz, 1995). Abundant research shows that race matters when whites make electoral calculations (Hutchings & Valentino, 2004). Evidence also suggests that whites perceive white candidates to be less liberal than Black candidates even if both have similar policy positions, further indicating a strong association between whiteness and partisanship (Jacobsmeier, 2014). Furthermore, fearing racial favoritism, whites perceived Black elected officials as more likely to favor Blacks over whites (Goldman, 2017), which is an individual political attitude based on white identity and ideology. White identity and ingroup processes influence vote choice (Petrow et al., 2018; Weller & Junn, 2018).

Whiteness as the Historical Connection

The issue of federalism, of course, connects the Fugitive Slave Act of 1850 and present-day state-level responses to enforcing immigration. As scholars have argued, both the Fugitive Slave Act of 1850 and Arizona's SB 1070 demonstrate the failure of federalism (McKanders, 2012). The Fugitive Slave Act of 1850 was Congress's way of appeasing slaveholding Southern whites who were threatening to go to war to maintain chattel slavery. However, Southern whites' economy fueled by slavery would have diminished, if not been obliterated, by secession, given that Union states would not have had to comply with fugitive slave laws, increasing the precarity of the slave economy. Congress held that immigration, the movement of people, is a federal power but created a cooperative system between the federal government and states, much like the cooperative system in place today between federal, state, and local governments to enforce immigration law. Under the 1850 Act, Congress authorized judges to appoint commissioners with the powers to arrest, imprison, or bail offenders of any crime against the United States, and it deemed escaping slavery to be such a crime (Fugitive Slave Act of 1850, Sec. 3). The federal government swore in state and local officials, including city policemen in Massachusetts, to arrest Thomas Sims, an escapee from Georgia (McKanders, 2012). Ignoring Massachusetts' personal liberty law, officials arrested Sims and returned him to Georgia. Today, the federal government allows for agreements between federal and state/local governments to enforce federal immigration law under Section 287(g) of the Immigration and Nationality Act (INA). Section 287(g) is the legal foundation for 287(g) MOAs and for programs like Secure Communities (Matos, 2018a).[19] It also holds that ICE has the power to interrogate any person believed to be a noncitizen. "Show me your papers" provisions use similar language as Section 287(g), and supporters have argued that the federal government failed to follow these provisions and so states had to pick up the slack to enforce immigration law (Rodriguez, 2008).

The connection between the Fugitive Slave Law and present-day immigration enforcement goes beyond federalism, however. I argue that the maintenance of white supremacy and resistance to it is the thread across time and space. In the same way that the antebellum South wanted to maintain slavery as an economically profitable labor-based system through fugitive slave laws and by other more violent means, other localities actively protected fugitive slaves through legislation.[20] Historical parallels can be fraught and often even dangerous in the cooptation or pushing aside of African American history and continued struggle (see Finkelman, 1992). Yet we witness patterns in present-day immigration enforcement that clearly resemble those of the Fugitive Slave Law, in that states continue to enforce laws from their own racialized legacies of controlling non-white mobility (while they use the labor of non-whites—in this case, undocumented immigrants), while others pass state-level sanctuary policies instead. At the district level, in both sets of states—those that passed anti-sanctuary and those that passed pro-sanctuary legislation—representatives whose constituents were majority non-Hispanic whites voted for the anti-sanctuary measure, votes that restrict non-white mobility and maintain the racial status quo.

Conclusion

In essence, the foundation of immigration in the United States is intricately connected to the control of Black bodies, as well as *other* non-white bodies deemed incompetent or morally questionable (Abrams, 2005, 2009), for the purpose of maintaining white supremacy. Chattel slavery was a system for this purpose. Hence, racial legacy is rooted in and measured by the systems in place to preserve white primacy. The conservation of white supremacy happens through social control, by way of inclusion or exclusion.[21] Controlling human mobility is a tool of exclusion and part and parcel of not only federal immigration law but also state-level immigration law.[22] A more nuanced look at district-level state politics indicates that the districts represented by non-Hispanic whites are continuing this history of social control through immigration politics.

Numerical white dominance in electoral districts is not ahistorical. The representation of non-Hispanic whites and the numerical dominance of whites in certain districts alone does not signal the politics of whiteness. The legacy of racial segregation, white flight, redlining, and racial covenants alongside whites' continued preference for white candidates, who represent their self-interest in maintaining the racial status quo, over non-white candidates all point to the politics of whiteness. These legacies connect whites' numerical dominance and electoral behavior to insidious and embedded ways in which white supremacy continues to play out in U.S. political systems. Today, the segregation of whites (and Blacks) in parts of the country is not a coincidence. Thus the election of certain candidates over others is ultimately and intimately related to white supremacy. Whites' individual political choices to elect representatives have macro-level outcomes that maintain a system of whiteness. This chapter is the culmination of the breadth and depth of how whiteness operates in immigration politics, how it structures it, and the consequences of whites' moral and immoral choices.

6
Conclusion
In Need of a Moral Reckoning

In his 1967 book *Where do we go from here: Chaos or community?* Martin Luther King (MLK) Jr. (2010 [1967]) described the dilemma white America faces: "the haunting ambivalence, the intellectual and moral recognition that slavery is wrong, but the emotional tie to the system so deep and pervasive that it imposes an inflexible unwillingness to root it out" (p. 81). In the preceding chapters, I have shown that all these decades later whites remain unwilling to uproot and sever their ties with the ideology of white supremacy. MLK Jr. envisioned the United States and white Americans working toward Democratic values and ideals and away from "the far country of racism." He was persistent in arguing that white America needed to look inward to uproot the emotional ties to the system and the system itself. It appears that the majority have yet to undertake this inward exploration: White Americans continue to be emotionally and morally tied to a system that does not necessitate their explicit participation—though many still do explicitly behave in white supremacist ways—but that certainly requires their complicity.

Immigration is just one area of many in which whites' complicity is evident. Analyzing immigration through the lens of whiteness yields important lessons for understanding U.S. immigration policy and politics. Immigration defines and redefines political membership and belonging. It is also, as Natalie Masuoka and Jane Junn (2013) argue, "the central engine for racial formation in the United States" (p. 189). Their data ties the immigration system to the persistence of white hegemony and, as they point out, immigration restriction actually drives the meaning of racial categories in the United States (p. 195). As a driver of demographic changes, immigration—and its restriction—is shaping the national conversation on race.

Preserving white supremacy has always been the intended outcome of immigration and naturalization policy in the United States, from the

Moral and Immoral Whiteness in Immigration Politics. Yalidy Matos, Oxford University Press.
© Oxford University Press 2023. DOI: 10.1093/oso/9780197656259.003.0007

1790 Naturalization Act that initiated the immigration restriction system to the Hart-Celler Act of 1965 to the Illegal Immigration Reform and Immigrant Responsibility Act of 1996. This book intervenes in our current understanding of contemporary immigration policy and politics, which emphasizes the effects of immigration on non-white bodies, and thus enables the invisibility of whiteness as structuring immigration law and attitudes. Most white Americans view and are encouraged to view immigration as about outgroups, but immigration policy and thus attitudes are primarily designed to maintain the racial status quo. For white Americans, that means it is designed to maintain the current dominant level of their ingroup.

Immigration law in the United States is structured by whiteness; hence immigration has been and continues to be a policy issue that is less about unauthorized immigrants and more about the maintenance of a "white democracy" (Olson, 2004). This has been one of the main arguments of this book. The regime of immigration law was designed to maintain a white electorate and thus to maintain policies that support white privilege. As Chapter 4 shows, those whites who are aware of their white privilege are the most willing to express progressive immigration attitudes. This admission by whites of their participation in this kind of system is key in understanding whites who hold progressive immigration attitudes and other progressive attitudes as well. However, as preceding chapters have shown, only a small minority of white Americans are willing to acknowledge and renounce such participation.

Most white Americans are either incapable or unwilling to admit to any kind of racial privilege. In fact, during the 2016 presidential election, the Republican nominee and eventual winner pandered to white voters (Casey Ryan, 2020; Lopez Bunyasi, 2019; Morgan & Lee, 2018; Sides, Tesler, & Vavreck, 2017; Strolovitch, Wong, & Proctor, 2017) using immigration to define ingroup membership (Matos & Miller, 2021). After eight years of a Black president and the white backlash of the 2016 presidential election, political science scholars have taken a renewed interested in white identity politics. Some scholars argue that Obama's presidency, given his blackness (not his inhumane immigration policy) and increases in immigration since 2000 have threatened whites' sense of group position and thus white identity has been more prevalent and activated since his presidency (Jardina, 2019; Schildkraut, 2017). In fact, scholarship on this topic prior to 2008 found white identity politics insignificant (Sears & Savalei, 2006; Wong & Cho, 2005). However, as I have argued in this book, this understanding of white public opinion and behavior is fraught. Whiteness has always been a part of how and why white people in the United States make decisions.

White public opinion and attitudes about immigration issues cannot be understood in the absence of historical and institutional context. The ways in which whiteness operated vis-à-vis immigration politics in the past relate to how it influences contemporary immigration attitudes. What Trump's 2016 presidential election campaign did was remind white Americans how to be ingroup members, including how to maintain their racial positioning (Matos & Miller, 2021). Immigration is inherently about whiteness—how to *do* whiteness—rather than whether to call oneself white or to express how salient being white is to one's identity, precisely because these expressions of white identity became eventually unnecessary. Once being white functioned normatively and implicitly, and whites were allowed a "natural" and "race-less" racial status, these expressions of white racial identity were no longer needed. What is needed, though, is the behavior that maintains positive group positioning. In fact, Chapter 2 and Chapter 3 show that white racial identity—how salient being white is to one's identity—inconsistently influences whites' immigration attitudes and behavior. The story of white Americans is one about a deep commitment to an ideology through attitudes and behavior, not a story about white racial identity.

As this book has shown, most whites stick to their group norms, voting to maintain their position rather than leveling the playing field. The fact that most white Americans express opposition to race-conscious policies and support for discriminatory policies indicates a political and moral choice—a choice to maintain a hierarchy that puts their own group above others rather than choosing to support more humane or redistributive policies. Political choices should not be distinguished from moral choices, as what is moral is political. These are choices white Americans have been making since long before 2008.

In this book, I offer a theoretical framework from which to understand white political attitudes and behavior. I argue that whites' political attitudes are not merely political but also moral. Examining immigration, I argue that whiteness structures immigration attitudes, these attitudes are moral choices, and, finally, psychological predispositions give meaning to the moral foundation undergirding whites' immigration attitudes. This framework extends well beyond immigration; it seems likely, given my findings, that whites will generally oppose any policy that does not support white supremacy, including protecting voting rights, police transparency, and strengthening the safety net. This opposition is embedded in whites' deep ties to the ideology of white supremacy.

In Chapter 2, I established that white racial identity and white group consciousness, as measured by asking whether whites need to work together, have very little bearing on their own on immigration attitudes and on redistributive policies like affirmation action. I did not find that whites whose white identity is important to them or whites with higher levels of group consciousness were dramatically different than other whites. However, Chapter 2 established that whiteness undergirds psychological predispositions. Whites who expressed more identity saliency had higher levels of racial resentment, moral traditionalism, anti-egalitarianism, and authoritarianism. However, upon further examination, among white non-racial identifiers, I found that higher levels of white group consciousness increased levels of the same predispositions. In other words, white racial identity on its own can easily be misconstrued. Another important finding of this chapter is that whites who express power-cognizance or an awareness of white privilege also express lower levels of racial resentment, moral traditionalism, anti-egalitarianism, and authoritarianism. These psychological predispositions, as I have argued, cannot be disassociated from whites' socialization as people who live in the world as white. Hence, they are important in any examination of white attitudes and behavior.

Whites' predisposed attitudes about equality, fairness, and racism are part of how white people behave and what predicates their political behavior. Whiteness is not natural; white children growing up in a white supremacist society have to learn to be white, how to embody and practice whiteness. This learning and socialization give rise to white people's predispositions that they then use to make social and political choices. Chapter 3 further shows that once we consider whites' predispositions, white racial identity is insignificant in almost all cases. White group consciousness remains significant in influencing some of white Americans' immigration attitudes, after taking into account their levels of predispositions, though not as significant as the predispositions themselves. This chapter also found that moral traditionalism is one of the most consistent and strongest predictors of restrictive immigration policies. Moreover, moral traditionalism superseded Democratic identification among whites in many instances. White Democrats who express higher levels of moral traditionalism also express more conservative immigration attitudes.

There is an intricate connection between immigration and white partisanship (Bowler, Nicholson, & Segura, 2006; Craig & Richeson, 2014; Dyck,
Johnson, & Wasson, 2012). Most white Americans who self-identify as
Republicans support punitive and restrictive immigration policies, while the
majority of white Democrats oppose such policies. However, as this book
suggests, for white Democrats, higher levels of certain predispositions—
namely racial resentment, beliefs about the traditional family, and an authoritarian personality—can suppress alignment with Democratic officials'
liberalization of immigrant policy. White Democrats, much like white
Republicans, need to contend with how they continue to choose whiteness if
a more just and equitable immigration policy is desired, though it is unclear
that this is, in fact, a desire of white Democrats. In fact, many Black Americans
in the 1960s felt that "their most troublesome adversary was not . . . the Ku
Klux Klan . . . but the white liberal who is more devoted to 'order' than to
justice, who prefers tranquility to equality" (King, 2010 [1967], p. 93). The
two-party system and ideologies behind Democratic and Republicans ideals
are rooted in whiteness. The two-party system itself was not instituted for
major changes but to maintain the status quo as much as possible. Hence
Democrats and Republicans are two sides of the same coin, the coin being
white supremacy. Because of this, white Democrats need to come to terms
with how their behavior or lack thereof helps maintain whiteness.

These results matter deeply for U.S. politics and the future of immigration policy. Scholars of U.S. public opinion are interested in understanding
the factors that play a role in the formulation of public opinion and political behavior. In political science, an emerging scholarship on white identity politics posits the importance of white racial identity for whites, often
characterizing the Obama presidency and the 2016 election as catalysts.
However, as Chapter 3 shows, white political behavior cannot be simplified
to questions that ask just about whites' identity saliency. Historically, given
their status as the dominant racial group in U.S. society, these questions are
irrelevant. Whites' behavior is influenced by preconceived ideas, norms, and
values that they have learned, and these predispositions are manifestations
of how whiteness operates, how it shows up in daily life. Without an examination of these predispositions, white identity politics is not complete, because the (im)moral choices whites make when visiting the voting polls or
supporting policies did not start with Obama's presidency, but date back to
the country's inception, when whiteness became a strategy for power. In this
sense, if white Americans are making decisions on immigration based on

predispositions, what we should be focused on is not how much or how little whites recognize their whiteness or deem it important, but how they perform that understanding through behavior. Whites' predispositions are inherently raced (as are all predispositions), given that predispositions are learned through socialization. Whites learn politics and intergroup and ingroup behavior through the lens of whiteness; thus, this chapter showcases that white identity, white group consciousness, and partisanship moderate the influence of predispositions on whites' immigration attitudes. More specifically, this chapter shows the importance of morally based values about the "right" social order.

Part of the utility of whiteness is the choice to elect representatives who serve as descriptive (also white) and, in many instances, substantive (aligned with their policy views) members of their communities. Examining state-level contemporary immigration legislation, I ground Chapter 5 in the historical link between the Fugitive Slave Law of 1850 and anti- and pro-sanctuary legislation to further argue for the importance of examining the role of whiteness in immigration politics and policy. These laws were and are designed to control the mobility of non-white people. In both cases conflicts over federalism were at issue in policies designed to maintain a white-over-non-white system of institutions and redistribution. The chapter broadens our understanding of the far-reaching influence of whites' moral choices. At the district level, in states that passed either pro- or anti-sanctuary immigration legislation, representatives who served more non-Hispanic whites were more likely to vote against sanctuary policies. I link this pattern to the history of these districts and communities as predominantly white. I end this chapter by returning to one of the primary arguments of the book: Immigration policy is a tool of white supremacy. Controlling non-white human mobility and labeling it "Immigration policy," electing those who support these kinds of legislation, and supporting these kinds of policies are all moral choices.

The good news for white people, though, is that they can make other choices. Awareness of white racial advantages among whites is politically important and pushes whites toward more progressive attitudes, as Chapter 4 finds. Furthermore, predispositions—byproducts of socialization—influence whether whites are pushed toward awareness of white privilege or a lack of awareness. When whites can admit that they have white advantages and privilege, they express more progressive immigration attitudes. When whites understand that they can make different choices, some do.

In the wake of the January 6, 2021, insurrection on the U.S. Capitol, members of the Republican Party did decide to make different choices. Some of those members have couched their stance on Trump's involvement in the January 6 insurrection and his subsequent attempts to overturn the 2020 election results in moral terms. Republican Senator Mitt Romney is one example. Even before the 2020 election, Romney had criticized Trump publicly (Romney, 2019). After the insurrection and during Trump's impeachment trial, Romney cast the only Republican vote to convict the president and remove him from office; he also demonstrated with Black Lives Matter protesters in July 2020. Romney explained the choice to defy Trump to a *New York Times* reporter: "I've learned that if you don't follow your conscience, it haunts you for a long, long time" (Leibovich, 2020). To be sure, Senator Romney has been on the wrong side of history on many occasions, and he bears responsibility for that. Romney's presence at a Black Lives Matter protest is symbolic in the face of his role in Congress, where he opposed progressive policies like the John Lewis Voting Rights Advancement Act and the Freedom to Vote Act, which he helped kill in January 2022, and eradicating qualified immunity for the police. This is not to make the argument or join scholars trying to disentangle white supremacy from white identity. The two are intricately connected and any work whose aim is to disassociate them is doing a disservice to individuals and groups who choose to repudiate white supremacy even when it is costly to their group. In other words, it is not enough for Romney, a white person, to attend a protest; his whiteness disables him to see the connection between his whiteness and his behavior in perpetuating white supremacy by opposing policies aimed at loosening the grip of white supremacy. But his remarks highlight the moral choices white Americans, particularly elected officials, make daily.

In her book *American while Black: African Americans, immigration, and the limits of citizenship* Niambi Michelle Carter (2019) details how Black Americans' understanding of how white supremacy informs immigration policies influences how they view immigration and immigrants. Even when immigration is costly to Black Americans because of their racial positioning in the United States, Black Americans understand liberal immigration policies as having to do with justice and "doing the right thing." She argues that this is not about altruism but rather stems from a knowledge of "the dangers of white supremacy" to themselves as well as to immigrants (p. 170). Instead of following in the footsteps of espousing the same views and behavior of white ethnic immigrants or of more recent immigrants, white and non-white alike, Black Americans have a deep understanding of whites' emotional ties to the system of white supremacy and know that aligning themselves with white supremacy is costly. Black Americans understand that allying themselves with this system or seeking active membership in whiteness will not accomplish equality, satisfaction, or quality of life because even if achievable there will always need to be a group at the bottom of the hierarchy. Black Americans could easily espouse anti-immigrant sentiments and punitive immigration attitudes because most have no ties to living immigrants and are also impacted by immigration (Carter, 2019), but this group's understanding that immigration is structured by white supremacy, along with their intimate knowledge of that system, keeps them from mimicking white attitudes on immigration. Black Americans are making different moral choices.

The issue of immigration, what politicians and pundits call the "immigration crisis," is really a crisis of white supremacy. If we were to take white supremacy out of our domestic and international policies, there would be fewer reasons why people all over the world, and especially in Central and South America and the Caribbean, would be forced to migrate. Although migration is a natural phenomenon, most migrants do not want to leave their home country. If it were not for extreme poverty, environmental chaos, and political and social instability, most people would decide to stay in their homeland. U.S. foreign policy has wreaked havoc on Central and South America and the Caribbean, especially in the countries the United States has invaded and where the United States has supported dictatorships and essentially white supremacy. Although there is no going back to a time before U.S. invasion and meddling, the solution to migration is to alleviate the impoverishment the United States helped create and continues to help perpetuate.

Through a deep moral compulsion some white people are making different moral choices; not nearly enough, however. A set of questions whites must answer for themselves comes from Toni Morrison, in a 1993 interview with Charlie Rose. As Morrison asked of whites, I too ask white Americans, and those invested in whiteness: "If I take your race away, and there you are, all strung out. And all you got is your little self, and what is that? What are you without racism?" What are you without whiteness?

This book explicitly allows for accountability to play a role in political science and the academy by highlighting and magnifying the concept of whites' moral choices, not just as individuals but as a group. To reject white supremacy and actively work against it means a sort of loss of identity for whites but a gain in moral life.

Survey Questionnaires

More information on the ANES surveys can be found at https://electionstudies.org/ including the extended questionnaire and codebook.

Dependent Variables

Police Checks. Some states have passed a law that will require state and local police to determine the immigration status of a person if they find that there is a reasonable suspicion he or she is an undocumented immigrant. Those found to be in the U.S. without permission will have broken state law. From what you have heard, do you favor, oppose, or neither favor nor oppose these immigration laws?

Immigration Levels. Should the number of new legal immigrants be increased a lot, increased a little, neither increased nor decreased, decreased a little, or decreased a lot?

Immigration Policy. Which comes closest to your view about what government policy should be toward unauthorized immigrants now living in the United States? (1) Make all unauthorized immigrants felons and send them back to their home country; (2) Have a guest worker program in order to work; (3) Allow to remain and eventually qualify for U.S. citizenship, if they meet certain requirement; or (4) Allow unauthorized immigrants to remain in the United States without penalties.

Birthright. Some people have proposed that the U.S. Constitution should be changed so that the children of unauthorized immigrants do not automatically get citizenship if they are born in this country. Do you favor, oppose, or neither favor nor oppose this proposal?

Border Wall. Do you favor, oppose, or neither favor nor oppose building a wall on the U.S. border with Mexico?

Border Security Spending. Should federal spending on tightening border security to prevent illegal immigration be increased, decreased, or kept about the same?

DREAM Act. There is a proposal to allow people who were illegally brought into the U.S. as children to become permanent U.S. residents under some circumstances. Specifically, citizens of other countries who illegally entered the U.S. before age 16, who have lived in the U.S. 5 years or longer, and who graduated high school would be allowed to stay in the U.S. as permanent residents if they attend college or serve in the military. From what you have heard, do you favor, oppose, or neither favor nor oppose this proposal?

Independent Variables

White Racial Identity Variables

White ID. A five-category variable ranging from zero (white is not at all important to self-identity) to five (white is extremely important to self-identity). "How important is being White to your identity?"

White Consciousness. A five-category variable asking: "How important is it that whites work together to change laws that are unfair to whites?"

White Linked Fate. "Do you think what happens generally to White people in this country will have something to do with what happens in your life?"

Jobs for Whites. A five-category variable asking: "How likely is it that many whites are unable to find a job because employers are hiring minorities instead?"

White Discrimination. How much discrimination is there in the United States today against each of the following groups?

Whites Better. In general, does the federal government [treat whites better than blacks, treat them both same, or treat blacks better than whites/treat blacks better than whites, treat them both the same, or treat whites better than blacks]?

Whites in Politics. Would you say that whites have [too much influence in American politics, just about the right amount of influence in American politics, or too little influence in American politics/too little influence in American politics, just about the right amount of influence in American politics, or too much influence in American politics]?

White Racial Advantage (2018 CCES). A five-point Likert scale asking respondents to agree or disagree: "White people in the U.S. have certain advantages because of the color of their skin."

Racism Rare (2018 CCES). A five-point Likert scale asking respondents to agree or disagree: "Racial problems in the U.S. are rare, isolated situations."

Predispositions

Racial Resentment. The racial resentment scale asks respondents to agree or disagree with four statements: (1) "Irish, Italians, Jewish and many other minorities overcame prejudice and worked their way up. Blacks should do the same without any special favors"; (2) "Generations of slavery and discrimination have created conditions that make it difficult for blacks to work their way out of the lower class"; (3) "Over the past few years, blacks have gotten less than they deserve"; (4) "It's really a matter of some people not trying hard enough; if blacks would only try harder they could be just as well off as whites."

Moral Traditionalism. The scale asks four questions: Do you agree strongly, agree somewhat, neither agree nor disagree, disagree somewhat, or disagree strongly with this statement? (1) "The world is always changing and we should adjust our view of moral behavior to those changes"; (2) "The newer lifestyles are contributing to the breakdown of our society"; (3) "We should be more tolerant of people who choose to live according to their own moral standards, even if they are very different from our own"; (4) 'This country would have many fewer problems if there were more emphasis on traditional family ties."

Authoritarianism. The scale asks four questions: "Which one you think is more important for a child to have? (1) Independence or Respect for elders; (2) Curiosity or Good manners; (3) Obedience or Self-reliance; and (4) Being considerate or Well-behaved."

Egalitarianism. The egalitarianism scale is based on respondents' agreement with six statements: (1) "Our society should do whatever is necessary to make sure that everyone has an equal opportunity to succeed"; (2) "We have gone too far in pushing equal rights in this country"; (3) "One of the big problems in this country is that we don't give everyone an equal chance"; (4) "This country would be better off if we worried less about how equal people are"; (5) "It is not really that big a problem if some people have more of a chance in life than others"; and finally (6) "If people were treated more equally in this country we would have many fewer problems." This scale is coded so that higher values indicate less egalitarianism.

Other Relevant Independent Variables

Feeling thermometers for Hispanics, Asians, undocumented immigrants, and Black Americans. A 100-point rating rescaled to range from zero (coldest) to one (warmest).

Latinos in Politics. Would you say that Hispanics have too much influence in American politics, just about the right amount of influence in American politics, or too little influence in American politics?

Job Threat. Now I'd like to ask you about immigration in recent years. How likely is it that recent immigration levels will take jobs away from people already here? Is it (1) extremely likely; (2) very likely; (3) somewhat likely; or (4) not at all likely?

Patriotism. The Patriotism scale is based on responses to four questions: (1) "How important is being an American to you personally?"; (2) "How do you feel about this country? Do you hate it, dislike it, neither like nor dislike it, like it, or love it?"; (3) "When you see the American flag flying does it make you feel extremely good, very good, moderately good, slightly good, or not good at all?"; (4) "How important is being American to your identity?"

National Economy. Now thinking about the economy in the country as a whole, would you say that over the past year the nation's economy has gotten better, stayed about the same, or gotten worse?

Lost Job (2018 CCES). Binary question asking respondents if they have lost a job.

Church Attendance. Lots of things come up that keep people from attending religious services even if they want to. Thinking about your life these days, do you ever attend religious services, apart from occasional weddings, baptisms, or funerals? [Yes, No]

Children. How many children or teenagers age 0 to 17 live in this household? [0, No children; 1, at least 1 child]

Notes

Introduction

1. Indeed, Citizenship and Immigration Services changed its mission statement in 2018 to emphasize the "nation's lawful immigration system" and no longer references a "nation of immigrants" (Gonzales, 2018).
2. Today, describing the United States as a "nation of immigrants" is generally considered to be pro-immigration, but historically this phrase was used to justify exclusion (Gabaccia, 2010).
3. Thank you to Kali Handelman for highlighting this point for me.
4. This narrative is what Davis and Ernst (2011, 2019) call racial spectacles, "narratives that obfuscate the existence of a white supremacist state power structure" (2019, p. 763). Instead of revealing the existence of white supremacy, white ethnics obscured it, signed on to it, and perpetuated it by actively presuming innocence while choosing to subordinate Black Americans for their own racial privilege.
5. This notion of "black-over-white victimization" elucidates what some white ethnics, especially those who trace their roots to "immigrant ghettoes," described in their writings as their experience alongside African Americans at African Americans' arrival to inner cities. The "victimization" is what white ethnics' thought was an erroneous conflation between themselves and "real" (read: white Anglo Saxon Protestant, WASP) whites (see Jacobson, 2006).
6. In the current formulation of race in the United States, as well as globally, a given white person will always be considered white and perceived as such. There are, of course, instances of white individuals passing as non-white and of non-white people passing as white due to their lighter skin tone. Nonetheless, whiteness as it is conceived in the United States and much of the world comes with privileges and rights that all white people have (even those passing as white) even if they have not asked for those privileges and rights.
7. Also partially quoted in Mills (1998, p. 158).
8. Importantly, whites will always be complicit in many ways in the system of white supremacy. However, actively rejecting white supremacy by electing certain kinds of candidates and supporting particular policies is better than nothing at all.

Chapter 1

1. For example, Niambi Carter (2019) examines Black Americans' attitudes toward immigrants and argues that their experiences of chattel slavery, Jim Crow, segregation, and institutional racism structure their attitudes toward immigrants. She articulates a theory of "conflicted nativism" in which Black Americans are positioned as Americans but not fully incorporated in the body politic in ways that shape their attitudes. In other words, for Black Americans the history of slavery and Jim Crow structures their attitudes, and this history will be necessarily different for white Americans as the main culprits of and beneficiaries of slavery and Jim Crow. Positionality matters for identity politics.

2. Here I have described the scant research within the realm of political science and white racial attitudes. There is an entire field of whiteness studies that interrogates the extent to which white identity exists, how it exists, what it means, and the role it has. Furthermore, there is extant scholarship on this topic in Black Studies, Ethnic Studies, History, and American Studies.

3. Kinder and Kam (2009) define ethnocentrism as: "a mental habit. . . . [A] predisposition to divide the human world into in-groups and out-groups. It is a readiness to reduce society to us and them. Or rather, it is a readiness to reduce society to us *versus* them" (p. 8).

4. Blumer's Sense of Group Position theory posits that the dominant group develops animosity toward subordinate group members from beliefs about the proper relationship between groups, and these feelings form the basis of racial prejudice (Bobo, Kluegel, & Smith, 1997).

5. Any examination of the production of white racial identity necessitates a foundation in colonialism and slavery. White U.S.-American identity was also created out of imperial terror toward the indigenous peoples of present-day North America.

6. Alien land laws passed in California in 1913; Arizona in 1917; Louisiana in 1921; New Mexico in 1922; Idaho, Montana, and Oregon in 1923; Kansas in 1925; and Utah and Wyoming in 1943; among others.

7. The 1917 Immigration Act also made "all idiots, imbeciles, feeble-minded persons, epileptics, [and] insane persons" ineligible to naturalize, as well as alcoholics, criminals, polygamists, anarchists, vagrants, beggars, prostitutes, persons deported who have sought re entry, and unaccompanied children under the age of 16, among other restrictions.

8. The homestead was an area of public land in the West granted to any U.S. citizen willing to settle on and farm the land. These acts were laws devised by the federal government in order to populate the land.

9. Act of Jan. 27, 1864, § 1, 1864 Wash. Laws 12, amended by Act of Jan. 29, 1886, § 1, 1885–86 Wash. Laws 102, and repealed by Act of Feb. 3, 1927, ch. 56, § 1, 1927 Wash. Laws 45.

10. Sess. II, Chap. 3; 1 stat 103. 1st Congress; March 26, 1790.

11. Although free white women were not excluded from the law explicitly, common law at the time entailed a transfer of a woman's civic identity and the use of her property

to her husband at marriage. Furthermore, citizenship could devolve only through the father. Legally, white immigrant women could naturalize; however, in practice married or widowed women were often granted derivative citizenship (derived from their spouses), while some women were barred altogether depending on the court's interpretation of the laws. For more on white women's citizenship during this time, see Kerber (1992).

12. In 1960, non-Hispanic whites made up 85% of the U.S. population, Hispanics made up 3.5%, and Asians made up 0.6%. In 2011, the numbers were 63%, 17%, and 5%, respectively (Taylor & Cohn, 2012).

13. The "Latino threat" narrative, as argued by Chavez and others, details the ways in which Latino immigration to the United States was often portrayed by the media as an invasion and as destroying the U.S. way of life.

14. Matthew Frye Jacobson's *Roots too: White ethnic revival in post–Civil Rights America* (2006) describes groups like Irish immigrants as "Ellis Island whites": whites or soon-to-be whites who came through Ellis Island when they immigrated to the United States. "Ellis Island whiteness" is a colorblind ideological narrative about mostly whites who immigrated through Ellis Island, but also includes those who immigrated after and through other ports of entry, as privilege-free people who endured discrimination, but worked hard for upward mobility and the "American Dream." This narrative conceals the structural nature of whiteness as the foundation of the American racial/social/economic hierarchy. It took hold during the Civil Rights Movement as a way to undermine the structural critiques of the Civil Rights Movement by claiming that hard work, the will to pull themselves up by their bootstraps, rather than the experience of racism or resources, distinguished white immigrants who rose socioeconomically from Black Americans who did not.

15. Both consisted of basically building a wall of Border Patrol agents along parts of the border to stop unauthorized immigration. The El Paso program reduced apprehensions by 76% in that subsection of the border and gained national attention that led to the implementation of the strategy in San Diego a year later (see Nevins, 2010).

16. The militia movement in the United States is a right-wing extremist movement with an anti-government ideology and a strong emphasis on paramilitary activity. It emerged in 1993–1994, saw a slump in the early 2000s, and experienced a revival starting in 2008. Trump's presidential election changed the emphasis of the movement, which supported his candidacy, from anti–federal government to searching for other enemies such as antifa. Antifa is an anti-fascist protest movement, which gained new prominence in the United States after the white supremacist Unite the Right rally in Charlottesville, Virginia, in August 2017 (see Anti-Defamation League (ADL), 2020).

17. By underclass, I mean a population burdened by a cycle of a socioeconomic precarity as well as a uniquely vulnerable population due to the threat of detention and deportation.

18. Indeed, the Personal Responsibility and Work Opportunity Reconciliation Act of 1996 also demonized immigrant and Black women and set boundaries for their access to public benefits and services.

19. As in white identity [white] as well as the practice of whiteness by whites [White].
20. Important to note is there are few, if any, white persons who are exclusively moral or immoral (and I would make this general argument for all people). For the purposes of this body of work, those white persons who are making moral choices about immigration can be making immoral choices as undergirded by whiteness in other ways, maybe even regarding other policies.
21. There is a real issue of impossibility about the extent to which white people can repudiate the system their own identity and existence is wrapped in, however. I would not go so far as to say it is permanently impossible.
22. Politically, non-extensionists were just that rather than abolitionists, though in some accounts they are lumped together with abolitionists.
23. Slavery normalized extramarital sex for white slaveholders who raped enslaved women.
24. Act of Mar. 26, 1790, ch. 3, § 1, 1 Stat. 103, 103 (repealed 1795).
25. Act of Jan. 29, 1795, ch. 20, § 1, 1 Stat. 414, 414 (repealed 1802).
26. Immigration law is not the only area of law that conflates morality with whiteness. For example, Wright-Schaner (2016) shows that the requirement for lawyers to demonstrate that they are of "good moral character" prior to admission to the Bar can be discriminatory and in instances racially discriminatory.
27. The prohibition against admission of prostitutes has long been used as a pretext to bar non-white women. For example, in the late 1800s and early 1900s, Japanese women were scrutinized by immigration officials and debarred or deported for suspected prostitution as were other categories of women (see Gardner, 2005).
28. This idea comes from Kwame Anthony Appiah's book *In my father's house* (Appiah, 1992).
29. The movement of women is more complicated. Non-white women's movement is limited and governed by the intersection of racial, gender, and moral scrutiny, whereas white women's movement is governed by gender without the scrutiny of race. Moreover, white women's movement is protected whereas that of non-white women is not.
30. Naomi Zack defines moral systems in society as "closely tied to understanding and agreement within groups, occurring at the same time, often defined by place. Mores and morals are thus concretely historical" (2011, p. xvi).
31. King (2010 [1967]) would argue poor whites will also be economically compensated by supporting policies that are beneficial to poor whites and Blacks.

Chapter 2

1. Only about 23% of the foreign-born population in the United States is undocumented, while most foreign-born individuals are naturalized U.S. citizens, lawful permanent residents, or have lawful temporary status, such as Deferred Action for Childhood Arrivals (DACA) or Temporary Protected Status (Budiman, 2020).

2. The party's policy proposals, according to Boissoneault (2017), included "deportation of foreign beggars and criminals; a 21-year naturalization period for immigrants; mandatory Bible reading in schools; and the elimination of all Catholics from public office." Boissoneault describes the reach of the Know Nothing party at its height in the 1850s as follows: "[it] included more than 100 elected congressmen, eight governors, a controlling share of half-a-dozen state legislatures from Massachusetts to California, and thousands of local politicians".

3. Framing policy debates is, of course, not just a right-wing strategy; however, the usage of the family unit and moral traditionalism is a uniquely conservative strategy aimed at primarily Southern, rural, and suburban whites.

4. In examining white and Black evangelicals, Allison Calhoun-Brown (1997) points out that for whites "doctrinal orthodoxy supported slavery, segregation, and inequality; for blacks, this same orthodoxy became the basis for the struggle against these injustices" (p. 116).

5. After 9/11, of course, a broader anti-immigrant sentiment proliferated, especially an anti-Muslim sentiment, that was inherently about national (identity) security (Alsultany, 2012; Kaplan, 2003; Sides & Gross, 2013).

6. Scholars have conceptualized the changes in whites' racial attitudes in many different ways using a variety of labels (Blumer, 1958; Bobo, 1988; Bobo & Kluegel, 1993; Bonilla-Silva, 2014; Dovidio, Evans, & Tyler, 1986; Katz & Hass, 1988; Kinder & Sanders, 1996; Kinder & Sears, 1981; McConahay, 1986; McConahay & Hough Jr., 1976; Pettigrew & Meertens, 1995); however, at the heart of the different concepts is an understanding that regardless of label, a new type of racism emerged post–civil rights.

7. Racial resentment is a reliable scale for non-white groups as well as white people (Henry & Sears, 2002; Kam & Burge, 2018); all exhibit some level of racial resentment (Nunnally & Carter, 2012; Orey, 2004; Smith, 2014).

8. I also only included respondents who are neither immigrants nor children of immigrants, because these groups would be less detached from their immigrant experience. Immigrants and children of immigrants may be less likely to shape their attitudes about immigration primarily around their racial identity.

9. I collapse "very important" and "extremely important" as both categories indicate a heightened level of social identity but consider "not at all important" and "a little important" to be meaningfully different.

10. For white racial identity, because it is an independent variable with two or more levels, with a continuous dependent variable, I used a one-way ANOVA; a Kruskal–Wallis test with ordinal/interval variables; and a chi-square test with categorical variables

11. I use these terms interchangeably throughout this book.

12. Members of all racial/ethnic groups tend to rate their own ingroup higher than outgroups.

13. Test based on the dummy categories of "not at all important" and "very or extremely important," which excludes the intervening categories of "a little" and "moderately important."

14. This nostalgia reappears in my own survey experiment in Chapter 4. There is also scholarship on white nostalgia across different fields that examines the different kinds of whites and nostalgic pasts (Anderson, 2005; Dickinson, 2006; Maly, Dalmage, & Michaels, 2013; McPherson, 2003; Price, 2018).

15. Tested using a simple logistic with the full continuous ethnocentrism variable. The test of the overall model is statistically significant, LR chi-squared 77.32, $p = 0.000$. Using the three-category ethnocentrism variables produces the same results ($\chi^2(2) = 82.79$, $p = 0.000$), with no difference between the second (neutral) and third (higher than neutral) categories.

16. A Kruskal–Wallis test using the three-category ethnocentrism test confirms this positive relationship ($\chi^2 = 230.36, p = 0.000$).

17. All predispositions are scaled to signal more conservative dispositions as higher numbers. Higher numbers for egalitarianism indicate greater opposition to egalitarianism.

18. The middle point for independents is 0.5; hence any under 0.5 are considered Democrats and any above 0.5 are considered Republicans.

19. Measures of power-cognizance are scaled so that the higher number (the dummy variable = 1) is the cognizant answers, while zero is the racially evasive answers.

Chapter 3

1. For example, scholars have argued that the lynching described in the short story is based on the lynching of Jesse Washington in Waco, Texas, and that the character Big Jim C., Jesse's colleague, is either a personification of Jim Crow laws or even a reference to Jim Clark, sheriff of Dallas County, Alabama, from 1955 to 1966 (Beckett, 2021; Buccola, 2019).

2. I created restrictive and progressive distinctions by each immigration-related policy preference, where police checks, border spending, and border wall are categorized as favor (restrictive)/oppose (progressive), immigration levels are measured by decreased a lot or a little (restrictive)/increased a lot or a little (progressive), and finally, policy is categorized by make immigrant felons and deport them (restrictive)/ allow to stay with no penalties (progressive). In 2004 and 2008, the immigration policy question asked respondents about the importance of controlling illegal immigration as a U.S. policy goal where "very important" is restrictive and "not important at all" is progressive.

3. Tables 3A.10 and 3A.11 in Appendix B show these results. Given data limitations, these models do not include all control variables shown in 2012 and 2016.

4. OR = odds ratio; CI = confidence interval.

5. There are only 148 unemployed persons in the ANES 2016, which limits the generalizability of this finding. These models can be found in Table 3A.15 in Appendix B.

6. Full models can be found in Table 3A.19 in Appendix B. The reference category is Democrats.

Chapter 4

1. White racial advantage is still significant across all four models, albeit with lower coefficients. The influence of white group consciousness measures are both significant in both models 3 and 4 though the direction stays consistent.
2. Unfortunately, the 2018 data do not allow me to test these models by controlling for white identification or group consciousness, since that question is missing from both the common content and the smaller module.

Chapter 5

1. This provision was the impetus for survey questions in the ANES asking respondents whether they supported or opposed the police stopping anyone they deemed reasonably suspicious of being in the country illegally, which I analyzed in Chapter 3.
2. Some individual counties and cities within these states as well as counties and cities in other states have also passed some kind of sanctuary policy.
3. About 40% of this chapter appeared in an article in the *American Behavioral Scientist* (July 2017, Sage Publications, https://doi.org/10.1177/0002764217720480). It is reprinted here with permission from the publisher.
4. In 2002, with the passage of the Homeland Security Act, INS ceased to exist and immigration naturalization and enforcement was split between Immigration and Customs Enforcement (ICE), Customs and Border Patrol (CBP), and U.S. Citizenship and Immigration Services (USCIS), all under the Department of Homeland Security.
5. In *Arizona et al. v. United States* (2012), Justice Kennedy states, "The Government of the United States has broad, undoubted power over the subject of immigration and the status of aliens," and cites the U.S. Constitution, Article 1, Section 8, Clause 4 and *Toll v. Moreno*, 458 U.S. 1, 10 (1982). On June 25, 2012, however, the U. S. Supreme Court issued decisions striking down three of the four provisions of SB 1070. All justices agreed to uphold the provision that allowed state police to investigate the immigration status of any person stopped, detained, or arrested if there is "reasonable suspicion" that the individual is in the country illegally, giving states this particular right. Thus, the bill was found unconstitutional in part, but the "show me your papers" provision was allowed, leading some sheriff's offices and counties to racially profile Latinos (see ACLU Foundation of Arizona, 2012; *Melendres v. Arpaio*, 2013).
6. In the 1980s, sanctuary referred to efforts by churches to provide "safe haven" and resources to Central American asylum seekers.
7. Utah passed both a restrictive SB 1070 copycat law, HB 497, and a guest worker program, HB 116, in 2011. HB 116 allowed undocumented immigrants who met certain requirements to apply for a work permit. While some people described the program as compassionate, the American Civil Liberties Union of Utah criticized it as exploitative.
8. The Georgia Security and Immigration Compliance Act (SB 529) requires that all public employers, contractors, and subcontractors register and comply with the

federal work authorization program operated by DHS to verify new employee work eligibility.

9. I excluded the District of Columbia and U.S. territories in this work as I am looking exclusively at state-level immigration legislation. Neither the District of Columbia nor U.S. territories are states, though presumably both are able to pass immigration legislation.

10. https://www.ncsl.org/research/immigration/immigration-laws-database.aspx

11. http://www.socialexplorer.com; I merged using STATA 14.

12. https://www.census.gov/geo/maps-data/data/tiger-line.html

13. A shapefile is geospatial vector data format for geographic information system (GIS) software.

14. GeoDa is a free and open source software tool that serves as an introduction to spatial data analysis, developed by Dr. Luc Anselin and his team. https://geodacenter.git hub.io.

15. All Fisher's exact tests had a p value of 0.000. The Fisher's exact tests were tested using dummy party and vote variables. In other words, any party affiliation other than the two prominent U.S. parties were marked as missing and any votes other than yea or nay were marked as missing for the purposes of this test.

16. Two members switched party affiliation from the Democratic Party following the 2012 elections: Richard Laird (District 37) became an independent and Alan Harper (District 61) joined the Republican Party; both voted to support HB 56.

17. Examining the upper chamber has a limitation, namely fewer districts to examine, and a much larger district may not show what a smaller geographic unit might.

18. Due to Washington's upper chamber districts and Vermont's multi-member district structure, examinations of party by district-level demographics are limited in these states.

19. Under the Secure Communities program, ICE agents can run federal immigration checks on every individual booked into a local county jail and then send fingerprints from the FBI to DHS.

20. This is not to argue that racism did not exist in the antebellum North. The North was not any less racist and also passed legislation that undercut free Blacks, so the history of the antebellum North is not without its own complexities and contradictions (see Browne (2015), who describes lantern laws in 19th century New York).

21. For example, poor and working-class whites were included into the white polity to circumvent class coalitions between poor whites and Blacks.

22. In fact, pre-1875 immigration law was just as concerned with intra-state and state-to-territory migration as international immigration (Abrams, 2009; Neuman, 1993).

Bibliography

Abbink, K., Freidin, E., Gangadharan, L., & Moro, R. (2018). The effect of social norms on bribe offers. *Journal of Law, Economics, & Organization, 34*(3), 457–474. doi:10.1093/jleo/ewy015

Abrajano, M., & Hajnal, Z. L. (2015). *White backlash: Immigration, race, and American politics.* Princeton, NJ: Princeton University Press.

Abrams, K. (2005). Polygamy, prostitution, and the federalization of immigration law. *Columbia Law Review, 105*(3), 641–716.

Abrams, K. (2009). The hidden dimension of nineteenth-century immigration law. *Vanderbilt Law Review, 62*(5), 1353–1418.

Acharya, A., Blackwell, M., & Sen, M. (2016). The political legacy of American slavery. *Journal of Politics, 78*(3), 621–641.

Acharya, A., Blackwell, M., & Sen, M. (2018). *Deep roots: How slavery still shapes Southern politics.* Princeton, NJ: Princeton University Press.

ACLU Foundation of Arizona. (2012). Request for public records re: Arizona Senate Bill 1070. Retrieved from https://www.aclu.org/legal-document/request-public-records-re-arizona-senate-bill-1070.

Adorno, T. W., Frenkel-Brunswik, E., Levinson, D. J., & Sanford, R. N. (1950). *The authoritarian personality.* New York: Harper and Row.

Akerlof, G. A., & Kranton, R. E. (2010). *Identity economics: How our identities shape our work, wages, and well-being.* Princeton, NJ: Princeton University Press.

Alamillo, R. (2019). Hispanics para Trump?: Denial of racism and Hispanic support for Trump. *Du Bois Review, 16*(2), 457–487. doi:10.1017/S1742058X19000328

Alexander, M. (2012). *The new Jim Crow: Mass incarceration in the age of colorblindness (Revised edition).* New York: The New Press. (Original work published in 2010).

Allen, T. (2012). *The invention of the white race* (2nd ed.). New York: Verso.

Allport, G. W. (1954). *The nature of prejudice.* Cambridge: Allison-Wesley.

Alsultany, E. (2012). *Arabs and Muslims in the media: Race and representation after 9/11.* New York: New York University Press.

Alvarez, P. (2017). The diversity visa program was created to help Irish immigrants. Retrieved from https://www.theatlantic.com/politics/archive/2017/11/diversity-visa-program/544646/.

American National Election Studies, University of Michigan, & Stanford University. (2017). ANES 2016 time series study. Retrieved from: www.electionstudies.org.

Andersen, M. L. (2003). Whitewashing race: A critical perspective on whiteness. In W. D. Ashley & B.-S. Eduardo (Eds.), *White out: The continuing significance of racism* (pp. 21–34). New York: Routledge.

Anderson, C. (2003). *Eyes off the prize: The United Nations and the African American struggle for human rights, 1944–1955.* Cambridge, UK: Cambridge University Press.

Anderson, D. (2005). Down memory lane: Nostalgia for the Old South in post-civil war plantation reminiscences. *Journal of Southern History, 71*(1), 105–136.

Ansley, F. L. (1989). Stirring the ashes: Race, class and the future of civil rights scholarship. *Cornell Law Review, 74*(6), 993–1077.

Anti-Defamation League (ADL). (2020). The militia movement (2020). Retrieved from https://www.adl.org/resources/backgrounders/the-militia-movement-2020.

Appiah, K. A. (1992). *In my father's house: Africa in the philosophy of culture.* London: Methuen.

Arizona et al. v. United States, 567, U.S. 387 (U.S. Supreme Court 2012).

Arora, M. (2020). Immigrant opposition in a changing national demographic. *Political Research Quarterly, 73*(2), 340–351. doi:10.1177/1065912919827107

Ayers, J. W., Hofstetter, C. R., Schnakenberg, K., & Kolody, B. (2009). Is immigration a racial issue? Anglo attitudes on immigration policies in a border county. *Social Science Quarterly, 90*(3), 593–610.

Baker, K. J. (2011). *Gospel according to the Klan: The KKK's appeal to Protestant America, 1915–1930.* Lawrence: University Press of Kansas.

Baldwin, J. (1965a). The American dream and the American Negro. *New York Times,* 32–33, 87–89. Retrieved from http://www.nytimes.com/images/blogs/papercuts/baldwin-and-buckley.pdf.

Baldwin, J. (1965b). *Going to meet the man.* New York: Dial Press.

Baldwin, J. (1998). On being "white" . . . and other lies. In D. R. Roediger (Ed.), *Black on white: Black writers on what it means to be white* (pp. 177–180). New York: Schocken Books.

Barreto, M. A., Cooper, B. L., Gonzalez, B., Parker, C. S., & Towler, C. (2011). The Tea Party in the age of Obama: Mainstream conservatism or out-group anxiety? In J. Go (Ed.), *Rethinking Obama (political power and social theory)* (Vol. 22, pp. 105–137). Bingley, UK: Emerald Group Publishing Limited.

Bashford, A. (2014). Immigration restriction: Rethinking period and place from settler colonies to postcolonial nations. *Journal of Global History, 9*(1), 26–48. doi:10.1017/S174002281300048X

Beckett, B. I. (2021). "Like a butterfly on a pin": Witnessing genealogies of whiteness in James Baldwin's "going to meet the man." *Alif: Journal of Comparative Poetics, 2021*(41), 73–109.

Beltrán, C. (2020). *Cruelty as citizenship: How migrant suffering sustains white democracy.* Minneapolis: University of Minnesota Press.

Berlant, L. (1997). *The queen of America goes to Washington City: Essays on sex and citizenship.* Durham, NC: Duke Univeristy Press.

Bicchieri, C., & Xiao, E. (2009). Do the right thing: But only if others do so. *Journal of Behavioral Decision Making, 22*(2), 191–208. doi:10.1002/bdm.621

Bierce, A. (2000). *The devil's dictionary.* South Bend: Infomotions, Inc.

Biss, E. (2015, Dec. 6). White debt. *New York Times Magazine.* Retrieved from https://www.nytimes.com/2015/12/06/magazine/white-debt.html.

Blumer, H. (1958). Race prejudice as a sense of group position. *Pacific Sociological Review, 1*(1), 3–7.

Bobo, L. (1988). Group conflict, prejudice, and the paradox of contemporary racial attitudes. In P. A. Katz & D. A. Taylor (Eds.), *Eliminating racism: Profiles in controversy* (pp. 85–116). New York: Plenum.

Bobo, L., & Hutchings, V. (1996). Perceptions of racial group competition: Extending Blumer's theory of group position to a multiracial social context. *American Sociological Review, 61,* 951–972.

Bobo, L., & Kluegel, J. R. (1993). Opposition to race-targeting: Self-interest, stratification ideology, or racial attitudes? *American Sociological Review, 58*(4), 443–464.

Bobo, L., Kluegel, J. R., & Smith, R. A. (1997). Laissez-faire racism: The crystallization of a kinder, gentler, antiblack ideology. In S. A. Tuch & J. K. Martin (Eds.), *Racial attitudes in the 1990s: Continuity and change* (pp. 15–42). Westport, CT: Praeger.

Bobo, L., & Smith, R. A. (1994). Antipoverty policies, affirmative action, and racial attitudes. In S. H. Danziger, G. D. Sandefur, & D. H. Weinberg (Eds.), *Confronting poverty: Prescriptions for change* (pp. 365–395). Cambridge, MA: Harvard University Press.

Boissoneault, L. (2017, Jan 26). How the 19th-century Know Nothing party reshaped American politics. Retrieved from https://www.smithsonianmag.com/history/imm igrants-conspiracies-and-secret-society-launched-american-nativism-180961915/.

Bonilla-Silva, E. (1997). Rethinking racism: Toward a structural interpretation. *American Sociological Review, 62*(3), 465–480.

Bonilla-Silva, E. (2014). *Racism without racists: Color-blind racism and the persistence of racial inequality in America* (4th ed.). Lanham, MD: Rowman & Littlefield Publishers.

Bonilla-Silva, E., Lewis, A., & Embrick, D. G. (2004). "I did not get that job because of a black man . . .": The story lines and testimonies of color-blind racism. *Sociological Forum (Randolph, NJ), 19*(4), 555–581. doi:10.1007/s11206-004-0696-3

Bowler, S., Nicholson, S. P., & Segura, G. M. (2006). Earthquakes and aftershocks: Race, direct democracy, and partisan change. *American Journal of Political Science, 50*(1), 146–159. doi:10.1111/j.1540-5907.2006.00175.x

Brader, T., Valentino, N. A., & Jardina, A. (2009). *Immigration opinion in a time of economic crisis: Material interests versus group attitudes.* Paper presented at the American Political Science Association (APSA) Annual Conference, Toronto, Canada.

Brader, T., Valentino, N. A., & Suhay, E. (2008). What triggers public opposition to immigration? Anxiety, group cues, and immigration threat. *American Journal of Political Science, 52*(4), 959–978.

Brandt, M. J., & Reyna, C. (2014). To love or hate thy neighbor: The role of authoritarianism and traditionalism in explaining the link between fundamentalism and racial prejudice. *Political Psychology, 35*(2), 207–223. doi:10.1111/pops.12077

Brandzel, A. L. (2016). *Against citizenship: The violence of the normative.* Champaign: University of Illinois Press.

Brandzel, A. L., & Desai, J. (2008). Race, violence, and terror: The cultural defensibility of heteromasculine citizenship in the Virginia Tech massacre and the Don Imus affair. *Journal of Asian American Studies, 11*(1), 61–85.

Branscombe, N. R., Doosje, B., & McGarty, C. (2002). Antecedents and consequences of collective guilt. In D. M. Mackie & E. R. Smith (Eds.), *From prejudice to intergroup emotions: Differentiated reactions to social groups* (pp. 49–66). New York: Psychology Press.

Branscombe, N. R., Ellemers, N., Spears, R., & Doosje, B. (1999). The context and content of social identity threat. In N. Ellemers, R. Spears, & B. Doosje (Eds.), *Social identity: Context, commitment, content* (pp. 35–58). Oxford: Blackwell.

Branscombe, N. R., Schmitt, M. T., & Schiffhauer, K. (2007). Racial attitudes in response to thoughts of white privilege. *European Journal of Social Psychology, 37*(2), 203–215. doi:10.1002/ejsp.348

Branton, R., Cassese, E. C., Jones, B. S., & Westerland, C. (2011). All along the watchtower: Acculturation fear, anti-Latino affect, and immigration. *Journal of Politics, 73*(3), 664–679.

Brewer, M. B. (1999). The psychology of prejudice: Ingroup love or outgroup hate? *Journal of Social Issues, 55*(3), 429–444. doi:10.1111/0022-4537.00126

Brewer, M. B. (2001). The many faces of social identity: Implications for political psychology. *Political Psychology, 22*(1), 115–125.

Brewer, M. B., & Gardner, W. (1996). Who is this "we"? Levels of collective identity and self representations. *Journal of Personality and Social Psychology, 71*(1), 83–93. doi:10.1037/0022-3514.71.1.83

Brewer, P. R. (2003). The shifting foundations of public opinion about gay rights. *Journal of Politics, 65*(4), 1208–1220.

Brewer Stewart, J. (1976). *Holy warriors: The abolitionists and American slavery.* New York: Hill and Wang.

Brewer Stewart, J. (1983). Young Turks and old turkeys: Abolitionists, historians, and aging processes. *Reviews in American History,* 11(2), 226-232. doi:10.2307/2702147

Brooks, C., & Manza, J. (1997). The social and ideological bases of middle-class political realignment in the United States, 1972–1992. *American Sociological Review, 62*(2), 191–208. doi:10.2307/2657299

Brown, C. L. (2012). *Moral capital: Foundations of British abolitionism.* Chapel Hill: University of North Carolina Press.

Browne, S. (2015). *Dark matters: On the surveillance of blackness.* Durham, NC: Duke University Press.

Buccola, N. (2019). *The fire is upon us: James Baldwin, William F. Buckley Jr., and the debate over race in America.* Princeton, NJ: Princeton University Press.

Budiman, A. (2020, Aug 20). Key findings about U.S. immigrants. Retrieved fromhttps://www.pewresearch.org/fact-tank/2020/08/20/key-findings-about-u-s-immigrants/.

Burke, P. J., & Reitzes, D. C. (1991). An identity theory approach to commitment. *Social Psychology Quarterly, 54*(3), 239–251. doi:10.2307/2786653

Burns, P., & Gimpel, J. G. (2000). Economic insecurity, prejudicial stereotypes, and public opinion on immigration policy. *Political Science Quarterly, 155*(2), 201–225.

Burton, O. (2015). To protect and serve whiteness. *North American Dialogue, 18*(2), 38–50. doi:10.1111/nad.12032

Carter, N. M. (2019). *American while Black: African Americans, immigration, and the limits of citizenship.* New York: Oxford University Press.

Cacho, L. M. (2012). *Social death: Racialized rightlessness and the criminalization of the unprotected.* New York: New York University Press.

Cain, B., Citrin, K., & Wong, C. (2000). *Ethnic context, race relations, and California politics.* San Francisco: Public Policy Institute of California.

Calcutt, L., Woodward, I., & Skrbis, Z. (2009). Conceptualizing otherness: An exploration of the cosmopolitan schema. *Journal of Sociology, 45*(2), 169–186. doi:10.1177/1440783309103344

Calhoun-Brown, A. (1997). Sojourners in the wilderness: The Christian right in comparative perspective. In C. E. Smidt & J. M. Penning (Eds.), *Religious forces in the modern political world* (pp. 115–137). Lanham: Rowman & Littlefield.

Camarota, S. A. (2012). *Immigrants in the United States: A profile of America's foreign-born population.* Washington, DC: Center for Immigration Studies. http://www.cis.org/sites/cis.org/files/articles/2012/immigrants-in-the-united-states-2012.pdf

Campbell, A., Converse, P. E., Miller, W. E., & Stokes, D. E. (1960). *The American voter.* New York: Wiley.

Campbell, A. L., Wong, C., & Citrin, J. (2006). "Racial threat," partisan climate, and direct democracy: Contextual effects in three California initiatives. *Political Behavior, 28*(2), 129–150. doi:10.1007/s11109-006-9005-6

Carmines, E. G., & Stimson, J. A. (1989). *Issue evolution: Race and the transformation of American politics.* Princeton, NJ: Princeton University Press.

Carter, N. M. (2019). *American while Black: African Americans, immigration, and the limits of citizenship.* New York: Oxford University Press.

Casellas, J. P., & Wallace, S. J. (2020). Sanctuary cities: Public attitudes toward enforcement collaboration between local police and federal immigration authorities. *Urban Affairs Review, 56*(1), 32–64. doi:10.1177/1078087418776115

Casey Ryan, K. (2020). Donald J. Trump and the rhetoric of white ambivalence. *Rhetoric & Public Affairs, 23*(2), 195–223. doi:10.14321/rhetpublaffa.23.2.0195

Chacón, J. A. (2006). Inventing an invisible enemy: September 11 and the war on immigrants. In J. Akers Chacón, M. Davis, & J. Cardona (Eds.), *No one is illegal: Fighting violence and state repression on the U.S.-Mexico border* (pp. 215–225). Chicago: Haymarket Books.

Chandler, C. R., & Tsai, Y.-M. (2001). Social factors influencing immigration attitudes: An analysis of data from the general social survey. *Social Science Journal, 38,* 177–188.

Chang, R. S. (1999). *Disoriented Asian Americans, law, and the nation-state.* New York: New York University Press.

Chappell, D. L. (1994). *Inside agitators: White southerners in the civil rights movement.* Baltimore: Johns Hopkins University Press.

Chavez, L. R. (2001). *Covering immigration: Popular images and the politics of the nation.* California: University of California Press.

Chavez, L. R. (2013). *The Latino threat: Constructing immigrants, citizens, and the nation.* Stanford: Stanford University Press.

Chong, D., & Druckman, J. N. (2007). Framing theory. *Annual Review of Political Science, 10,* 103–126.

Chong, D., & Druckman, J. N. (2011). Identifying frames in political news. In E. P. Bucy & R. L. Holbert (Eds.), *The sourcebook for political communication research: Methods, measures, and analytical techniques* (pp. 238–267). New York: Routledge.

Chouinard, V. (2001). Legal peripheries: Struggles over disabled Canadians' places in law, society and space. *Canadian Geographer, 45*(1), 187–192.

Chudy, J., Piston, S., & Shipper, J. (2019). Guilt by association: White collective guilt in American politics. *Journal of Politics, 81*(3), 968–981. doi:10.1086/703207

Citrin, J., Green, D. P., Muste, C., & Wong, C. (1997). Public opinion toward immigration reform: The role of economic motivations. *Journal of Politics, 59*(3), 858–881.

Citrin, J., Reingold, B., & Green, D. P. (1990). American identity and the politics of ethnic change. *Journal of Politics, 52*(4), 1124–1154.

Citrin, J., & Sides, J. (2008). Immigration and the imagined community in Europe and the United States. *Political Studies, 56*(1), 33–56. doi:10.1111/j.1467-9248.2007.00716.x

Ciuk, D. J. (2017). Democratic values? A racial group-based analysis of core political values, partisanship, and ideology. *Political Behavior, 39*(2), 479–501. doi:10.1007/s11109-016-9365-5

Cohrs, J. C., & Stelzl, M. (2010). How ideological attitudes predict host society members' attitudes toward immigrants: Exploring cross-national differences. *Journal of Social Issues, 66*(4), 673–694.

Colbern, A. (2017). *Today's runaway slaves: Unauthorized immigrants in a federalist framework* (Doctoral dissertation). Retrieved from ProQuest Dissertations Publishing. (Order No. 10280090).

Collingwood, L., & Gonzalez O'Brien, B. (2019). *Sanctuary cities: The politics of refuge*. New York: Oxford University Press.

Conover, P. J. (1988). Feminists and the gender gap. *Journal of Politics, 50*(4), 985–1010. doi:10.2307/2131388

Conover, P. J., & Feldman, S. (1986). Morality items of the 1985 pilot study. https://elec tionstudies.org/wp-content/uploads/2018/07/nes002251.pdf.

Corbin, C. M. (2017). Terrorists are always Muslim but never white: At the intersection of critical race theory and propaganda. *Fordham Law Review, 86*(2), 455–485.

Corrigan v. Buckley, 271 U.S. 323 (1926).

Courtwright, D. T. (2013). Morality, public policy, and partisan politics in American history: An introduction. *Journal of Policy History, 25*(1), 1–11. doi:10.1017/ s0898030612000322

Craig, M. A., & Richeson, J. A. (2014). On the precipice of a "majority-minority" America: Perceived status threat from racial demographic shift affects white Americans' political ideology. *Psychological Science, 25*(6), 1189–1197.

Cramer, K. J. (2016). *The politics of resentment: Rural consciousness in Wisconsin and the rise of Scott Walker*. Chicago: University of Chicago Press.

Cresswell, T. (2006). The right to mobility: The production of mobility in the courtroom. *Antipode, 38*(4), 735–754.

Croll, P. R. (2007). Modeling determinants of white racial identity: Results from a new national survey. *Social Forces, 86*(2), 613–642. doi:10.1093/sf/86.2.613

Das, A. (2020). *No justice in the shadows: How America criminalizes immigrants*. New York: Bold Type Books.

Davis, A. M., & Ernst, R. (2011). Racial spectacles: Promoting a colorblind agenda through direct democracy. *Studies in Law, Politics and Society, 55*, 133–171.

Davis, A. M., & Ernst, R. (2019). Racial gaslighting. *Politics, Groups, and Identities, 7*(4), 761–774. doi:10.1080/21565503.2017.1403934.

Dawson, M. C. (1994). A Black counterpublic?: Economic earthquakes, racial agenda(s), and Black politics. *Public Culture, 7*(1), 195–223. doi:10.1215/08992363-7-1-195

Dawson, M. C. (1994). *Behind the mule: Race and class in African-American politics*. Princeton, NJ: Princeton University Press.

De Genova, N. (2007). The production of culprits: From deportability to detainability in the aftermath of "homeland security." *Citizenship Studies, 11*(5), 421–448.

DeSante, C. D., & Smith, C. W. (2018). Fear, institutionalized racism, and empathy: The two dimensions of whites' racial attitudes. Paper presented at the American Political Science Association, Boston, MA.

DeSante, C. D., & Smith, C. W. (2020). Fear, institutionalized racism, and empathy: The underlying dimensions of whites' racial attitudes. *PS: Political Science & Politics, 53*(4), 639–645. doi:10.1017/S1049096520000414

DeSante, C. D., & Smith, C. W. (2020). *Racial stasis: The millenial generation and the stagnation of racial attitudes in American politics*. Chicago: University of Chicago Press.

Devos, T., & Banaji, M. (2005). American = white? *Journal of Personality and Social Psychology, 88*(3), 447–466.

Dickinson, G. (2006). The Pleasantville effect: Nostalgia and the visual framing of (white) suburbia. *Western Journal of Communication, 70*(3), 212–233. doi:10.1080/10570310600843504

Dillon, M. (1969). The abolitionists: A decade of historiography, 1959–1969. *Journal of Southern History, 35*(4), 500. doi:10.2307/2206837

Dixon, D., & Gelatt, J. (2005). Immigration enforcement spending since IRCA. Retrieved from https://www.migrationpolicy.org/research/immigration-enforcement-spend ing-irca.

Dixon, J. C. (2006). The ties that bind and those that don't: Toward reconciling group threat and contact theories of prejudice. *Social Forces, 84*(4), 2179–2204. doi:10.1353/sof.2006.0085

Dovidio, J. F., Evans, N., & Tyler, R. B. (1986). Racial stereotypes: The contents of their cognitive representations. *Journal of Experimental Social Psychology, 22*(1), 22–37.

Dred Scott v. Sandford, 60 U.S. 393 (1857).

Du Bois, W. E. B. (1966). *Black reconstruction in America, 1860–1880*. New York: Russell & Russell.

Duckitt, J., Bizumic, B., Krauss, S. W., & Heled, E. (2010). A tripartite approach to right-wing authoritarianism: The authoritarianism-conservatism-traditionalism model. *Political Psychology, 31*(5), 685–715. doi:10.1111/j.1467-9221.2010.00781.x

Dustmann, C., & Preston, I. P. (2007). Racial and economic factors in attitudes to immigration. *B.E. Journal of Economic Analysis & Policy, 7*(1), 62. doi:10.2202/1935-1682.1655

Dyck, J. J., Johnson, G. B., & Wasson, J. T. (2012). A blue tide in the golden state: Ballot propositions, population change, and party identification in California. *American Politics Research, 40*(3), 450–475. doi:10.1177/1532673X11427948

Ebonya, W. (2006). How Black candidates affect voter turnout. *Quarterly Journal of Economics, 121*(3), 973–998. doi:10.1162/qjec.121.3.973

Eckhouse, L. (2018). White riot: Race, institutions, and the 2016 U.S. Election. *Politics, Groups & Identities, 8*(2), 1–12. doi:10.1080/21565503.2018.1442725

Edsall, T. B., & Edsall, M. D. (1991). *Chain reaction: The impact of race, rights, and taxes on American politics*. New York: Norton.

Eichstedt, J. L. (2001). Problematic white identities and a search for racial justice. *Sociological Forum, 15*(3), 445–470.

Ellison, C. G., Shin, H., & Leal, D. L. (2011). The contact hypothesis and attitudes toward Latinos in the United States. *Social Science Quarterly, 92*(4), 938–958.

Enos, R. D. (2017). *The space between us: Social geography and politics*. Cambridge, UK: Cambridge University Press.

Espenshade, T. J., & Calhoun, C. (1993). An analysis of public opinion toward undocumented immigration. *Population Research and Policy Review, 12*(3), 189–224.

Espenshade, T. J., & Hempstead, K. (1996). Contemporary American attitudes toward U.S. immigration. *International Migration Review, 30*(2), 535–570.

Esses, V. M., Dovidio, J. F., & Hodson, G. (2002). Public attitudes toward immigration in the United States and Canada in response to the September 11, 2001 "attack on America." *Analyses of Social Issues and Public Policy, 2*(1), 69–85.

Esses, V. M., Dovidio, J. F., Jackson, L. M., & Armstrong, T. L. (2001). The immigration dilemma: The role of perceived group competition, ethnic prejudice, and national identity. *Journal of Social Issues, 57*(3), 389–412.

Esses, V. M., Jackson, L. M., & Armstrong, T. L. (1998). Intergroup competition and attitudes toward immigrants and immigration: An instrumental model of group conflict. *Journal of Social Issues, 54*(4), 1998.

Facchini, G., Mayda, A. M., & Puglisi, R. (2017). Illegal immigration and media exposure: Evidence on individual attitudes. *IZA Journal of Development and Migration, 7*(1), 1–36. doi:10.1186/s40176-017-0095-1

Fair Housing Administration. (1936). Underwriting manual. Retrieved from http://urbanoasis.org/projects/fha/FHAUnderwritingManualPtI.html.

Feldman, S. (1988). Structure and consistency in public opinion: The role of core beliefs and values. *American Journal of Political Science, 32*(2), 416–440.

Filindra, A. (2019). Is "threat" in the eye of the researcher? Theory and measurement in the study of state-level immigration policymaking. *Policy Studies Journal, 47*(3), 517–543. doi:10.1111/psj.12264

Finkelman, P. (1992). Fugitive slaves, midwestern racial tolerance, and the value of "justice delayed." *Iowa Law Review, 78*(1), 141.

Fiorina, M. P., Abrams, S. J., & Pope, J. (2006). *Culture war?: The myth of a polarized America* (2nd ed.). New York: Pearson Longman.

Flagg, B. J. (1993). "Was blind, but now I see": White race consciousness and the requirement of discriminatory intent. *Michigan Law Review, 91*(5), 953–1017. doi:10.2307/1289678

Flores, R. D., & Schachter, A. (2018). Who are the "illegals"? The social construction of illegality in the United States. *American Sociological Review, 83*(5), 839–868. doi:10.1177/0003122418794635

Fraga, L. R., Garcia, J. A., Hero, R., Jones-Correa, M., Martinez-Ebers, V., & Segura, G. M. (2010). *Latino lives in America: Making it home.* Philadelphia: Temple University Press.

Frank, T. (2004). *What's the matter with Kansas?: How conservatives won the heart of America* (1st ed.). New York: Metropolitan Books.

Frankenberg, R. (1993). *White women, race matters: The social construction of whiteness.* Minneapolis: University of Minnesota Press.

Freeman, J. (1986). The political culture of the Democratic and Republican Parties. *Political Science Quarterly, 101*(3), 327. doi:10.2307/2151619

Gabaccia, D. R. (2010). Nations of immigrants: Do words matter? *Pluralist, 5*(3), 5–31. doi:10.1353/plu.2010.0011

Garcia, R. J. (1995). Critical race theory and Proposition 187: The racial politics of immigration law. *Chicano-Latino Law Review, 17*, 118–154.

García Bedolla, L., & Haynie, K. L. (2013). The Obama coalition and the future of American politics. *Politics, Groups, and Identities, 1*(1), 128–133. doi:10.1080/21565503.2012.758593

Gardner, M. M. (2005). *The qualities of a citizen: Women, immigration, and citizenship, 1870–1965.* Princeton, NJ: Princeton University Press.

Garrison, W. L. (1850). *The Liberator.* Worcester, MA: American Antiquarian Society Historical Periodicals Collection. https://www.americanantiquarian.org.

Garrison, W. L. (1995). *William Lloyd Garrison and the fight against slavery: Selections from The Liberator.* Boston: Bedford Books of St. Martin's Press.

Gerster, P., & Cords, N. (Eds.). (1989). *Myth and southern history: The new south* (2nd ed. Vol. 2). Champaign: University of Illinois Press.

Gest, J. (2016). *The new minority: White working class politics in an age of immigration and inequality*. New York: Oxford University Press.

Gilens, M. (1996). Race coding and white opposition to welfare. *American Political Science Review, 90*(3), 599–604.

Gilens, M. (1999). *Why Americans hate welfare: Race, media, and the politics of antipoverty policy*. Chicago and London: University of Chicago Press.

Gimpel, J. G., & Schuknecht, J. E. (2009). *Patchwork nation: Sectionalism and political change in American politics*. Ann Arbor: University of Michigan Press.

Gjelten, T. (2015). *A nation of nations: A great American immigration story*. Riverside: Simon & Schuster.

Gold, A. R. (1989, Mar 17). City's Irish newcomers are illegal, but not alien. *New York Times*, p. A12. Retrieved from https://www.nytimes.com/1989/03/17/us/boston-jour nal-city-s-irish-newcomers-are-illegal-but-not-alien.html.

Goldman, S. K. (2017). Explaining white opposition to Black political leadership: The role of fear of racial favoritism. *Political Psychology, 38*(5), 721–739. doi:10.1111/pops.12355

Gonzales, R. (2018, Feb 22). America no longer a "nation of immigrants," USCIS says. Retrieved from https://www.npr.org/sections/thetwo-way/2018/02/22/588097749/america-no-longer-a-nation-of-immigrants-uscis-says.

Gotanda, N. (1991). A critique of "our constitution is color-blind." *Stanford Law Review, 44*(1), 1–68.

Graham, J., Haidt, J., & Nosek, B. A. (2009). Liberals and conservatives rely on different sets of moral foundations. *Journal of Personality and Social Psychology, 96*(5), 1029–1046. doi:10.1037/a0015141

Green, D. P., Palmquist, B., & Schickler, E. (2002). *Partisan hearts and minds: Political parties and the social identities of voters*. New Haven, CT: Yale University Press.

Greene, S. (1999). Understanding party identification: A social identity approach. *Political Psychology, 20*(2), 393–403. doi:10.1111/0162-895x.00150

Gregory, J. N. (2005). *The southern diaspora: How the great migrations of Black and white southerners transformed America*. Chapel Hill: University of North Carolina Press.

Griffith, B., & Vaughan, J. M. (2020, Mar 23). Map: Sanctuary cities, counties, and states. Retrieved from https://cis.org/Map-Sanctuary-Cities-Counties-and-States.

Grossman, M., & Hopkins, D. A. (2016). *Asymmetric politics: Ideological Republicans and group interest Democrats*. New York: Oxford University Press.

Gulasekaram, P., & Ramakrishnan, S. K. (2015). *The new immigration federalism*. New York: Cambrige University Press.

Gurin, P., Miller, A. H., & Gurin, G. (1980). Stratum identification and consciousness. *Social Psychology Quarterly, 43*(1), 30–47. doi:10.2307/3033746

Ha, S. E. (2010). The consequences of multiracial contexts on public attitudes toward immigration. *Political Research Quarterly, 63*(1), 29–42.

Hainmueller, J., & Hiscox, M. J. (2010). Attitudes toward highly skilled and low-skilled immigration: Evidence from a survey experiment. *American Political Science Review, 104*(1), 61–84.

Hair, J. F., Black, W. C., Black, B., Babin, B. J., & Anderson, R. E. (2010). *Multivariate data analysis* (7th ed.). London: Pearson Education.

Hancock, A.-M. (2004). *The politics of disgust: The public identity of the welfare queen*. New York: NYU Press.

Haney Lopez, I. (2006). *White by law: The legal construction of race*. New York: NYU Press.

Hanson, G. H., Scheve, K., & Slaughter, M. J. (2007). Public finance and individual preferences over globalization strategies. *Economics & Politics, 19*(1), 1–33. doi:10.1111/j.1468-0343.2007.00300.x

Harris, C. I. (1993). Whiteness as property. *Harvard Law Review, 106*(8), 1707–1791. doi:10.2307/1341787

Harrold, S. (2001). *American abolitionists*. Harlow, England: Longman.

Hartmann, D., Gerteis, J., & Croll, P. R. (2009). An empirical assessment of whiteness theory: Hidden from how many? *Social Problems, 56*(3), 403–424. doi:10.1525/sp.2009.56.3.403

Hartmann, D., Gerteis, J., & Edgell, P. (2010). *American mosaic project survey, 2003*. Minnesota: University of Minnesota. (ICPSR 28821).

Harvey, J. (2007). *Whiteness and morality: Pursuing racial justice through reparations and sovereignty*. New York: Palgrave Macmillan US.

Haynes, C., Merolla, J. L., & Ramakrishnan, S. K. (2016). *Framing immigrants: News coverage, public opinion, and policy*. New York: Russell Sage Foundation.

Heersink, B., & Jenkins, J. A. (2020a, Feb 7). The Republican Party is white and Southern. How did that happen? Retrieved from https://www.washingtonpost.com/politics/2020/02/07/republican-party-is-white-southern-how-did-that-happen/.

Heersink, B., & Jenkins, J. A. (2020b). *Republican Party politics and the American South, 1865–1968*. Cambridge, UK: Cambridge University Press.

Heersink, B., & Jenkins, J. A. (2020c). Whiteness and the emergence of the Republican Party in the early twentieth-century South. *Studies in American Political Development, 34*(1), 71–90. doi:10.1017/s0898588x19000208

Helms, J. E. (1990). *Black and white racial identity: Theory, research, and practice*. New York: Greenwood Press.

Henry, P. J., & Sears, D. O. (2002). The symbolic racism 2000 scale. *Political Psychology, 23*(2), 253–283.

Henry, W. (1990). Beyond the melting pot. *Time, 135*(15), 28.

Hernández, K. L. (2017). *City of inmates: Conquest, rebellion, and the rise of human caging in Los Angeles*. North Carolina: UNC Press.

Hero, R. E., & Tolbert, C. J. (1996). A racial/ethnic diversity interpretation of politics and policy in the states of the U.S. *American Journal of Political Science, 40*(3), 851–871. doi:10.2307/2111798

Hickel, F. R., Alamillo, R., Oskooii, K., & Collingwood, L. (2021). The role of identity prioritization: Why some Latinx support restrictionist immigration policies and candidates. *Public Opinion Quarterly, 84*(4), 860–891. doi:10.1093/poq/nfaa048

Higham, J. (1958). *Strangers in the land: Patterns of American nativism, 1860–1925*. New Brunswick, NJ: Rutgers University Press.

Hill Collins, P. (2000). *Black feminist thought: Knowledge, consciousness, and the politics of empowerment* (Rev. 10th anniversary ed.). New York: Routledge.

Hing, B. O. (1993). *Making and remaking Asian America through immigration policy, 1850–1990*. Stanford, CA: Stanford University Press.

Hing, B. O. (2009). Institutional racism, ICE raids, and immigration reform. *University of San Francisco Law Review, 44*(2), 307–352.

Hochschild, A. R. (2016). *Strangers in their own land: Anger and mourning on the American right*. New York: New Press.

Hogg, M. A., Terry, D. J., & White, K. M. (1995). A tale of two theories: A critical comparison of identity theory with social identity theory. *Social Psychology Quarterly, 58*(4), 255–269. doi:10.2307/2787127

Hogg, M. A., Turner, J. C., & Davidson, B. (1990). Polarized norms and social frames of reference: A test of the self-categorization theory of group polarization. *Basic & Applied Social Psychology, 11*(1), 77–100. doi:10.1207/s15324834basp1101_6

Hood, M. V., & Morris, I. L. (1997). ¿amigo o enemigo?: Context, attitudes, and Anglo public opinion toward immigration. *Social Science Quarterly, 78*(2), 309–323.

Hood, M. V., & Morris, I. L. (1998). Give us your tired, your poor, . . . But make sure they have a green card: The effects of documented and undocumented migrant context on Anglo opinion toward immigration. *Political Behavior, 20*(1), 1–15.

Hood, M. V., & Morris, I. L. (2000). Brother, can you spare a dime? Racial/ethnic context and the Anglo vote on Proposition 187. *Social Science Quarterly, 81*(1), 194–206.

Hopkins, D. J. (2010). Politicized places: Explaining where and when immigrants provoke local opposition. *American Political Science Review, 104*(1), 40–60.

Horst, U., Kirman, A., & Teschl, M. (2007). *Changing identity: The emergence of social groups.* Economics Working Paper 0078. Institute for Advanced Study, School of Social Science.

Hosang, D. (2010). *Racial propositions: Ballot initiatives and the making of postwar california.* Berkeley: University of California Press.

Huddy, L., Feldman, S., & Cassese, E. (2007). On the distinct political effects of anxiety and anger. In W. R. Neuman, G. E. Marcus, A. Crigler, & M. MacKuen (Eds.), *The affect effect: Dynamics of emotion in political thinking and behavior* (pp. 202–230). Chicago: University of Chicago Press.

Huddy, L., & Khatib, N. (2007). American patriotism, national identity, and political involvement. *American Journal of Political Science, 51*(1), 63–71.

Hughes, M. (1997). Symbolic racism, old-fashioned racism, and whites' opposition to affirmative action. In S. A. Tuch & J. A. Martin (Eds.), *Racial attitudes in the 1990s: Continuity and change* (pp. 45–75). Westport, CT: Praeger.

Huston, J. (1990). The experiential basis of the northern antislavery impulse. *The Journal of Southern History, 56*(4), 609. doi:10.2307/2210930

Hutchings, V. L., & Valentino, N. A. (2004). The centrality of race in American politics. *Annual Review of Political Science, 7*(1), 383–408. doi:10.1146/annurev.polisci.7.012003.104859

Hutchings, V. L., & Wong, C. (2014). Racism, group position, and attitudes about immigration among Blacks and whites. *Du Bois Review, 11*(2), 419. doi:10.1017/S1742058X14000198

Igartua, J. J., & Cheng, L. (2009). Moderating effect of group cue while processing news on immigration: Is the framing effect a heuristic process? *Journal of Communication, 59*, 726–749.

Ignatiev, N., & Garvey, J. (Eds.). (1996). *Race traitor.* New York: Routledge.

Jackson, K. T. (1985). *Crabgrass frontier: The suburbanization of the United States.* New York: Oxford University Press.

Jacobsmeier, M. L. (2014). From Black and white to left and right: Race, perceptions of candidates' ideologies, and voting behavior in U.S. House elections. *Political Behavior, 37*(3), 595–621. doi:10.1007/s11109-014-9283-3

Jacobson, M. F. (1998). *Whiteness of a different color: European immigrants and the alchemy of race.* Cambridge, MA: Harvard University Press.

Jacobson, M. F. (2006). *Roots too: White ethnic revival in post-Civil Rights America*. Cambridge, MA: Harvard University Press.

Jacobson, R. D. (2008). *The new nativism: Proposition 187 and the debate over immigration*. Minneapolis: University of Minnesota Press.

Jardina, A. (2019). *White identity politics*. Cambridge, UK: Cambridge University Press.

Jardina, A., Kalmoe, N., & Gross, K. (2021). Disavowing white identity: How social disgust can change social identities. *Political Psychology, 42*(4), 619–636. doi:10.1111/pops.12717

Johnson, D. M. (2001). The AEDPA and the IIRIRA: Treating misdemeanors as felonies for immigration purposes. *Journal of legislation, 27*(2), 477–491.

Johnson, K. R. (2004). *The "huddled masses" myth: Immigration and civil rights*. Philadelphia: Temple University Press.

Jones, B., & Martin, D. (2017). Path-to-citizenship or deportation? How elite cues shaped opinion on immigration in the 2010 U.S. House elections. *Political Behavior, 39*(1), 177–204. doi:10.1007/s11109-016-9352-x

Juarez, M., Gomez-Aguinaga, B., & Bettez, S. P. (2018). Twenty years after IIRIRA: The rise of immigrant detention and its effects on Latinx communities across the nation. *Journal on Migration and Human Security, 6*(1), 74–96. doi:10.14240/jmhs.v6i1.113

Kam, C. D., & Burge, C. D. (2018). Uncovering reactions to the racial resentment scale across the racial divide. *Journal of Politics, 80*(1), 314–320. doi:10.1086/693907

Kanter, R. M. (1968). Commitment and social organization: A study of commitment mechanisms in utopian communities. *American Sociological Review, 33*(4), 499–517. doi:10.2307/2092438

Kanter, R. M. (1972). *Commitment and community: Communes and utopias in sociological perspective*. Cambridge, MA: Harvard University Press.

Kaplan, A. (2003). Homeland insecurities: Reflections on language and space. *Radical History Review, 85*(1), 82–93. doi:10.1215/01636545-2003-85-82

Katz, I., & Hass, R. G. (1988). Racial ambivalence and American value conflict: Correlational and priming studies of dual cognitive structures. *Journal of Personality and Social Psychology, 55*(6), 893–905. doi:10.1037/0022-3514.55.6.893

Katz, M. B. (Ed.) (1993). *The "underclass" debate: Views from history*. Princeton, NJ: Princeton University Press.

Keith, R. (1997). *Voting hopes or fears?: White voters, Black candidates, and racial politics in America*. Oxford: Oxford University Press.

Kendi, I. X. (2016). *Stamped from the beginning: The definitive history of racist ideas in America*. New York, NY: Nation Books.

Kerber, L. K. (1992). The paradox of women's citizenship in the early republic: The case of Martin vs. Massachusetts, 1805. *American Historical Review, 97*(2), 349–378. doi:10.2307/2165723

Key, V. O. (1949). *Southern politics in state and nation*. New York: Alfred A. Knopf.

Kim, C. J. (2000). *Bitter fruit: The politics of Black-Korean conflict in New York City*. New Haven, CT: Yale University Press.

Kinder, D. R., & Kam, C. D. (2009). *Us against them: Ethnocentric foundations of American opinion*. Chicago: University of Chicago Press.

Kinder, D. R., & Sanders, L. (1996). *Divided by color: Racial politics and democratic ideals*. Chicago: University of Chicago Press.

Kinder, D. R., & Sears, D. O. (1981). Prejudice and politics: Symbolic racism versus racial threats to the good life. *Journal of Personality and Social Psychology, 40*(3), 414–431. doi:10.1037/0022-3514.40.3.414

Kinder, D. R., & Sears, D. O. (Eds.). (1985). *Public opinion and political action* (3rd ed.). New York: Random House.

Kinder, D. R., & Winter, N. (2001). Exploring the racial divide: Blacks, whites, and opinion on national policy. *American Journal of Political Science, 45*(2), 439–456. doi:10.2307/2669351

King, D. (2002). *Making Americans: Immigration, race, and the origins of the diverse democracy.* Cambridge, MA: Harvard University Press.

King, M. L. Jr. (2010 [1967]). *Where do we go from here: Chaos or community?* Boston: Beacon Press.

Knoll, B. R. (2013). Implicit nativist attitudes, social desirability, and immigration policy preferences. *International Migration Review, 47*(1), 132–165. doi:10.1111/imre.12016

Knoll, B. R., Redlawsk, D. P., & Sanborn, H. (2010). Framing labels and immigration policy attitudes in the Iowa caucuses: "Trying to out-Tancredo Tancredo." *Political Behavior, 33*(3), 433–454.

Knowles, E. D., & Peng, K. (2005). White selves: Conceptualizing and measuring a dominant-group identity. *Journal of Personality and Social Psychology, 89*(2), 223–241. doi:10.1037/0022-3514.89.2.223

Knuckey, J., & Kim, M. (2020). The politics of white racial identity and vote choice in the 2018 midterm elections. *Social Science Quarterly, 101*(4), 1584–1599. doi:10.1111/ssqu.12809

Lahav, G., & Courtemanche, M. (2012). The ideological effects of framing threat on immigration and civil liberties. *Political Behavior, 34*, 477–505.

Lakoff, G., & Ferguson, S. (2006). The framing of immigration. Retrieved fromhttps://escholarship.org/uc/item/0j89f85g.

Langer, G., & Cohen, J. (2005). Voters and values in the 2004 election. *Public Opinion Quarterly, 69*(5), 744–759. doi:10.1093/poq/nfi060

Lassiter, M. D. (2006). *The silent majority: Suburban politics in the sunbelt South.* Princeton, NJ: Princeton University Press.

Law, A. O. (2017). The Irish roots of the diversity visa lottery. Retrieved from https://www.politico.com/magazine/story/2017/11/01/diversity-visa-irish-history-215776.

Lazarus, M. L., III. (1989). An historical analysis of alien land law: Washington Territory & State 1853–1889. Symposium: Washington legal history. *University of Puget Sound Law Review, 12*(2), 197–246.

Lee, J. C.-S., & Appiah, K. A. (1994). Navigating the topology of race. *Stanford Law Review, 46*(3), 747–780. doi:10.2307/1229107

Lee, Y., & Ottati, V. (2002). Attitudes towards U.S. immigration policy: The role of in-group–out-group bias, economic concern, and obedience to law. *Journal of Social Psychology, 142*(5), 617–634.

Leach, C. W., Van Zomeren, M., Zebel, S., Vliek, M. L. W., Pennekamp, S. F., Doosje, B., . . . Spears, R. (2008). Group-level self-definition and self-investment: A hierarchical (multicomponent) model of in-group identification. *Journal of Personality and Social Psychology, 95*(1), 144–165. doi:10.1037/0022-3514.95.1.144

Leibovich, M. (2020, Jul 23). A club of G.O.P. political heirs push back on Trump. Retrieved from https://www.nytimes.com/2020/07/16/us/politics/trump-republicans.html?campaign_id=9&emc=edit_nn_20220511&instance_id=61016&nl=the-morning&regi_id=134902338&segment_id=91882&te=1&user_id=645a820770830e52a7a803bbe51a6eb9.

Lewis, A. E. (2004). "What group?" Studying whites and whiteness in the era of "colorblindness." *Sociological Theory, 22*(4), 623–646. doi:10.1111/j.0735-2751.2004.00237.x

Lipset, S. M., Lazarsfeld, P. F., Barton, A. H., & Linz, J. (1954). *The psychology of voting: An analysis of voting behavior. The handbook of social psychology* (Vol. II, pp. 1124–1554). Reading, MA: Addison-Wesley.

Lipsitz, G. (1998). *The possessive investment in whiteness: How white people profit from identity politics.* Philadelphia: Temple University Press.

Loewen, J. W. (2005). *Sundown towns: A hidden dimension of American crow.* New York: The New Press.

Lopez, I. H. (1997). *White by law: The legal construction of race.* New York: NYU Press.

Lopez Bunyasi, T. (2015). Color-cognizance and color-blindness in white America: Perceptions of whiteness and their potential to predict racial policy attitudes at the dawn of the twenty-first century. *Sociology of Race and Ethnicity, 1*(2), 209–224. doi:10.1177/2332649214553446

Lopez Bunyasi, T. (2019). The role of whiteness in the 2016 presidential primaries. *Perspectives on Politics, 17*(3), 679–698. doi:10.1017/S1537592719001427

Magnuson, E., & Painton, P. (1989, Mar 30). The re-greening of America: A new wave of Irish immigrants is showing its muscle. *Time, 133,* 30–31.

Maly, M., Dalmage, H., & Michaels, N. (2013). The end of an idyllic world: Nostalgia narratives, race, and the construction of white powerlessness. *Critical Sociology, 39*(5), 757–779. doi:10.1177/0896920512448941

Marquez, T., & Schraufnagel, S. (2013). Hispanic population growth and state immigration policy: An analysis of restriction (2008–12). *Publius: The Journal of Federalism, 43*(3), 347–367. doi:10.1093/publius/pjt008

Mason, L. (2018). *Uncivil agreement: How politics became our identity.* Chicago: University of Chicago Press.

Massey, D. S. (2009). Racial formation in theory and practice: The case of Mexicans in the United States. *Race and Social Problems, 1*(1), 12–26. doi:10.1007/s12552-009-9005-3

Massey, D. S., & Denton, N. A. (1993). *American apartheid: Segregation and the making of the underclass.* Cambridge, MA: Harvard University Press.

Massey, D. S., & Pren, K. A. (2012). Unintended consequences of US immigration policy: Explaining the post-1965 surge from Latin America. *Population and Development Review, 38*(1), 1–29. doi:10.1111/j.1728-4457.2012.00470.x

Masuoka, N. (2006). Together they become one: Examining the predictors of panethnic group consciousness among Asian Americans and Latinos. *Social Science Quarterly, 87*(5), 993–1011.

Masuoka, N., & Junn, J. (2013). *The politics of belonging: Race, public opinion, and immigration.* Chicago: University of Chicago Press.

Mathias, C. (2019, Nov 4). Go back to your country, they said. Retrieved from https://www.huffpost.com/feature/go-back-to-your-country.

Matos, Y. (2018a, Jan 9). How America's 1996 immigration act set the stage for increasingly localized and tough enforcement. Retrieved from https://scholars.org/brief/how-americas-1996-immigration-act-set-stage-increasingly-localized-and-tough-enforcement.

Matos, Y. (2018b). Immigration within contemporary political discourse. In H. V. Miller & A. Peguero (Eds.), *Routledge handbook on immigration and crime* (pp. 220–235). New York: Routledge.

Matos, Y. (2020). The American "dream": Understanding white Americans' support for the Dream Act and punitive immigration policies. *Perspectives on Politics, 19*(2), 1–20. doi:10.1017/S1537592720002492

Matos, Y., & Miller, J. L. (2021). The politics of pronouns: How Trump framed the ingroup in the 2016 presidential election. *Politics, Groups, and Identities,* (Online First), 1–19. doi:10.1080/21565503.2021.2007964

Maxwell, A., & Shields, T. (2019). *The long southern strategy: How chasing white voters in the South changed American politics.* New York: Oxford University Press.

Mayda, A. M. (2006). Who is against immigration? A cross-country investigation of individual attitudes toward immigrants. *The Review of Economics and Statistics, 88*(3), 510–530. doi:10.1162/rest.88.3.510

McCall, G. J., & Simmons, J. L. (1966). *Identities and interactions.* New York: Free Press.

McClain, P., Carew, J. D. J., Walton, E. Jr., & Watts, C. S. (2009). Group membership, group identity, and group consciousness: Measures of racial identity in American politics? *Annual Review of Political Science, 12*(1), 471–485. doi:10.1146/annurevpolsci10072805102452

McClosky, H., & Zaller, J. (1984). *The American ethos: Public attitudes toward capitalism and democracy.* Cambridge, MA: Harvard University Press.

McConahay, J. B. (1986). Modern racism, ambivalence, and the modern racism scale. In J. F. Dovidio & S. Gaertner (Eds.), *Prejudice, discrimination, and racism* (pp. 91–125). Orlando: Academic Press.

McConahay, J. B., & Hough Jr, J. C. (1976). Symbolic racism. *Journal of Social Issues, 32*(2), 23–45.

McDermott, M. L. (2016). Race and gender cues in low-information elections. *Political Research Quarterly, 51*(4), 895–918. doi:10.1177/106591299805100403

McGhee, H. C. (2021). *The sum of us: What racism costs everyone and how we can prosper together.* New York: One World.

McIntosh, P. (1989, July/Aug, 10–12). White privilege: Unpacking the invisible knapsack. *Peace and Freedom.*

McKanders, K. M. (2012). Immigration enforcement and the fugitive slave acts: Exploring their similarities. *Catholic University Law Review, 61*(4), 953.

McPherson, T. (2003). *Reconstructing Dixie: Race, gender, and nostalgia in the imagined South.* Durham, NC: Duke University Press.

Melendres v. Arpaio, No. 2:07-cv-02513-GMS (United States District Court, D. Arizona 2013).

Mettler, S. (2011). *The submerged state: How invisible government policies undermine American democracy.* Chicago: University of Chicago Press.

Metzl, J. M. (2019). *Dying of whiteness: How the politics of racial resentment is killing America's heartland.* New York: Basic Books.

Middleton, S. (1993). *The Black Laws in the old Northwest: A documentary history.* Westport, CT: Greenwood Press.

Miller, A. H., Gurin, P., Gurin, G., & Malanchuk, O. (1981). Group consciousness and political participation. *American Journal of Political Science, 25*(3), 494–511. doi:10.2307/2110816

Miller, E. T. (2020). Race, class, patriotism, and religion in early childhood: The formation of whiteness. In S. K. McManimon, Z. A. Casey, & C. Berchini (Eds.), *Whiteness at the table: Antiracism, racism, and identity in education* (pp. 1–20). Lanham, MD: Lexington Books.

Mills, C. W. (1997). *The racial contract.* Ithaca, NY: Cornell University Press.

Mills, C. W. (1998). White right: The idea of a *Herrenvolk* ethics. In *Blackness visible: Essays on philosophy and race* (pp. 139–166). Ithaca, NY: Cornell University Press.

Mohl, R. A. (2002). The nuevo New South: Hispanic migration to Alabama. *Migration World Magazine, 30*(3), 14–18.

Monogan, J. E. (2011). Replication data for: The politics of immigrant policy in the 50 U.S. states, 2005–2011. Retrieved from: https://doi.org/10.7910/DVN/AE1LSM.

Monogan, J. E. (2013). The politics of immigrant policy in the 50 US states, 2005–2011. *Journal of Public Policy, 33*(1), 35–64. doi:10.1017/S0143814X12000189

Moreno, P. D. (2013). *The American state from the Civil War to the New Deal: The twilight of constitutionalism and the triumph of progressivism.* Cambridge, UK: Cambridge University Press.

Morgan, S., & Lee, J. (2018). Trump voters and the white working class. *Sociological Science, 5*(10), 234–245. doi:10.15195/v5.a10

Morrison, T. (1992). *Playing in the dark: Whiteness and the literary imagination.* New York: Vintage Books.

Mutz, D. C. (2018). Status threat, not economic hardship, explains the 2016 presidential vote. *Proceedings of the National Academy of Sciences of the United States, 115*(19), E4330. doi:10.1073/pnas.1718155115

Myrdal, G. (1962). *An American dilemma: The Negro problem and modern democracy* (20th anniversary ed.). New York: Harper & Row.

Negrón, R. (2019, Sep 30). A nation of immigrants or a nation of laws? Retrieved from https://www.diggitmagazine.com/column/nation-immigrants-or-nation-laws.

Neuman, G. (1993). The lost century of American immigration law (1776–1875). *Columbia Law Review, 93*(8), 1833. doi:10.2307/1123006

Neundorf, A., & Smets, K. (2017). *Political socialization and the making of citizens*: Oxford: Oxford University Press.

Nevins, J. (2010). *Operation Gatekeeper and beyond: The war on "illegals" and the remaking of the U.S.-Mexico boundary* (2nd ed.). New York: Routledge.

Newman, B. J. (2012). Acculturating contexts and Anglo opposition to immigration in the United States. *American Journal of Political Science, 57*(2), 374–390.

Newman, B. J., Johnson, C. D., Strickland, A. A., & Citrin, J. (2012). Immigration crackdown in the American workplace: Explaining variation in e-verify policy adoption across the U.S. States. *State Politics & Policy Quarterly, 12*(2), 160–182.

Newton, L. (2008). *Illegal, alien, or immigrant: The politics of immigration reform.* New York: New York University Press.

Ngai, M. M. (2004). *Impossible subjects: Illegal aliens and the making of modern America.* Princeton, NJ: Princeton University Press.

Nobles, M. (2000). *Shades of citizenship: Race and the census in modern politics.* Stanford, CA: Stanford University Press.

Novak, M. (1972). *The rise of the unmeltable ethnics; politics and culture in the seventies.* New York: Macmillan.

Nunnally, S., & Carter, N. (2012). Moving from victims to victors: African American attitudes on the "culture of poverty" and Black blame. *Journal of African American Studies, 16*(3), 423–455. doi:10.1007/s12111-011-9197-7

Nussbaum, M. (2016). *Anger and forgiveness: Resentment, generosity, justice.* New York: Oxford University Press.

Oakes, P. J., Haslam, S. A., & Turner, J. C. (1994). *Stereotyping and social reality.* Oxford, UK: Blackwell.

Olivas, M. A. (2007). Immigration-related state and local ordinances: Preemption, prejudice, and the proper role for enforcement. *University of Chicago Legal Forum, 2007*(1), 27–56.

Oliver, E. J., & Wong, J. (2003). Intergroup prejudice in multiethnic settings. *American Journal of Political Science, 47*, 567–582.

Oliver, M. L., & Shapiro, T. M. (1995). *Black wealth/white wealth: A new perspective on racial inequality.* New York: Routledge.

Olson, J. (2004). *The abolition of white democracy.* Minneapolis: University of Minnesota Press.

Omi, M., & Winant, H. (2015). *Racial formations in the United States* (3rd ed.). New York: Routledge.

Opotow, S. (1990). Moral exclusion and injustice: An introduction. *Journal of Social Issues, 46*(1), 1–20. doi:10.1111/j.1540-4560.1990.tb00268.x

Orey, B. D. A. (2004). Explaining Black conservatives: Racial uplift or racial resentment? *The Black Scholar, 34*(1), 18–22. doi:10.1080/00064246.2004.11413241

Oshatz, M. (2008). The problem of moral progress: The slavery debates and the development of liberal protestantism in the United States. *Modern Intellectual History, 5*(2), 225–250. doi:10.1017/S1479244308001637

Oshatz, M. (2011). *Slavery and sin: The fight against slavery and the rise of liberal protestantism.* New York: Oxford University Press.

Pantoja, A. (2006). Against the tide? Core American values and attitudes toward US immigration policy in the mid-1990s. *Journal of Ethnic and Migration Studies, 32*(3), 515–531.

Parker, C. S., & Barreto, M. A. (2013). *Change they can't believe in: The Tea Party and reactionary politics in America.* Princeton, NJ: Princeton University Press.

Parker, C. S., Sawyer, M. Q., & Towler, C. (2009). A Black man in the White House?: The role of racism and patriotism in the 2008 presidential election. *Du Bois Review, 6*(1), 193–217. doi:10.1017/S1742058X09090031

Parker, K. M. (2015). *Making foreigners: Immigration and citizenship law in America, 1600–2000.* Cambridge, UK: Cambridge University Press.

Pérez, E. O. (2010). Explicit evidence on the import of implicit attitudes: The IAT and immigration policy judgments. *Political Behavior, 32*(4), 517–545.

Pérez, E. O. (2016). Unspoken politics: Implicit attitudes and political thinking. Cambridge, UK: Cambridge University Press.

Pérez, E. O., Kuo, E. E., Russel, J., Scott-Curtis, W., Muñoz, J., & Tobias, M. (2021). The politics *in* white identity: Testing a racialized partisan hypothesis. *Political Psychology.* doi:10.1111/pops.12788

Perry, P. (2001). White means never having to say you're ethnic: White youth and the construction of "cultureless" identities. *Journal of Contemporary Ethnography, 30*(1), 56–91. doi:10.1177/089124101030001002

Perry, P. (2002). *Shades of white: White kids and racial identities in high school.* Durham, NC: Duke University Press.

Petrow, G., Transue, J., & Vercellotti, T. (2018). Do white in-group processes matter, too? White racial identity and support for Black political candidates. *Political Behavior, 40*(1), 197–222. doi:10.1007/s11109-017-9422-8

Pettigrew, T. F. (1981). The mental healh aspect. In B. P. Bowser & R. G. Hunt (Eds.), *Impacts of racism on white Americans* (pp. 97–118). Beverly Hills, CA: Sage.

Pettigrew, T. F., & Meertens, R. W. (1995). Subtle and blatant prejudice in Western Europe. *European Journal of Social Psychology, 25*, 57–76.

Pettigrew, T. F., Wagner, U., & Christ, O. (2007). Who opposes immigration? Comparing German with North American findings. *Du Bois Review, 4*(1), 19–39.

Pew Research Center. (2018, Aug 9). *An examination of the 2016 electorate, based on validated voters.* Retrieved from https://www.pewresearch.org/politics/2018/08/09/an-examination-of-the-2016-electorate-based-on-validated-voters/.

Pew Research Center. (2019). Most border wall opponents, supporters say shutdown concessions are unacceptable. Retrieved from https://www.pewresearch.org/politics/2019/01/16/most-border-wall-opponents-supporters-say-shutdown-concessions-are-unacceptable/.

Phoenix, D. L. (2019). *The anger gap: How race shapes emotion in politics.* Cambridge, UK: Cambridge University Press.

Powell, A. A., Branscombe, N. R., & Schmitt, M. T. (2005). Inequality as ingroup privilege or outgroup disadvantage: The impact of group focus on collective guilt and interracial attitudes. *Personality & Social Psychology Bulletin, 31*(4), 508–521. doi:10.1177/0146167204271713

Price, B. (2018). Material memory: The politics of nostalgia on the eve of MAGA. *American Studies, 57*(1/2), 103–137. doi:10.1353/ams.2018.0027

Public Religion Research Institute (PRRI). (2019a). Data shows how passionate and partisan Americans are about the border wall. Retrieved from https://www.prri.org/spotlight/data-shows-how-passionate-and-partisan-americans-are-about-the-border-wall/.

Public Religion Research Institute (PRRI). (2019b). PRRI 2019 American values survey. Retrieved from https://www.prri.org/research/fractured-nation-widening-partisan-polarization-and-key-issues-in-2020-presidential-elections/.

Quadagno, J. S. (1996). *The color of welfare: How racism undermined the war on poverty.* New York: Oxford University Press.

Ramakrishnan, K., & Wong, T. K. (2010). Partisanship, not Spanish: Explaining municipal ordinances affecting undocumented immigrants. In M. Varsanyi (Ed.), *Taking local control: Immigration policy activism in U.S. cities and states* (pp. 73–96). Palo Alto, CA: Standord University Press.

Ramakrishnan, S. K. (2005). *Democracy in immigrant America: Changing demographics and political participation.* Stanford, CA: Stanford University Press.

Ramakrishnan, S. K., & Baldassare, M. (2004). *The ties that bind: Changing demographics and civic engagement in California.* San Francisco: Public Policy Institute of California.

Riera, P. (2016). Tactical voting. In Oxford Handbooks Editorial Board (Ed.), *Oxford handbook topics in politics.* Oxford Academic. Retrieved from https://doi.org/10.1093/oxfordhb/9780199935307.013.55.

Rimal, R. N. (2008). Modeling the relationship between descriptive norms and behaviors: A test and extension of the theory of normative social behavior (TNSB). *Health Communication, 23*(2), 103–116. doi:10.1080/10410230801967791

Rocha, R. R., & Espino, R. (2009). Racial threat, residential segregation, and the policy attitudes of Anglos. *Political Research Quarterly, 62*(2), 415–426.

Rodriguez, C. M. (2008). The significance of the local in immigration regulation. *Michigan Law Review, 106*(4), 567–642.

Roediger, D. R. (2005). *Working toward whiteness: How America's immigrants became white: The strange journey from Ellis Island to the suburbs.* New York: Basic Books.

Roediger, D. R. (2007). *The wages of whiteness: Race and the making of the American working class* (2nd ed.). New York: Verso.

Rogers, K., & Fandos, N. (2019, July 14). Trump tells Congresswomen to "go back" to the countries they came from. Retrieved from https://www.nytimes.com/2019/07/14/us/politics/trump-twitter-squad-congress.html.

Rogers, R. W., & Prenticedunn, S. (1981). Deindividuation and anger-mediated interracial aggression—unmasking regressive racism. *Journal of Personality and Social Psychology, 41*(1), 63–73. doi:10.1037/0022-3514.41.1.63

Romney, M. (2019, Jan 1). Mitt Romney: The president shapes the public character of the nation. Trump's character falls short. Retrieved from https://www.washingtonpost.com/opinions/mitt-romney-the-president-shapes-the-public-character-of-the-nation-trumps-character-falls-short/2019/01/01/37a3c8c2-0d1a-11e9-8938-5898adc28fa2_story.html.

Sabia, D. (2010). The anti-immigrant fervor in Georgia: Return of the nativist or just politics as usual? *Politics & Policy, 38*(1), 53–80.

Scammon, R. M., & Wattenberg, B. J. (1970). *The real majority.* New York: Coward-McCann.

Scheve, K. F., & Slaughter, M. J. (2001). Labor market competition and individual preferences over immigration policy. *Review of Economics and Statistics, 83*(1), 133–145.

Schickler, E. (2016). *Racial realignment: The transformation of American liberalism, 1932–1965.* Princeton, NJ: Princeton University Press.

Schildkraut, D. J. (2011). *Americanism in the twenty-first century: Public opinion in the age of immigration.* New York: Cambridge University Press.

Schildkraut, D. J. (2017). White attitudes about descriptive representation in the US: The roles of identity, discrimination, and linked fate. *Politics, Groups & Identities, 5*(1), 84–106. doi:10.1080/21565503.2015.1089296

Schildkraut, D. J. (2019). The political meaning of whiteness for liberals and conservatives. *The Forum, 17*(3), 421–446. doi:10.1515/for-2019-0028

Schrag, P. (2010). *Not fit for our society: Nativism and immigration.* Berkeley: University of California Press.

Schuman, H., Steeh, C., & Bobo, L. D. (1985). *Racial attitudes in America: Trends and interpretations.* Cambridge, MA: Harvard University Press.

Sears, D. O. (1986). College sophomores in the laboratory: Influences of a narrow data base on psychology's view of human nature. *Journal of Personality and Social Psychology, 51*(3), 515–530.

Sears, D. O., & Funk, C. L. (1999). Evidence of the long-term persistence of adults' political predispositions. *Journal of Politics, 61*(1), 1–28. doi:10.2307/2647773

Sears, D. O., Henry, J. P., & Kosterman, R. (2000). Egalitarian values and contemporary racial politics. In D. O. Sears, J. Sidanius, & L. Bobo (Eds.), *Racialized politics: The debate about racism in America,* (pp. 75–118). Chicago: University of Chicago Press.

Sears, D. O., & Savalei, V. (2006). The political color line in America: Many "peoples of color" or Black exceptionalism? *Political Psychology, 27*(6), 895–924. doi:10.1111/j.1467-9221.2006.00542.x

Sears, D. O., Sidanius, J., & Bobo, L. (Eds.). (2000). *Racialized politics: The debate about racism in America.* Chicago: University of Chicago Press.

Sears, D. O., & Valentino, N. A. (1997). Politics matters: Political events as catalysts for preadult socialization. *The American Political Science Review, 91*(1), 45–65. doi:10.2307/2952258

Segrest, M. (2019). *Memoir of a race traitor* (2nd ed.). New York: The New Press.

Shapiro, H. (1988). *White violence and Black response: From Reconstruction to Montgomery.* Amherst: University of Massachusetts Press.

Shapiro, T. M. (2017). *Toxic inequality: How America's wealth gap destroys mobility, deepens the racial divide, and threatens our future.* Boulder: Basic Books.

Shear, M. D., Benner, K., & Schmidt, M. S. (2020, Oct 28). "We need to take away children," no matter how young, Justice Dept. officials said. Retrieved from https://www.nytimes.com/2020/10/06/us/politics/family-separation-border-immigration-jeff-sessions-rod-rosenstein.html.

Sherif, M. (1965). *The psychology of social norms.* New York: Octagon Books.

Sibley, D. (1995). *Geographies of exclusion: Society and difference in the West.* New York: Routledge.

Shor, B., & McCarty, N. (2011). The ideological mapping of American legislatures. *American Political Science Review, 105*(3), 530–551. doi:10.1017/S0003055411000153

Sidanius, J. (1993). The psychology of group conflict and the dynamic of oppression: A social dominance perspective. In S. Iyengar & W. J. McGuire (Eds.), *Explorations in political psychology* (pp. 183–219). Durham, NC: Duke University Press.

Sidanius, J., Feshbach, S., Levin, S., & Pratto, F. (1997). The interface between ethnic and national attachment: Ethnic pluralism or ethnic dominance? *Public Opinion Quarterly, 61*(1), 102–133. doi:10.2307/2749514

Sidanius, J., & Pratto, F. (1999). *Social dominance: An intergroup theory of social hierarchy and oppression.* New York: Cambridge University Press.

Sides, J., & Gross, K. (2013). Stereotypes of Muslims and support for the war on terror. *Journal of Politics, 75*(3), 583–598. doi:10.1017/S0022381613000388

Sides, J., Tesler, M., & Vavreck, L. (2017). How Trump lost and won. *Journal of Democracy, 28*(2), 34–44. doi:10.1353/jod.2017.0022

Sides, J., Tesler, M., & Vavreck, L. (2019). *Identity crisis: The 2016 presidential campaign and the battle for the meaning of America.* Princeton, NJ: Princeton University Press.

Sigelman, C. K., Sigelman, L., Walkosz, B. J., & Nitz, M. (1995). Black candidates, white voters: Understanding racial bias in political perceptions. *American Journal of Political Science, 39*(1), 243–265. doi:10.2307/2111765

Skitka, L. J., Hanson, B. E., Washburn, A. N., & Mueller, A. B. (2018). Moral and religious convictions: Are they the same or different things? *PLoS One, 13*(6), e0199311. doi:10.1371/journal.pone.0199311

Smith, C. W. (2014). Shifting from structural to individual attributions of Black disadvantage: Age, period, and cohort effects on Black explanations of racial disparities. *Journal of Black Studies, 45*(5), 432–452. doi:10.1177/0021934714534069

Smith, J. R., & Terry, D. J. (2003). Attitude-behaviour consistency: The role of group norms, attitude accessibility, and mode of behavioural decision-making. *European Journal of Social Psychology, 33*(5), 591–608. doi:10.1002/ejsp.172

Smith, L. (1949). *Killers of the dream* (1st ed.). New York: W. W. Norton.

Smith, R. M. (2003). *Stories of peoplehood: The politics and morals of political membership.* Cambridge, UK: Cambridge University Press.

Sniderman, P. M., Hagendoorn, L., & Prior, M. (2004). Predisposing factors and situational triggers: Exclusionary reactions to immigrant minorities. *American Political Science Review, 98*(1), 35–49. doi:10.1017/S000305540400098X

Soss, J., Fording, R. C., & Schram, S. F. (2011). *Disciplining the poor: Neoliberal paternalism and the persistent power of race.* Chicago: University of Chicago Press.

Southern Poverty Law Center. (2020). Family separation under the Trump Administration—a timeline. Retrieved from https://www.splcenter.org/news/2020/06/17/family-separation-under-trump-administration-timeline.

Southern Poverty Law Center. (2021). Civil rights martyrs. Retrieved from https://www.splcenter.org/what-we-do/civil-rights-memorial/civil-rights-martyrs.

Staff. (2020, Sep 22). "Go back to Africa": Woman faces up to 7 years in bottle attack on Black NYC jogger. Retrieved from https://www.nbcnewyork.com/news/local/suspect-arrested-in-racist-ranting-bottle-attack-on-black-jogger-in-queens/2628693/.

Steinberg, S. (1995). *Turning back: The retreat from racial justice in American thought and policy.* Boston: Beacon Press.

St-Esprit, M. (2018, Jan 29). Targeted by a white supremacist in Pittsburgh for being a "race traitor." Retrieved from https://www.publicsource.org/targeted-by-a-white-supremacist-in-pittsburgh-for-being-a-race-traitor/.

Stimson, J. A. (2004). *Tides of consent: How public opinion shapes American politics.* Cambridge, UK: Cambridge University Press.

Strolovitch, D. Z., Wong, J. S., & Proctor, A. (2017). A possessive investment in white heteropatriarchy? The 2016 election and the politics of race, gender, and sexuality. *Politics, Groups, and Identities, 5*(2), 353–363. doi:10.1080/21565503.2017.1310659

Stryker, S. (1968). Identity salience and role performance: The relevance of symbolic interaction theory for family research. *Journal of Marriage and Family, 30*(4), 558–564. doi:10.2307/349494

Sugrue, T. J. (1996). *The origins of the urban crisis race and inequality in postwar detroit.* Princeton, NJ: Princeton University Press.

Sullivan, M. J. (2019). *Earned citizenship.* New York: Oxford University Press.

Sumner, W. G. (1906). *Folkways: A study of the sociological importance of usages, manners, customs, mores, and morals.* Boston: Ginn and Company.

Sumner, W. G. (1913). *War, and other essays.* New Haven, CT: Yale University Press.

Tajfel, H. (Ed.) (1978). *Differentiation between social groups: Studies in the social psychology of intergroup relations.* New York: Academic Press.

Tajfel, H. (1981). *Human groups and social categories: Studies in social psychology.* Cambridge, UK: Cambridge University Press.

Tajfel, H., & Turner, J. C. (1979). An integrative theory of intergroup conflict. In W. G. Austin & S. Worchel (Eds.), *The social psychology of intergroup relations* (pp. 33–98). Monterey, CA: Brooks/Cole.

Tajfel, H., & Turner, J. C. (1986). The social identity theory of intergroup behavior. In S. Worchel & W. G. Austin (Eds.), *Psychology of intergroup relations* (pp. 7–24). Chicago: Nelson Hall.

Takaki, R. T. (1989). *Strangers from a different shore: A history of Asian Americans* (1st ed.). Boston: Little Brown.

Taylor, P., & Cohn, D. V. (2012). A milestone en route to a majority minority nation. Retrieved from http://www.pewsocialtrends.org/2012/11/07/a-milestone-en-route-to-a-majority-minority-nation/?src=rss_main.

Terkildsen, N. (1993). When white voters evaluate Black candidates: The processing implications of candidate skin color, prejudice, and self-monitoring. *American Journal of Political Science, 37*(4), 1032–1053. doi:10.2307/2111542

Tesler, M. (2012a). The return of old-fashioned racism to white Americans' partisan preferences in the early Obama era. *Journal of Politics, 75*(1), 110. doi:10.1017/s0022381612000904

Tesler, M. (2012b). The spillover of racialization into health care: How President Obama polarized public opinion by racial attitudes and race. *American Journal of Political Science, 56*(3), 690–704. doi:10.1111/j.1540-5907.2011.00577.x

Tesler, M. (2016a, Aug 16). Donald Trump is making the border wall less popular. Retrieved from https://www.washingtonpost.com/news/monkey-cage/wp/2016/08/16/donald-trump-is-making-the-border-wall-less-popular/.

Tesler, M. (2016b). *Post-racial or most-racial?: Race and politics in the Obama era.* Chicago: University of Chicago Press.

Tesler, M., & Sears, D. O. (2010). *Obama's race: The 2008 election and the dream of a post-racial america.* Chicago: The University of Chicago Press.

Thandeka. (1999). *Learning to be white: Money, race, and god in America.* New York: Continuum.

Theiss-Morse, E. (2009). *Who counts as an American? The boundaries of national identity.* New York: Cambridge University Press.

Tichenor, D. J. (2002). *Dividing lines: The politics of immigration control in America.* Princeton, NJ: Princeton University Press.

Tichenor, D. J., & Filindra, A. (2012). Raising Arizona v. United States: Historical patterns of American immigration federalism. *Lewis & Clark Law Review, 16*(4), 1247.

Tolbert, C. J., & Grummel, J. A. (2003). Revisiting the racial threat hypothesis: White voter support for California's Proposition 209. *State Politics & Policy Quarterly, 3*(2), 183–192.

Transue, J. E. (2007). Identity salience, identity acceptance, and racial policy attitudes: American national identity as a uniting force. *American Journal of Political Science, 51*(1), 78–91. doi:10.1111/j.1540-5907.2007.00238.x

Tuch, S., & Hughes, M. (2011). Whites' racial policy attitudes in the twenty-first century: The continuing significance of racial resentment. *Annals of the American Academy of Political and Social Science, 634*, 134–152. doi:10.1177/0002716210386

Turner, J. C. (1975). Social comparison and social identity: Some prospects for intergroup behaviour. *European Journal of Social Psychology, 5*(1), 1–34.

Turner, J. C., Hogg, M. A., Oakes, P. J., Reicher, S., & Wetherell, M. (1987). *Rediscovering the social group: A self-categorization theory.* New York: Basil Blackwell.

Turner, J. C., Oakes, P. J., Haslam, S. A., & McGarty, C. (1994). Self and collective: Cognition and social-context. *Personality and Social Psychology Bulletin, 20*(5), 454–463. doi:10.1177/0146167294205002

USCIS. (2022). Policy manual. Retrieved from https://www.uscis.gov/policy-manual/volume-12-part-f-chapter-1.

Valentino, N. A., Brader, T., & Jardina, A. (2013). Immigration opposition among U.S. whites: General ethnocentrism or media priming of attitudes about Latinos? *Political Psychology, 34*(2), 149–166.

Viroli, M. (1997). *For love of country: An essay on patriotism and nationalism.* New York: Oxford University Press.

Volle, J. J. (2019). *The original Know-Nothings: Donald Trump and the Know-Nothing movement.* Cham, Switzerland: Palgrave Macmillan.

Walker, H. L. (2020). *Mobilized by injustice: Criminal justice contact, political participation, and race.* Oxford: Oxford University Press.

Wallace, G. P. R., & Wallace, S. J. (2020). Who gets to have a dream? Examining public support for immigration reform. *International Migration Review, 54*(2), 527–558. doi:10.1177/0197918319833924

Wallace, S. J. (2014). Papers please: State-level anti-immigrant legislation in the wake of Arizona's SB 1070. *Political Science Quarterly, 129*(2), 261–291. doi:10.1002/polq.12178

Walster, E., Berscheid, E., & Walster, G. W. (1973). New directions in equity research. *Journal of Personality and Social Psychology, 25*(2), 151–176. doi:10.1037/h0033967

Walton, H. (1975). *Black Republicans: The politics of the black and tans.* Metuchen, NJ: Scarecrow Press.

Ward, D. (1985). Generations and the expression of symbolic racism. *Political Psychology, 6*(1), 1. doi:10.2307/3791267

Waters, M. C. (1994). Ethnic and racial identities of second-generation Black immigrants in New York City. *International Migration Review, 28*(4), 795. doi:10.2307/2547158

Weller, N., & Junn, J. (2018). Racial identity and voting: Conceptualizing white identity in spatial terms. *Perspectives on Politics, 16*(2), 436–448. doi:10.1017/S1537592717004285

Wessler, S. F. (2011). Bills modeled after Arizona's SB 1070 spread through states. Retrieved from https://colorlines.com/article/bills-modeled-after-arizonas-sb-1070-spread-through-states/.

White, I. K., & Laird, C. N. (2020). *Steadfast Democrats: How social forces shape black political behavior.* Princeton, NJ: Princeton University Press.

Wiegman, R. (2012). *Object lessons.* Durham, NC: Duke University Press.

Wilcox, C., & Robinson, C. (2010). *Onward Christian soldiers? The religious right in American politics* (4th ed.). Boulder, CO: Westview Press.

Wilderson, F. B. (2015). *Incognegro: A memoir of exile and apartheid.* Durham, NC: Duke University Press.

Williams, J. (2010, Apr 03). Tea Party anger reflects mainstream concerns. *Wall Street Journal.* Retrieved from https://www.wsj.com/articles/SB10001424052702304252704575155942054483252.

Winant, H. (2004a). Behind blue eyes: Whiteness and contemporary U.S. Racial politics. In M. Fine, L. Weis, L. Powell Pruitt, & A. Burns (Eds.), *Off white: Readings on power, privilege, and resistance* (pp. 3–16). New York: Routledge.

Winant, H. (2004b). *The new politics of race: Globalism, difference, justice.* Minneapolis: University of Minnesota Press.

Winders, J. (2007). Bringing back the border: Post 9/11 politics of immigration, borders, and belonging in the contemporary US south. *Antipode, 39*(5), 920–942.

Winter, D. G. (2003). Personality and political behavior. In D. O. Sears, L. Huddy, & R. Jervis (Eds.), *Oxford handbook of political psychology* (pp. 110–145). New York: Oxford University Press.

Winter, N. J. G. (2008). *Dangerous frames: How ideas about race & gender shape public opinion.* Chicago: University of Chicago Press.

Wishnie, M. (2001). Laboratories of bigotry? Devolution of the immigration power, equal protection, and federalism. *New York University Law Review, 76*(2), 493–569.

Wong, C. (2010). *Boundaries of obligation in American politics: Geographic, national, and racial communities.* Cambridge, UK; New York: Cambridge University Press.

Wong, C., & Cho, G. E. (2005). Two-headed coins or Kandinskys: White racial identification. *Political Psychology, 26*(5), 699–720. doi:10.1111/j.1467-9221.2005.00440.x

Wong, T. K. (2017, Jan 26). The effects of sanctuary policies on crime and the economy. Retrieved from https://www.americanprogress.org/issues/immigration/reports/2017/01/26/297366/the-effects-of-sanctuary-policies-on-crime-and-the-economy/.

Wright-Schaner, S. (2016). The immoral character of "good moral character": The discriminatory potential of the bar's character and fitness determination in jurisdictions employing categorical rules preventing or impeding former felons from being barred. *Georgetown Journal of Legal Ethics, 29*(4), 1427–1442.

Yadon, N., & Ostfeld, M. C. (2020). Shades of privilege: The relationship between skin color and political attitudes among white Americans. *Political Behavior, 42*(4), 1369–1392. doi:10.1007/s11109-020-09635-0

Yancy, G. (2004). *What white looks like: African-American philosophers on the whiteness question.* London: Taylor and Francis.

Yeatman, A. (2003). Global ethics, Australian citizenship and the "boat people"—a symposium. *Journal of Sociology, 39*(1), 15–22. doi:10.1177/0004869003039001309

Yinger, J. (1985). Ethnicity. *Annual Review of Sociology, 11*, 151–180.

Zack, N. (2011). *The ethics and mores of race: Equality after the history of philosophy.* Lanham, MD: The Rowman & Littlefield Publishing Group.

Zaller, J. R. (1992). *The nature and origins of mass opinion.* Cambridge, UK: Cambridge University Press.

Index

For the benefit of digital users, indexed terms that span two pages (e.g., 52–53) may, on occasion, appear on only one of those pages.

Black Lives Matter, 190
blackness, 1, 7–8, 13–14, 27, 105–6, 154,
    156–57, 185–86
black-over-white victimization, 5–6,
    197n.5
Black studies, 198n.2
Blumer, Herbert, 31, 53, 198n.4
bootstrap ideology, 149, 199n.14
border spending, 97, 98*f*, 110, 202n.2
border wall. *See* Mexico–US border wall
Brewer, Marilynn B., 52–53, 65–66, 93
"browning of America," 39
Buckley, William F., Jr., 92
Bush, George H. W., 4–5
Bush, George W., 110

California, 30, 159*t*, 201n.2
    alien land laws in, 35, 198n.6
    and American Party, 201n.2
    immigration laws in, 30, 154–55, 157–
        58, 159*t*, 172*t*, 174, 177–78, 179
    Los Angeles, 160
    migrants in, 164
    San Diego, 39–40, 199n.15.
        See also Proposition 187 (1994, CA)
    SB 54 (2017, CA)
Catholicism, 57, 201n.2
Census, 53, 70, 164–65
Central Americans, 203n.6
Chaney, Early, 14
Chicano Movement, 37
Chinese Exclusion Act (1882), 35
Christianity, 3–4. *See also* Catholicism
    evangelicals
    Protestantism
    Unitarians
Church of Creativity, 14
citizenship, 91, 132–33, 142–43, 174, 193
    birthright, 82–83, 94–95, 97, 98*f*, 101–3,
        102*f*, 104, 106*t*, 107, 109–10, 109*t*,
        111, 114–15, 114*t*, 193
    derivative, 198–99n.11
    and egalitarianism, 64
    gendered, 198–99n.11
    and good moral character, 46–47
    and moral traditionalism, 60
    in Naturalization Law (1790), 35–36
    normative, 6–7

paths to, 34, 38–39, 60, 77, 101–3,
    129–30, 145, 151
proof of, 154
racialized, 2–3, 6–7, 11, 34–36, 42, 47–49
shadow, 6–7
and white racial identity, 76*t*, 77.
    See also naturalization
civil rights, 4–5, 44, 91, 128
    and colorblindness, 27, 130
    and Democratic Party, 18–19
    post-, 27, 28, 36–42, 49–50, 55, 61–62
    pre-, 34–36
    and race neutrality, 11
    and race traitors, 14
    and racial resentment, 61–62
    and whiteness, 25–26, 28, 36–42, 49–50,
        55
Civil Rights Movement, 25–26, 34, 36–37,
    58, 61–62, 130
    and Ellis Island whiteness, 199n.14
Clark, Jim, 202n.1
class, 43, 194
    Black working class, 15
    colonial upper class, 12
    racialized, 45–46, 72–73, 204n.21
    and whiteness, 12
    white working class, 10, 12, 15, 58, 149
Clay, Henry, 153
Clinton, Bill, 38–39
Cold War, 11
Collaborative Multiracial Post-Election
    Survey (CMPS), 70*t*, 73, 87, 88*t*
collective identity, 52–53, 65
colonialism/imperialism, 44
    British, 12, 22
    settler colonialism, 27, 33
    US, 55–56, 165
    and white racial identity, 198n.5
Colorado: immigration laws in, 159*t*, 167,
    172*t*, 173–74, 177–78, 179.
        See also HB 1124 (2019, CO)
colorblind discourse, 11, 27, 36, 42, 151
    and anti-racism, 23
    and authoritarianism, 61
    and egalitarianism, 63–64
    and Ellis Island whiteness, 199n.14
    and immigration policy, 42, 55–56
    and race cognizance, 70–71, 130–31, 132